3

FOTO**TORST**

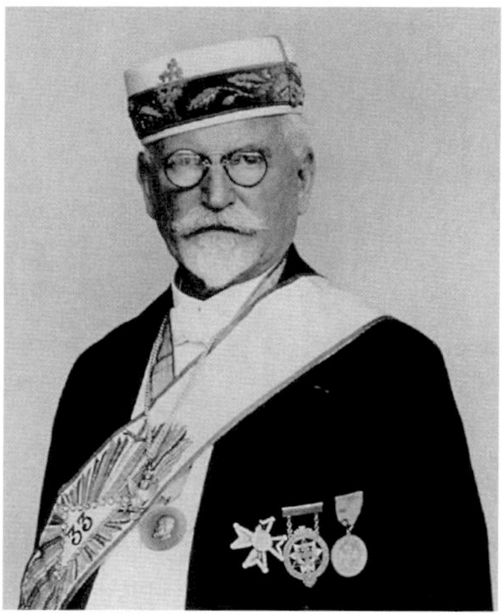

JOSEF MOUCHA

Alfons **Mucha**

TORST

Acknowledgements
The publisher expresses his sincere thanks to *Mucha Trust, The Museum of Decorative Arts in Prague, Jana Orlíková, Pavel Scheufler, and Jiří Řapek*

ISBN 80-7215-250-5

"A picture, I would say, acts aggressively: it enters the soul, without consideration, through an open window. The observer can do whatever he wants with it. He can ignore it, prevent it from entering his consciousness, or, led by its outer appearance, he can stop in front of the work and perhaps even seek its content and meaning and, eventually, find in it the essence, of either beauty or truth, on account of which the work came into being."

Alfons Mucha [1]

The author of a volume on Mucha's prints from the period 1895–1905 called Alfons Maria Mucha (1860–1939) the best known Czech artist in the world.[2] Today, as we enter the twenty-first century, he remains the most famous Czech artist of the Art Nouveau period. He achieved fame mostly because of his posters, particularly those for the theater of Sarah Bernhardt. Beginning with the lithograph *Gismonda* (designed in 1894), which made him famous overnight, Mucha used his great sense of decorative line and harmonious color to create clear composition, simply described figures, striking detail and ornament, pleasing pastels, and an erotic undercurrent that remained within the bounds of good taste. But Mucha's posters were not merely a way of achieving fame; they enabled his legacy to return from the chasm of condemnation into which it had been cast by the proponents of rationalistic Constructivism, Functionalism, and the *Neue Sachlichkeit.* His commissioned artwork survived the era of disfavor and went on to evoke an interest in the many concealed levels of his outstanding talent. This talent ran in all directions: book illustration, drawings for periodicals, oil portraits on commission, ornamental panels, advertisements, jewelry, decorative little statues, architectural designs, and a way of making industrially manufactured products untypical (regardless of whether they were biscuit boxes, postage stamps, or banknotes). The avant-garde of the first Czechoslovak Republic could not bear him for another reason: the approval he later met with from official circles was visible to all, day in, day out; and the establishment of the new state also took a particular liking to the reincarnation of the Art Nouveau (Sezessionist) style, which came to be called Art Deco.

On the other hand, in the years 1895–1903, Mucha was an indispensable activist of the movement that set the tone from Paris during La Belle Epoque. The wide range of his expression did not lack its own style. It is no accident, therefore, that for many of the artist's contemporaries one way of describing the new art (Art Nouveau) was "le style Mucha" – at least in the city on the Seine, the international metropolis of the arts and culture at the time. Apart from designs for luxury goods, Mucha published large handbooks which, with their models, expanded the range of techniques available to Art Nouveau artists. The publications *Documents décoratifs* (1902) and *Figures décoratives* (1905) are handbooks codifying not so much the author's style (that had already been done) as the parameters of the Art Nouveau style. They were actually instructions for how to apply to three-dimensional work rules which had been discovered during graphic design. Mucha himself tested the practicability of such an approach with the realization of various projects for the Paris International Exhibition in 1900. In exquisite hand-books he summarized his experience, which could be applied not only to ornamentation or figure drawing. Most of all he devoted himself to the poster – in other words, to a continuously accessible street gallery that inspired the latest fashions and general taste of the *Fin de siècle.* Into the gaily decorated boulevards of Paris, five years before the end of the nineteenth century, he brought the balanced sense of proportions of his own range of colors.

Alfons Mucha began as an illustrator of journals and books. But before he established himself in this thankless task, which, owing to his fastidiousness, took an incredible amount of time, he spent years as an apprentice and student in Vienna, Munich, and Paris. Whereas in the Austro-Hungarian metropolis he worked as a helper in a stage-design workshop, in Munich in the mid-1880s the ideal of serious painting, academic historicism, began to appeal to him. The Munich School helped to prepare him for what was at that time the most serious career conceivable, though his talent as a graphic artist remained stronger. His first professional experience had influenced him so much, in fact, that it remained a source from which he would always draw. His jobs for theaters in Paris and New York brought him one kind of success, but it was habits acquired from the first apprenticeships that actually robbed him of the success he had hoped to achieve with the fulfilment of his life's great endeavor, the painting of the monumental cycle called the *Epic of the Slavs* (1911–28).[3]

He considered his masterpieces – usually pastel, though sometimes also combined with charcoal drawing – to be the most private of matters.[4] Mucha was not concerned exclusively with creating pleasingly attractive female figures surrounded with intertwining decorative ornaments, which are now known to everybody; he was also interested in achieving the energetically drawn expression of dark impressions, such as those evoked by *Zimní ležení u hořícího města* [A winter encampment by a burning town], *Prosba* [The request], or *Absint* [Absinthe].[5] From the depths of gushing expressiveness there sometimes radiates in the middle of the pictures a mysteriously emerging dim light – for instance in *Vize* [The vision], done in pastel on grey paper, or *Dvojice se světlem* [A couple in the light], done in pastel and black chalk on blue paper. The unfinished (and undated) versions of sketches for Eugène Manuel's *Poésies du foyer et de l'école* (published in 1893) are equally phantasmic.

The posters and panels in the reprints of a wide range of sizes constitute, a century later, almost standard decoration of Euro-American interiors, from frequently visited establishments to offices and households. That would have been a source of great satisfaction for a member of the Société Internationale de l'Art Populaire, an organization founded by the physician, lawyer, poet, and author of a book on William Morris, Henri Cazalis (1840–1909), which aimed to enlighten the poor and make their lives more beautiful.[6]

Original Muchas are priceless parts of private and public collections and permanent exhibitions all over the world. In Prague, thanks to his family, a Mucha Museum was opened in 1998. Among its valuable exhibits is a selection of photographs – items that the painter would never have expected to see exhibited. Even less would he have expected a second monograph of photos. The first was published in London and New York by his son Jiří Mucha with Graham Ovenden (who wrote the Forewords to the volumes published by Academy Photographic Editions). The 1974 publication is an album of ninety-three photographs; the front of the dust-jacket bears a print by Mucha, while the back – from the commercial point of view less important – bears one of his photographs; it is meant to be, among other things, a humorous borrowing of Mucha's design for a permanent cover for the journal *L'Art Photographique* (first published in July 1899) but the idea is spoilt by an unsuitable typeface. All the prints in the book come from the collection of Jiří Mucha. He provided the photos, facts about them (including their dates), but the decisive information in the commentary, which describes the importance of Alfons Mucha's photographs, is hidden: though Jiří Mucha is not even a co-author of the text, his influence is evident. Similarly, Jiří Mucha is directly responsible for the second selection of photographs by his father. In the late 1970s he provided Jiří Řapek, an art historian employed at the time by the Museum of Applied Arts in Prague, with three suitcases of negatives amounting to about 1,500 shots. The following quotation indicates just how complicated it was to identify the subject matter of the photos and their dates of origin. "The album of models," said Jiří Mucha, "was a sample book for my father, which he used as a memory aid. Consequently, it is impossible to date a drawing on the basis of a photograph, but, on the other hand, they often do help to date works which we often see in the background of the photographs. It is a priceless aid not only for determining the time when a photograph was made, but also for identifying some drawings or lithographs."[7]

The new contact prints or enlargements from the old and very high-contrast negatives were made by Miloslav Šebek in three sets, which then made their way to places far apart from each other – from Havana to Munich, Bologna, and Moscow. One of the sets was eventually entrusted to Alfons Mucha's hometown, Ivančice, Moravia. The Museum of Applied Arts in Prague has a unique set of prints made by the artist himself. It was acquired in the early 1970s by Anna Fárová, the person responsible for reestablishing the photography collection there, and she immediately gave Mucha the place of honor among eleven photographers in the exhibition "Outstanding Czech Photographers."[8] At the next exhibition of these unique pieces, Jan Mlčoch, its curator, remarked that these period contact prints ranked among the most exclusive items in the collection of the Museum of Applied Arts.[9]

In general, the work of all great artists, providing it bears the marks of their spirit, is usually published in total. Mucha cannot be an exception. And yet there is also an additional, separate reason for publishing a monograph of his photographs; namely, to chart out the history of this medium in Czech art, and go somewhat beyond an interest only in an artist who aspired to a permanent place in the hall of fame of all periods and styles.

Alfons Mucha's attitude toward photography was strictly utilitarian. Consequently, he involuntarily avoided the assessment found in the note-books of the leading Czech literary critic F. X. Šalda, who wrote in the early 1930s about the "gilded and star-studded Mucha, with whom we were already over-saturated by the end of the last century."[10] Mucha's uncontrived, forward-looking photography should surprise nobody, not even when seen in comparison with the anachronistic nature of his late paintings. He had a similar approach to cinematography. "In 1895 he became acquainted with the Lumière brothers," wrote Jiří Mucha in a biography of his father, "attracted by the idea that he would be able to study motion precisely captured in all its phases."[11] Alfons Mucha organized meetings in his studio with celebrities and apart from concerts or recitals he also used film projection. This led him to consider, as he put it, "how to compose scenes, where the motion would be real and the framework fictive."[12] He saw the camera as a functional instrument that allowed him to make an exact record of what he saw. A comparison of the seated model in the preparatory photograph with the finished sculpture, *Vyšívačka* [The embroiderer] (1899), provides a superb example of Mucha's use of photography for documentation.

Over the years, Mucha worked with at least six different cameras. From the beginning he was aware that a moment in time could not be fully captured with a drawing and he saw the advantages of photography. Among the first shots, taken in the 1880s, are the memorable views from the windows of rented rooms, where he sat drawing. The artist's sketchbook, of course, continued to fill up with countless sketches. Apart from them, however, Mucha began to put together a photography album. He systematically assembled visual notes made on journeys, together with souvenirs from his visits home – *Jihomoravské vinobraní* [South Moravian grape harvest] (1886). He also photographed ordinary walks through the Luxembourg Gardens or, for instance, while skating. He recorded the surroundings in which he was staying and studios where he worked and received important guests. He did not neglect to include in this optical diary portraits of his fellow artists, especially those who left for France following their studies in Munich (Karel Václav Mašek and Luděk Marold) and, later, Paul Gauguin. Other shots document typical moments of his life as an artist, and, with time, as a father and husband. Alfons Mucha also liked to photograph himself – more than once with a sly smile and staring waggishly into the camera, but also addressing some un- known audience in the distant future.

Far more often than merely as a recording device Mucha used photography to find solutions for his work. In this case, of course, arranged scenes in the studio predominated. Of the numerous parallels in the history of photography done by painters the most interesting comparison is with the costume scenes of the English pictorialist of the "First Wave", Henry Peach Robinson (1830–1901) – with the reservation that Mucha insisted on finishing a picture using the traditional media of the artist, whereas the artist of *Fading Away* (1858) preferred to use a composite of negatives.

Mucha's early photos from the streets could have been made while collecting material for his genre drawings, which were published as an accompaniment to light reading. After all, the earliest of Mucha's magazine illustrations demonstrate the comparison with "moments from real life."[13] In any case, the painter occasionally returned to photography right up to the end of his life.

When taking photographs Mucha had only his own needs in mind. His photos were not governed by the rules recognized by leading photographers of the day, although, as the artist of graphic designs, he worked with magazines that focused on the shifts in the social ambitions of photography: apart from the cover for *L'Art Photographique* (1899), he also designed the frontispiece for the Czech literary journal *Lumír* (1898).[14] Mucha did not consider himself a photographer and consequently had no photographer as his ideal.[15] The merit of his photos resides in the fact that they were made without any training or ambitions in a field whose problems and complexity held little attraction for him. Though self-taught as photographer, Mucha, whether intentionally or not, played a highly important role in the history of the medium.

In his day initiatives to use the medium for art spread rapidly, though views persisted concerning the impossibility of that notion. Photography continued to serve as a synonym for "derivation." The leading Czech writer Jan Neruda, for instance, stated in 1868: "Are we to reject the photograph because it is not a work of art? Surely not. It mediates for us a pictorial knowledge of things which we should otherwise know only after great sacrifice."[16] But in the international atmosphere of *fin-de-siècle* Paris, Mucha established the Czech tradition of art photography in a way that ignored the artistic creed he had seen in the work of others, for instance, Edward Steichen (who had also made Mucha's portrait).[17] At the Paris International Exhibition, in 1900, contemporary photography, including Czech, was abundantly represented. But Mucha's idealistically based individuality had no reason not to agree with Neruda, though much had been changing with the times. Just as in Euro-American culture in general, so too in the Bohemian Lands the Art Nouveau model of sophisticated photography was accompanied by making photographic prints that were comparable to works of art. With the so-called "noble prints" (though not only with them) the photographer tried to attain the status of the artist, an honor that was usually accorded only to the creator of an unrepeatable artefact touched by an inspired hand.[18] This sort of self-confirmation was, of course, unnecessary for Mucha. The personal visual diary of his Munich days achieved the status of a professional aid in the French metropolis. Among painters at the *Fin de siècle* the camera became more widespread on account of its practicality: it was used by a great number of artists, including Degas, Gauguin, Toulouse-Lautrec, Renoir, Bonnard, Vuillard, Munch, Matisse, Fortuny, Eakins, and Kirchner.[19] Models had to be paid for their time – in the case of illustrations, expenditures on models, at least in the early days, comprised half of Mucha's fees; whereas the deft camera was immediately able to capture all the necessary but fleeting details of positions of the moving figure (including the complex tension in the phases of a ballerina's dance), which could not be imitated by posing. For that purpose Mucha employed either specialists or whoever was at hand. He had no qualms about using even himself.

Photography also had a slightly bizarre use for Mucha. It was employed to depict the emanations of the soul during hypnotic seances organized by Mme Lina de Ferkel, the astrologer Camille Flammarion, and Colonel Albert de Rochas d'Aiglun. The last named published a report of these activities in an 1899 issue of *Nature* and accompanied a book of his studies with photographs from Mucha's studio.[20]

In extreme cases Mucha used photography directly as a descriptive guideline when making sketches for his larger work. With the help of a grid he transferred from the photograph to the canvas the folds of drapery, foreshortened bent extremities, and complicated musculature and proportions in general. It has been convincingly demonstrated that Mucha also tried out the color scheme of a composition first on a photograph.[21] He also experimented with lighting and exposure times, manufactured a self-releasing shutter, and revealed the effect of the model's movement in front of the camera, as well as the movement of the camera itself, for instance in *Jihofrancouzská krajina z vlaku* [The south of France, landscape from a train] (c. 1900). His repeated making of prints from negatives with technological defects is evidence that Mucha approved of the factor of chance and was well aware of the magic of the unexpected. This includes failures caused by damaging the emulsion of incautiously dried and stored negatives: part of an original print (*Komedie* [Comedy], 1908), which was published by Fárová in her *Osobnosti české fotografie* [Outstanding Czech Photographers], consists of the accidental transfer of a bit of newsprint. The clashes between uncontrived backgrounds and compositions subordinated to the lofty idea of some future work became the norm. For the sake of precise outline in a planned drawing Mucha sometimes shaded the environment with a white surface – either behind the whole figure, or at least behind a sharply observed detail. Sometimes, models suggest the raising of imaginary attributes, which are conjured up for them only later by the artist's pencil.

Mucha did not hesitate to make a great departure in his drawings from poses chosen for photographs. Often, however, he was able to anticipate the final result with such precision that the photographs and the drawings which resulted from them, or a combination of several photographs, are clearly identifiable.[22] The surviving photographs either confirm the faithfulness of the pictures to their models, or, on the other hand, document cases where the model for a poster of a theater performance was some alter ego who bore no resemblance whatsoever to the leading lady. The photographic preparations in this case augment a vivid imagination that was supported by great skill. "In my father's case," recalled Jiří Mucha, "an absolutely regular procedure for work gradually developed. Every new job was first sketched out, then – unless he already had a suitable photograph – he made a photographic record based on the drawing. [...] But he didn't take photographs of models only for a drawing he may have had in mind. He also improvised in front of the camera, using several variants, and in this way created a copious archive."[23]

The miraculously instant picture, as it was described by Degas, was an immediate inspiration to the Impressionists, who found specific phenomena in the photographs: a looser composition, the hitherto unimaginable severing of figures at the edge of the picture, and the merging of the background in a shallow depth of focus. Whereas the Impressionists tried, at least illusively, to kindle in the mind of the viewer Corot's slogan "Give in to your first impression!", Alfons Mucha declared a rather different strategy. An explanation for the origin of Mucha's typically dynamic compositions was put forth by his son, Jiří Mucha: "Every photographic sketch clearly reveals its provenance. Each displays an entirely recognizable style, even a painterly technique, flatness or three-dimensionality, emphasis on color or line, and decorative nature or hard reality. Throughout his life, my father made this sort of photograph, so that eventually I, too, had to step in front of the camera. The procedures were always long and arduous before I assumed the correct position and before Father, with the enthusiasm of a man launching a rocket, pressed the shutter release."[24]

Fárová ranked Alfons Mucha among the leading figures in the history of photography, arguing that the style of the fine artist made its way into his works with this auxiliary medium to such an extent that they "sometimes involuntarily become finished photographic pieces in their own right."[25] And, indeed, Mucha's photos do not lack aesthetic self-sufficiency. In them he was able to exploit the sense of eloquence found in attitude and gesture, which he had learnt and then cultivated with drawing. The snapshots from Tsarist Russia, however, surpassed the standards of his usual travel photos. This is explained in the monograph by Jana Brabcová, an expert on Mucha and curator of exhibitions of his work, who states: "We know of many photographs from Mucha's Russian sojourn, which have been presented as his work. From information provided by Alfons Mucha's wife, however, we see that the shots were taken by the French photographer who had accompanied Mucha to Russia."[26] Nevertheless, the ultimate aim of the photographs, namely to provide models for the realization of some of the painter's plans, was present from the beginning to such an extent that it determined both the selection and the presentation of the models for the canvas he was about to paint. And it is because of Mucha's direction that these shots have a place in a monograph dedicated to his photography: it is for the same reason that even the self-portraits not necessarily taken by Mucha himself are included here. The backgrounds of the figures photographed in Moscow generally played no important role: they are usually out of focus (with the exception of the silhouette of the Church of St Basil, which later dominated the painting). Nevertheless, the set of photographs from the study trip to Russia is a treasury of historical facts, and is therefore of universal importance. The pair of photo-taking foreigners (Mucha and the anonymous Frenchman) attracted attention – after all, tourism in those parts was highly unusual in 1913. Though some photos were made without onlookers, it seems that they were not made clandestinely. The camera draws inquisitive looks, sometimes friendly, sometimes not so friendly. Here a little group poses informally, there a huddled beggar covers her face with a scarf. The painter later faithfully captured the proverbial Russian resignation to the apparently supreme and, in the logic of things, unalterable decisions of higher authorities. Here, in any case, Mucha clearly perceived the pilgrims in their peasant clothes, with bundles and walking sticks, as a social class. They are precisely the sort of figures he needed for the purposes he described, in 1919, in the commentary to his painting *Zrušení nevolnictví na Rusi* [The abolition of serfdom in Russia] (1914): "The common people remain, they discuss, think, thank God, give their blessing, and have yet to understand their new-found freedom."[27]

The importance of the Russian excursion is also revealed by another reminiscence, which was articulated, ten years after the journey, in a large oil painting. It expresses the psychology of being freed from one's lot on Earth and accepting Fate, which is leading one to an unavoidably worse end. The title of the painting kept changing: *Rusko* [Russia], *Hvězda* [Star], *Sibiř* [Siberia], *Zimní noc* [Winter night], and even the improbable *Enigmatická žena v divočině* [Enigmatic woman in the wilderness] (1923).

The twenty-part *Epic of the Slavs,* however, came somewhat late. The link between the illusory and the symbolic meanings of the colors and subject matter was intended to be abstract, not to prolong historicizing academic pseudo-Realism; yet, the apotheosis of Slavdom, executed in larger-than-life dimensions, comes across as banal. The ideological charge of the confrontation between Pan-Slavism and Germandom is neutralized when one compares the *Epic* with the designs for the decorative panels of the German Theater in New York, which were carried out with the same technique and, what is most important, with a similar mannerism. Its literary interpretation, rather than the work itself, is what conveys Mucha's intended meanings:

the painting *Zrušení nevolnictví na Rusi,* for instance, is subtitled *Svobodná práce – osnovou států* [Unshackled labor: the basis of the state].[28] The photographs, by contrast, have maintained their freshness, and, what is more, have demonstrated their ability to be contemporary. Suffice it to mention the shots depicting one of the studios that had just been set up after having been moved from one continent to another: among its furnishings were heavy boxes full of negatives from the ever growing glass archive. (The photo of the chock-a-block studio in rue du Val-de-Grâce, by the way, expands the range of Mucha postcards.) The chaotic space – with house plants everywhere, drapery flowing down from the ceiling, an extravagant throne, a rotating mirror, skulls, and a bizarrely attired idol – resembles a liquid Surrealist still-life with the figures of an athlete, an elephant, Christ, a stuffed polar bear, a harmonium, a horse's head with bridle, devotional articles, light fixtures, books, and the mantle of the fireplace with a photo gallery.

In Mucha's lifetime the photograph still bore the incontestable hallmark of authenticity. Its superhuman precision had a particular appeal, especially for Mucha the painter, who was so focused on the ideal of beauty that he tended to lose sight of objective reality. Mucha's life was full of surprising scenes (sometimes even of an anecdotal character) into which he would plunge with a chronic unawareness. "My father," Jiří Mucha wrote, "had a truly fantastic ability to mix one person up with another [...]. It was something he was so accustomed to that once, in New York, instead of going to a party being held in his honor, he stumbled into somebody else's house, where by coincidence there also happened to be guests. He stayed there two hours, and didn't find it the least bit odd that he didn't know a single person there."[29]

It was women, above all, which Mucha "elevated and turned into impersonal bearers of all beauty."[30] When sketching, if the face of the model excited him too much, he covered it with a veil. When taking photographs, however, not only did he not do that, but some of his lithographs make full use of the bewitching looks of the models who had first been captured in photographs. The eyes, fixed firmly on the lens (and bound by the necessity not to move during the long exposure times then required in the studio), suddenly send out a signal to the viewer of the poster, the calendar, or the panel – for instance, *Rose* (1897) and *Emerald* (1900). Though Mucha's renowned beauties are sensual, their main purpose is not to allure with provocative expressions. Their effectiveness is achieved by mixing an imagined vision and an anatomically precise rendering. If one senses that one is undressing a *fin-de-siècle* pin-up girl with one's eyes, then one has found oneself in the train of the artist's photographic vision: the exalted pose was first frozen by the camera so that the delineation of the clothes in the painting suggest the nakedness beneath them. Here, too, is the source of the profane level of Mucha's nudes as collections of erotic diversions and curiosities.[31]

Mucha's photographs represent a contribution to the history of photography not only because they suggest the penetration of artistic thinking into a related discipline, no matter how much they draw the greater part of their charm from the artist's initial intention. In the changed cultural context of today, we accept the photographs as miniatures in their own right. They are full of an appealing dynamic, rawness, and authenticity, which the artist could not have employed as directly had he used any other medium. With the matter-of-fact spirit of photography – often the opposite of the refinement found in fine art – Mucha touches upon the fact that at the *Fin de siècle* the principal task of art was to break with the past and discover the way to approach the future. We are particularly sensitive to that fact, because at the turn of the millennium we, too, must take positions. Alfons Mucha was active at the boundary between two eras and he represented two stages of civilization. In the search for a new classicism he related, as an artist, to tradition. Interest in his photographic legacy demonstrates that it is not the particular painting but the photograph that preceded it, which contains not only the subject matter but also the meaning that it was intended to convey.

Endnotes

1 Alfons Mucha, *Slovanská epopeje*, Prague: Česká grafická unie, 1930, p. 3.
2 Jana Brabcová, *Alfons Mucha*, Prague: Panorama 1980, unpaged.
3 See the entry for Alfons Mucha in *Ottův slovník naučný nové doby. Dodatky k velikému Ottovu slovníku naučnému IV/1*, Prague: Novina, 1936, p. 377.
4 See Petr Wittlich, *Alfons Mucha. Pastely, plakáty, kresby a fotografie. Výstava v Císařské konírně Pražského hradu*, London: Mucha Foundation, 1994, p. 18.
5 Jana Brabcová places this stage of his work in the period of the Faustian scenes made during his Munich sojourn. See her "Hledání další cesty," in Jiří Kotalík (ed.), *Alfons Mucha (1860–1939)*, Prague: National Gallery, 1980, p. 85.
6 Compare William Morris's public lecture, in 1877, "The Decorative Arts". See also Alfons Mucha, *Tři projevy o životě a díle* [Three speeches about life and work], Brno: Brněnský klub, 1936, p. 9: "Art is the only sustenance of the hungry and thirsty souls here on Earth. Whoever feeds them with rubbish reaps all possible illnesses in the soul of man."
7 Jiří Mucha, untitled and undated typescript, pp. 4–5. As the study is introduced with a remark about "ninety-five years since the Munich photographs," it is fair to deduce that the article was written in 1981. A shorter version was published as the introduction to the catalogue *Alfons Mucha fotografem*, in June 1982. The exhibition in the Cheb Museum was organized by the Museum of Applied Arts, Prague. The author of its catalogue and conception was the curator Jiří Řapek. Thanks to him, too, we were able to determine the dates and subject matter of a large part of the photos. (Among other things, he discovered that Mucha had in various years dressed his models in the same costumes out of his own wardrobe.) Řapek is also owed our gratitude for having lent us the typescript by Jiří Mucha, which is important for determining the beginning of Alfons Mucha's photographic work and it corrects errors in previous publications. According to the monograph by Graham Ovenden, Mucha made his first photographs on 7 x 7 cm negatives while working in Vienna; cf. *Tržní náměstí ve Vídni* [A market square in Vienna] (1880). The photographs and their titles were used by Vladimír Remeš when discussing Ovenden's book in "Alfons Mucha jako fotograf," *Revue Fotografie*, 1977. Vol. 21, no. 4, p. 23; the error also made its way into other literature, for instance Daniela Mrázková and Vladimír Remeš, *Tschechoslowakische Fotografen 1900–1940*, Leipzig: VEB Fotokinoverlag, 1983, p. 10; Daniela Mrázková, *Příběh fotografie*, Prague: Mladá fronta, 1985, p. 28; Daniela Mrázková and Vladimír Remeš, *Cesty česko-slovenské fotografie*, Prague: Mladá fronta, 1989, pp. 34–5; and Pavel Scheufler's entry on Mucha in *Encyklopedie českých a slovenských fotografů*, Prague: ASCO 1993, pp. 244–5; another photo from the same series, with the title *Munich* (1880), was published with the article by Jiří Mucha, "Alfons Mucha," *Fotografie*, 1979. Vol. 23, no. 3, p. 54. Not till the Cheb catalogue *Alfons Mucha fotografem*, prepared in collaboration with Jiří Mucha, do we find a photo of an identical environment, which was identified as *Pohled z okna pokoje Alfonse Muchy v Mnichově v sousedství Amalienstrasse* [View from Alfons Mucha's window, near Amalienstrasse, Munich] (1886).
In the typescript, Jiří Mucha remarked: "My father's first photographs were made in Munich ninety-five years ago. We don't know what kind of camera he used back then, but we assume he borrowed it and, from the window of his room, took photographs of life in Amalienstrasse.

[…] He must have returned the square-format camera to its owner, because no photographs survived from the period when he was studying at the Académie Julian and later at the Académie Colarossi, 1887–92."

8 Anna Fárová, *Osobnosti české fotografie I/ze sbírek Uměleckoprůmyslového musea v Praze*, catalogues of the Gallery of Fine Art, Roudnice nad Labem, 1973, and of the Museum of Applied Arts, Prague, 1974.

9 See Jan Mlčoch, press release for the exhibition *Alfons Mucha: Fotografické studie*, Galerie Josefa Sudka, Prague, 3 June 1998. During this exhibition of twenty-one originals, several photos were identified thanks to the work of the curators Jan Mlčoch and Petr Štembera. The press release, however, makes the erroneous claim that the event was probably the "first ever independent exhibition of original photographs of this world-class artist"; the journal *Československá fotografie* had, in 1978, reported on an exhibition of forty photographs in the Italian Cultural Institute; the title of the exhibition remains unknown, but the photographs came from the estate of the architect Paolo Porthoghesi, who brought them from Italy and exhibited them in Prague during his lectures there.

10 Quoted from Jiří Kotalík, "Alfons Mucha a české umění," in Kotalík (ed.), *Alfons Mucha (1860–1939)*, p. 38.

11 Jiří Mucha, *Alfons Mucha*, Prague: Mladá fronta, 1982, p. 228.

12 Ibid. The insight of the observation becomes clear when comparing the formulation of the problem with the views in Vlastimil Jiřík, "Vztah výtvarných oborů k prostoru a času. Několik poznámek k uměleckohistorickému pojmu prostoru a času," *Filosofický časopis*, 1982. Vol. 30, no. 3, pp. 490–5. Alfons Mucha did eventually get round to arranging a *tableaux vivante*; see Jiří Mucha, *Alfons Mucha*, pp. 416–21.

13 Mucha, *Alfons Mucha*, p. 87. See also Antonín Dufek, "Společnost před kamerou I. Žánr a reportáž v XIX. století," *Československá fotografie*, 1976. Vol. 27, no. 6, p. 269.

14 Josef Václav Sládek, a poet and the publisher-editor of the literary journal *Lumír*, was also a passionate photographer who, like Mucha, had an international outlook. Cf. J. V. Sládek, "Fotografie momentní," *Lumír*, 1886. Vol. 14, září, pp. 431–2: "Cameras are lately becoming more widespread in our country too. The ranks of amateurs are growing. Regrettably, their equipment is usually so miserable that it is almost impossible even to think about a fine-grained picture."

15 It does not mean that he did not have successors. See Antonín Nový, *Mucha Girls* (1974), in *Encyklopedie českých a slovenských fotografů*, Prague: ASCO 1993, pp. 259–60, with references to other literature.

16 Quotation taken from Jan Neruda, "Umění není fotografie," in Vladimír Dostál (ed.), *Čítanka z dějin české a slovenské estetiky XIX. století*, Prague: Československý spisovatel, 1972, p. 104. See also Pavel Scheufler, *Pražské fotografické ateliéry 1839–1918. II/ 1889–1918*, Prague: Muzeum hlavního města Prahy, 1989, p. 29: "In photography, however, the directness of the visual message of the nude was extremely arousing and was, it was thought at the time, incapable, in view of the nature of photography, of artistic stylization. [...] Not till work in the spirit of pictorialism did these pieces achieve general respect and the possibility of presenting the public with photographic nudes." An attitude similar to Neruda's is evident later in the thinking of V. V. Štech, Josef Čapek, and Karel Teige. See also Antonín Dufek, "Fotografie dvacátých let," in *Dějiny českého výtvarného umění 1890–1938 (IV/2)*, Prague: Academia 1998, pp. 213–4.

17 See Anna Fárová, *Osobnosti české fotografie I/ ze sbírek Uměleckoprůmyslového musea v Praze*, Prague: Uměleckoprůmyslové museum, 1974.

18 See Antonín Dufek, "Fotografie 1890–1918," in *Dějiny českého výtvarného umění 1890–1938 (IV/1)*, Prague: Academia, 1998, p. 195, and below. The twisted path from this second wave of pictorialism to the next stage is well illustrated by the story of Edward Steichen, who met Mucha immediately after his arrival in Paris in 1900. See also Jiří Mucha, *Alfons Mucha*, 1982, p. 252, and René d'Harnoncourt, *Steichen Fotograf*, Prague: Galerie „d", 1969. For a useful definition of the term "Sezessionist pictorialism" see Antonín Dufek, "Piktorialismus a jeho prehistorie v českých zemích," *Československá fotografie*, 1976. Vol. 27, no. 4, p. 173; Vladimír Birgus, "Piktorialismus, čili zmatek nad zmatek," *Československá fotografie*, 1980. Vol. 31, no. 10, p. 446; Antonín Dufek, "Z historie české fotografie (od r. 1890 do r. 1918)," *Fotografie*, 1984. Vol. 28, no. 4, p. 36; Scheufler, *Pražské fotografické ateliéry 1839–1918. II/ 1889–1918*, p. 15.

19 See Michel Frizot, *Histoire de voir. Le médium des temps modernes (1880–1939)*, Paris: Centre National de la Photographie, 1989, p. 26; Elvire Perego, "Privatsphäre und geheime Gärten. Der Künstler als Amateurfotograf," in Michel Frizot (ed.), *Neue Geschichte der Fotografie*, Cologne: Könemann, 1998, p. 336. The Czech scene is described in Pavel Scheufler, *Přehled vývoje fotografie v Praze v letech 1839–1918 II/ 1889–1918*, Prague: Státní pedagogické nakladatelství, 1991, pp. 62–4.

20 Albert de Rochas d'Aiglun, *Les sentiments, la musique et le geste*, Grenoble: H. Falque et F. Perrin, 1900. This side of Mucha's work is well explained in the catalogue by Petr Wittlich, *Alfons Mucha. Pastely, plakáty, kresby a fotografie. Výstava v Císařské konírně Pražského hradu*, London: Mucha Foundation, 1994, pp. 18–19.

21 Jana Brabcová, "Cesta ke slávě," in Kotalík (ed.), *Alfons Mucha (1860–1939)*, 1980, p. 42. The photograph of the facade of the Fouquet jewelers, completed by hand and included in this volume, is also interesting.

22 For a comparison of the photographic and graphic legacy of Alfons Mucha see Jiří Mucha, Marina Henderson, and Aaron Scharf, *Alfons Mucha: Posters and Photographs*, London: Academy Editions, 1971.

23 Jiří Mucha, typescript, pp. 4–5.

24 Mucha, *Alfons Mucha*, pp. 108–9.

25 Fárová, *Osobnosti české fotografie I/ ze sbírek Uměleckoprůmyslového musea v Praze*, 1973, unpaged.

26 Jana Brabcová, *Alfons Mucha*, Prague: Svoboda 1996, p. 72.

27 Alfons Mucha, *Katalog výstavy obrazů Alfonse M. Muchy z cyklu Slovanská epopeje*, Prague: Klementinum, 1919, unpaged.

28 Mucha, *Slovanská epopeje*, p. 43.

29 Mucha, *Alfons Mucha*, p. 84.

30 Ibid., p. 187.

31 Just how long Mucha's photographs of nudes remained unique in Czech photography is clear from the article that begins with the following sentence: "The nude in photography, not to mention the original Czech nude, is a kind of Cinderalla." See Viktor R., "O fotografickém aktu u nás," *Fotografický obzor*, 1934. Vol. 42, no. 7, pp. 101–3. The publication of the first nude was achieved by František Drtikol in the same journal but in 1911. Mucha preceded the artists of *Česká fotografická moderna* [Czech modern photography] by one generation. See the catalogue of works by Vladimír Jindřich Bufka, František Drtikol, Karel (Carol) Novák, and Josef Anton Trčka, compiled and edited by the curators Zdeněk Kirschner and Josef Kroutvor in the Museum of Applied Arts, Prague, 1989.

„Obraz působí, řekl bych, agresivně: bez ohledu vniká otevřeným okem do duše. Jest věcí pozorovatele, aby s ním naložil po své vůli. Může jej přejít, nepřipouštěje si ho do vědomí, anebo sveden vnějškem díla zastaví se před ním a snad i pátrá po jeho obsahu a významu a nakonec i najde v něm ono jadérko, buď krásy nebo pravdy, kvůli němuž povstalo.“

Alfons Mucha[1]

„Alfons Maria Mucha (1860–1939) je nesporně ve světě nejznámější český výtvarný umělec,“ vepsala začátkem roku 1980 Jana Brabcová do záhlaví sborníku reprodukcí grafických prací z let 1895–1905.[2] S neoslabenou charakteristikou vstupuje tento secesní tvůrce i do 21. století. Proslulost mu vynesly především plakáty, zvláště pro divadlo Sarah Bernhardtové. Počínaje litografií Gismonda (návrh 1894), která ho přes noc proslavila, zhodnotil Mucha vlohy pro dekorativní účin lineárního členění a barevné harmonizace plochy: přehledná kompozice, jednoznačné vymezení postavy, výrazné detaily a ornamenty, příjemné pastelové ladění, decentní erotický podtext. Plakáty Muchovu slávu více než jen založily. Dovolily návrat celého jeho odkazu z propasti odsudku, do níž byl uvržen vyznavači racionalistického konstruktivismu, funkcionalismu a nové věcnosti. Zakázková produkce přežila éru nepřízně a vyvolala zájem o veškeré zasuté vrstvy vynikajícího talentu. Ten expandoval v mnoha směrech: knižní ilustrace, kresby pro periodika, zakázkové portrétní olejomalby, ozdobná panneau, reklamy, klenoty, dekorační sošky, architektonické návrhy, ozvláštňování průmyslově vyráběných předmětů – od krabic na sušenky po státně šířené tisky československých poštovních známek a bankovek. Proto také nemohla avantgarda za první republiky Muchu vystát: měla jeho pozdní oficialitu dennodenně na očích – spolu s reinkarnací secesní setby zvané dnes art deco, s níž se identifikoval établissement nového státního útvaru...

Na druhé straně byl Alfons Mucha v letech 1895–1903 nepominutelným aktivistou hnutí, které z Paříže udávalo tón takzvané belle époque. Široký rejstřík jeho projevů rozhodně nepostrádá svébytnost rukopisu. Nikoli náhodou bylo před sto lety pro mnohé autorovy současníky synonymem nového umění heslo le style Mucha, alespoň ve městě nad Seinou, tehdy ovšem světové kulturní metropoli. Vedle návrhů designu pro výrobce luxusního zboží vydával Mucha obsáhlé manuály, modelově rozvíjející rejstřík secesního instrumentáře. Documents décoratifs (1902) a Figures décoratives (1905) jsou atlasy kodifikující nikoli už autorský styl, nýbrž některé z parametrů slohu. Byly vlastně návodem na přelití zákonitostí objevených při grafické práci do praktického systému tří rozměrů. Mucha si nosnost takového postupu sám ověřil realizací rozličných projektů při pařížské Světové výstavě 1900. Ve výpravných příručkách tedy shrnul zkušenost určenou netoliko dekorativní ornamentice nebo figurální kresbě. Nejbezprostřednější a nejcitelnější působiště si ovšem zjednával na plakátovacích plochách – jinak řečeno v nepřetržitě přístupné pouliční galerii inspirující módu a obecný vkus na zlomu dvou věků: do křiklavě dekorovaných pařížských bulvárů vnesl pět let před koncem 19. století uměřenost vlastní barevné škály.

Alfons Mucha začínal jako časopisecký a knižní ilustrátor. Než se však zavedl v této nevděčné úloze, při jeho pečlivosti pohlcující nezměrné množství času, prošel tovaryšskými a studentskými léty ve Vídni, Mnichově a Paříži. Působil-li v rakousko-uherské metropoli coby pomocná síla v malírně scénických staveb, zhlédl se v Mnichově poloviny 80. let 19. století v ideálu seriózní malby, totiž v historizujícím akademismu. Mnichovským školením se připravoval k tenkrát nejvážnější myslitelné dráze, leč grafické předpoklady zůstaly silnější. První profesní zkušenosti si zafixoval natolik, že z nich napořád čerpal. Zatímco při divadelních angažmá pařížských i newyorských sklízel úspěch, stály ho nakonec návyky prvotní průpravy kýženou odezvu při naplnění životního předsevzetí – monumentálního souboru Slovanská epopej (1911–1928).[3]

Vrcholné projevy – zpravidla pastely, někdy kombinované s kresbou uhlem – považoval umělec za privatissima.[4] Alfons Mucha se nezabýval výhradně líbezně přitažlivými ženskými figurami, obklopenými spletí dekorativních ornamentů, jež jsou notoricky známé, nýbrž také energicky črtanými výrony temných dojmů, jaké přináší Zimní ležení u hořícího města, Prosba nebo Absint.[5] Z hloubi prýštící expresivitu někdy prozařuje uprostřed samotných obrazů tajuplně se vzmáhající přísvit – třeba v pastelu na šedém papíře, zvaném Vize, anebo ve Dvojici se světlem provedené pastelem a černou křídou na modrý papír. Přízračné jsou rovněž nedotažené (a nedatované) verze náčrtů ilustrací ke knize Poésies du foyer et de l'école Eugèna Manuela (vyšla 1893).

Plakáty a panneau v novotiscích nejrůznějších velikostí tvoří po stu letech běžnou dekoraci euroamerických interiérů – od hojně navštěvovaných podniků přes prostředí pracovišť až po domácnosti. Toť velké zadostiučinění členu Société Internationale de l'Art Populaire, organizace zřízené lékařem, právníkem a básníkem Henrim Cazalisem za účelem osvěty a zkrášlování života nemajetných vrstev.[6]

Originály děl Alfonse Muchy jsou ceněnou součástí soukromých i veřejných sbírek a stálých expozic v České republice i v cizině. V Praze bylo péčí rodiny otevřeno Mucha museum (1998), mezi jehož exponáty po zásluze patří také výběr fotografií – položka, jíž by se malíř sotva nadál. Tím méně by očekával již druhou ryze fotografickou monografii. Tu první vydal v Londýně a v New Yorku roku 1974 autorův syn Jiří spolu s Grahamem Ovendenem, autorem předmluv ke svazkům Academy Photographic Editions. Tehdejší album o třiadevadesáti fotografických vyobrazeních nese na přední straně přebalu Muchovo dílo grafické, zatímco fotografie se ukrývá na zadní straně – z prodejního hlediska zanedbávané. Jinak se má jednat o vtipné převzetí Muchova návrhu stabilní obálky časopisu L'Art Photo-graphique, jenž začal vycházet v červenci 1899, avšak nápad je degradován nepatřičnou typografií... Vše, co kniha zprostředkovává obrazově, pochází ze sbírky Jiřího Muchy. Dodal především snímky, jejich identifikaci a datování. V komentáři, objevujícím význam fotografické tvorby Alfonse Muchy, má rozhodující slovo skrytě: přestože není spoluautorem textu, jeho vliv na něj je zřetelně znát. A Jiří Mucha se zprostředkovaně zasloužil i o druhý výbor z fotografického díla svého otce. Koncem 70. let totiž poskytl ke zpracování historikovi umění Jiřímu Řapkovi, působícímu tehdy v pražském Uměleckoprůmyslovém museu, tři kufry negativů čítající na 1500 záběrů. Jak složitě postupovalo odhadování námětů a určování období vzniku snímků, naznačí následující citát: „Alba modelů byla pro otce vzorníkem, ke kterému se uchyloval tak jako k paměti. Proto je na jedné straně nemožné datovat podle fotografie kresbu, ale naopak fotografie pomáhají datovat práce, které často vidíme v pozadí. Je to neocenitelná pomůcka nejen pro stanovení doby, kdy fotografie vznikla, ale i pro identifikaci některých kreseb nebo litografií."[7]

Novodobé kontakty či zvětšeniny ze starých, velmi kontrastně vyvolaných negativů byly pořízeny Miloslavem Šebkem ve třech sadách, aby putovaly na nejrůznější místa – od Havany přes Mnichov a Bolognu až do Moskvy. Jedno vyhotovení bylo posléze svěřeno městu Ivančice, rodišti Alfonse Muchy. Uměleckoprůmyslové museum v Praze má ve svých sbírkách jedinečné provedení pozitivů samotným umělcem. Získala je počátkem 70. let Anna Fárová, obnovitelka tamní fotografické sbírky, která také Alfonsi Muchovi přidělila čelné místo v přehlídce jedenácti autorů s názvem Osobnosti české fotografie.[8] Při dalším výstavním zveřejnění těchto unikátů poznamenal Jan Mlčoch, že patří k „nejexkluzivnějším sbírkovým předmětům“ Uměleckoprůmyslového musea.[9]

Od důležitých autorů bývá nakonec publikováno vše, co je nadáno pečetí jejich ducha, a Muchův případ nemůže být výjimkou. A přece má jeho fotografická monografie pro ohledání historie příslušného média v české kultuře také samostatný smysl, do jisté míry mimoběžný zájmu o výtvarníka aspirujícího na definitivu ve dvoraně slávy všech dob a stylů.

K fotografování se Alfons Mucha stavěl naprosto účelově. Mimovolně se tudíž v této oblasti vyhnul diagnóze Šaldova zápisníku, kde se počátkem 30. let píše o „pozlátkovém a hvězdičkovém Muchovi, kterým jsme byli přesyceni již na konci minulého století“.[10] Muchovo nevyumělkovaně progresivní fotografování by nemělo překvapit ani ve srovnání s anachroničností pozdního malířského díla. Stejně jasnozřivě nahlížel kinematografii. „Již někdy v roce 1895 se seznámil s bratry Lumièrovými,“ zaznamenal syn Jiří v otcově životopisu, „vábenpředstavou, že bude moci studovat věrně zachycený pohyb ve všech jeho fázích…“[11] Alfons Mucha pořádal ve svém ateliéru dostaveníčka celebrit a vedle koncertů či recitací využíval také filmových projekcí, pod jejichž dojmem se zabýval otázkou – jeho vlastními slovy řečeno – „jak komponovat scény, kde by byl pohyb skutečný a rámec fiktivní“.[12] Ve fotografické kameře shledával funkční nástroj, dovolující exaktní záznam. Vzornou pracovní dokumentací je komparace modelky sedící pro plastiku Vyšívačka (1899) s dohotoveným návrhem.

Postupem času pracoval Mucha s nejméně šesti různými fotoaparáty. Nezastupitelnost momentky kresbou a odlišné přednosti dokumentů získaných mechanickým průmětem si od počátku plně uvědomoval: mezi první záběry z 80. let 19. století patří pamětihodné pohledy z oken pronajatých pokojů, u nichž kreslíval. Malířské skicáky přirozeně nepřestal plnit nesčíslnými náčrty. Vedle nich si ovšem napříště zakládal fotografická alba. Soustavně shromažďoval vizuální poznámky z cest, případně suvenýry z návštěv domoviny – Jihomoravské vinobraní (1886). Fotografoval i na všedních procházkách Lucemburskou zahradou anebo třeba při bruslení. Zaznamenával podoby prostředí, v němž přebýval, ateliéry, kde pracoval a přijímal význačné hosty. Do optického památníku neopomenul zařadit podobizny souputníků, zejména těch, kteří se po studiích v Mnichově odebrali do Francie – Karla Václava Maška a Luďka Marolda. Stejně samozřejmě později přibude Paul Gauguin. Jiné záběry dokumentují příznačné okamžiky tvůrčího a časem též rodinného života. Ostatně sám Alfons Mucha se rád zvěčňoval – nejednou s potutelným pohledem šibalsky upřeným do kamery, potažmo však adresovaným neznámému publiku ve vzdálené budoucnosti.

Nad upomínkovým užíváním média mnohonásobně převažuje fotografování jako východisko k další práci. Vzhledem k Muchově orientaci dominují ateliérová aranžmá. Z četných paralel v historii fotografií produkovaných malíři je nejzajímavější srovnání s kostýmními inscenacemi anglického piktorialisty takzvané první vlny Henryho Peache Robinsona (1830–1901) – s tou výhradou, že Mucha lpěl na finalizaci obrazu tradičními výtvarnými prostředky, zatímco autor Fading Away (1858) a dalších děl dával přednost montážím negativů.

Muchovy rané pouliční záběry mohly vznikat při sběru materiálu k žánrovým kresbám, publikovaným jako doprovod kratochvilného čtení. Vždyť nejstarší Muchovy magazínové ilustrace vystihuje srovnání s „momentkami ze skutečného života".[13] K fotografickému žánru se ostatně malíř až do konce života příležitostně vracel.

Alfons Mucha míval při fotografování na mysli výhradně vlastní potřeby. Jeho záběry nebyly závislé na pravidlech vyznávaných příslušníky dobové fotografické elity, třebaže jako autor grafických návrhů spolupracoval s časopisy, které posunům společenských ambicí fotografování věnovaly pozornost: pro L'Art Photographique navrhl obálku (1899), pro Lumír frontispice (1898).[14] Mezi fotografy se Mucha nepočítal a nenásledoval žádný tímto stavem ceněný osobnostní vzor.[15] Přednost Muchových snímků spočívá v tom, že vznikaly bez jakéhokoli školení či ambicí v oboru, jehož problémy a pokročilost nebyly pro autora přitažlivé. Leč samorostlou fotografickou prací Mucha volky nevolky naplňoval velice důležitý historický moment.

V jeho době se rapidně šířily iniciativy využít předpokladů média artistně, byť zároveň přetrvávaly názory, že to není možné; fotografie nadále sloužila jako synonymum odvozeniny: „...fotografovaný obraz není dílem uměleckým," tvrdil roku 1868 Jan Neruda: „Máme odvrhnout fotografii proto, že není tím uměleckým dílem? Zajisté že ne; ona zprostředkuje nám obrazné seznání věcí, jichž bychom velikými jen oběťmi takto seznávati mohli."[16] V mezinárodní atmosféře velkoměstské Paříže éry fin du siècle otevřel Mucha českou tradici umění fotografie způsobem nedbajícím o konfesi, s níž se obeznámil nejenom v pojetí Edwarda Steichena, jímž byl portrétován.[17] Na Světové výstavě roku 1900 v Paříži byla dobová fotografie bohatě předvedena, včetně české. Leč Muchova idealisticky založená individualita neměla důvod nesouhlasit s Nerudou, byť se časem mnohé měnilo. Stejně jako v euroamerické kultuře vůbec, provázelo secesní model sofistikované fotografie i v českých zemích připodobňování pozitivů k výtvarným dílům. Takzvanými ušlechtilými tisky (i když nikoli výhradně jimi) se fotografové snažili získat postavení umělců, přiznávané obvykle tvůrcům neopakovatelných, inspirovanou rukou dotýkaných artefaktů.[18] Takového sebepotvrzení nebylo Muchovi samozřejmě zapotřebí. Jeho osobní vizuální záznamník z mnichovských studií ve francouzské metropoli jednoduše povýšil na profesionálně užívanou pomůcku. Fotografický aparát se mezi malíři koncem 19. století šířil právě pro svou praktičnost: sáhli po něm Degas, Gauguin, Toulouse-Lautrec, Renoir, Bonnard, Vuillard, Munch, Matisse, Fortuny, Eakins, Kirchner a mnozí další.[19] Modelům bylo třeba platit – v případě ilustrací pohlcovaly náklady polovinu z prvních Muchových honorářů. Zato pohotový aparát dokázal naráz zachytit veškeré potřebné detaily rychle pomíjivých – a pózováním tak jako tak nenapodobitelných – poloh pohybujících se postav (včetně složitých pnutí, jaká provázejí třeba taneční fáze baletních figur). Za tím účelem Mucha angažoval buď specialisty, anebo kohokoli z okolí. Nerozmýšlel se postavit před kameru i sám sebe.

Bizarní bylo nasazení fotografie k znázornění emanací ducha za hypnotických seancí pořádaných s paní Linou de Ferkel, hvězdářem Camille Flammarionem a plukovníkem Albertem de Rochas d'Aiglun, jenž vydal o těchto aktivitách roku 1899 zprávu v časopise Nature a snímky z Muchova ateliéru doprovodil i knižní zpracování svých nálezů.[20]

Fotografií používal Alfons Mucha v krajních případech přímo jako deskriptivního vodítka při skicování rozměrnějších formátů. Pomocí sítě přenášel ze snímků ohyby drapérií, perspektivní zkreslení pokrčených končetin, hru svalstva a proporce vůbec. Jana Brabcová dokládá, že si „na fotografie kompozičního rozvrhu zkoušel barevná řešení“.[21] Experimentoval také s osvětlením a s délkou expozice, zkonstruoval si samospoušť a poznal efektnost pohybu modelu před aparátem, stejně jako rozhýbání komory samotné – Jihofrancouzská krajina z vlaku (kolem 1900). Opakovaná pozitivní zpracování negativů poznamenaných technologickými chybami jsou dodatečným přitakáním účinkům náhod a osvědčují autorův smysl pro kouzlo neočekávaného. K věci patří i zkraty způsobené poškozením emulze nešetrně sušených a skladovaných negativů: součástí jednoho z originálních pozitivů, publikovaného již Annou Fárovou v Osobnostech české fotografie, je obtisk novinové sazby (Komedie, 1908)... Obyčejem jsou srážky nekašírovaného pozadí s kompozicemi vedenými vznešenou představou budoucího díla. Ve prospěch obrysové přesnosti plánovaného výkresu bývá občas prostředí odstíněno bílou plochou – buď za celou postavou, anebo alespoň za ostřeji sledovaným detailem. Příležitostně modelky naznačují pozdvihování imaginárních atributů, které jim přičaruje až umělcova tužka.

Autorovi nedělalo nejmenší problém výrazně se kresbou od pózy zvolené pro fotografování uchýlit, často však předjímal finále natolik přesně, že jsou snímky a jejich grafické dotažení či kombinace více záběrů jednoznačně identifikovatelné.[22] Dochované fotografie buď stvrzují věrnost obrazů modelům, anebo naopak dokumentují případy, kdy pro plakát na představení pózovalo protagonistce docela nepodobné alter ego. Fotografická příprava tedy umocňuje bohatou představivost podloženou zručností: „Postupně se u otce,“ vzpomíná Jiří Mucha, „vyvinula zcela pravidelná pracovní metoda. Jakoukoliv novou práci si nejprve načrtl. Pak – pokud již neměl vhodnou fotografii – si podle kresby pořídil fotografický záznam. [...] Nefotografoval ale modely pouze pro určitou plánovanou kresbu. Improvizoval před kamerou různé varianty a vytvářel si tak bohatý archiv.“[23]

Zázračně okamžitý obraz, jak charakterizoval fotografii Edgar Degas, měl přímý inspirativní vliv na impresionisty, těžící z momentek specifické úkazy: uvolněné kompozice, nevypočitatelné přetínání postav okraji obrazu, splývání pozadí v mělké hloubce ostrosti... Jestliže se impresionisté snažili slogan Camille Corota „poddat se prvnímu dojmu“ alespoň iluzivně roznítit v představě diváka, vyznával Alfons Mucha poněkud jinou strategii. Vznik dynamických, typicky muchovských kompozic přibližuje Jiří Mucha takto: „Každý obrázek“ [rozumí se zde fotografická skica] „neomylně prozrazuje svůj původ, na každém je již zcela zjevný styl, dokonce i malířská technika, plošnost nebo trojrozměrnost, důraz na barvu nebo na linii, dekorativnost nebo tvrdá realita. Takové fotografie si otec pořizoval celý život, takže jsem nakonec musel nastoupit před kameru i já. Byly to vždycky dlouhé a obtížné procedury, než jsem vystihl patřičnou polohu a než otec se zaujetím odpalovače kosmické rakety stiskl spoušť.“[24]

Anna Fárová zařadila Alfonse Muchu mezi prvořadé osobnosti historie fotografie s odůvodněním, že výtvarný sloh pronikl do jeho prací s pomocným médiem natolik, až se „bezděčně [...] občas stávají svébytnými fotografickými realizacemi“.[25] Muchovy snímky věru nepostrádají estetickou soběstačnost. A odpozorovaný, kresbou kultivovaný smysl pro výmluvnost postoje i gesta zhodnocuje autor také v momentkách. Nad obvyklý standard Muchových cestopisných záběrů ovšem vyniká „reportáž“ z carského Ruska. Vysvětlení lze nalézt v monografii od Jany Brabcové, která uvádí: „Je známo mnoho fotografií z ruského pobytu, jež jsou vydávány za práci Muchovu, podle záznamů paní Muchové však snímky pořídil francouzský fotograf, který Muchu do Ruska doprovázel.“[26] Nicméně konečný účel fotografií jakožto předloh k realizaci určitého malířského záměru byl od počátku přítomen v té míře, že udával jak výběr, tak podání modelů pro chystané plátno. A je to vliv Muchovy režie, pro nějž mají tyto záběry místo v monografii jeho fotografií: stejně tak zařazujeme autoportréty, u nichž je sporné, zda je mohl exponovat samospouští... Pozadí figur fotografovaných v Moskvě obvykle nehrálo valnou roli: bývá neostré – s výjimkou siluety chrámu Vasila Blaženého, následně vévodící také malbě. I tak je však soubor snímků ze studijní cesty do Ruska konzervou historických reálií obecného významu. Tandem fotografujících cizinců přitahoval zvýšenou pozornost – vždyť turismus nebýval v oněch končinách roku 1913 zažitou zvyklostí. I když některé záběry vznikly nepozorovaně, nezdá se, že by se fotografování odbývalo skrytě. Kameře jsou věnovány zpytavé pohledy – někdy vstřícnější, někdy méně... Skupinky místy improvizovaně pózují, schoulená žebračka si šátkem zakrývá tvář... Malíř posléze věrně vystihl ruskou odevzdanost vůči zdánlivě svrchovaným – a v logice věci pak neovlivnitelným – úradkům. Ale venkovsky vybavení poutníci s tlumoky a cestovními holemi, to jsou už na první pohled mimořádně jasně viděné sociální typy. Zrovna takové je Mucha potřeboval pro své záměry, popsané v komentáři k Zrušení nevolnictví na Rusi (1914): „Lid zůstává – rokuje – přemýšlí – Bohu děkuje – blahořečí – své nové svobodě avšak ještě nerozumí.“[27] Naléhavost ruské exkurze prozrazuje také další reminiscence, tentokrát artikulovaná s desetiletým odstupem v rozměrném oleji, jenž vyjadřuje psychologii úlevy od pozemského údělu, nechávající osud přecházet v nevyhnutelně nejhorší konec. Název kolísá od Ruska přes Hvězdu, Sibiř a Zimní noc až po málo pravděpodobnou Enigmatickou ženu v divočině (1923).

Dvacetidílná Slovanská epopej však přišla pozdě. Třebaže nemělo spojení iluzivnosti se symbolickými významy (barev, námětů i jejich nositelů) prodlužovat historizující akademický pseudorealismus, nýbrž abstrahovat, působí v nadživotních měřítcích vyvedená apoteóza Slovanstva plochým dojmem. Ideologickou nálož konfrontace panslavismu s germánstvím oslabuje srovnání Epopeje s návrhy dekorativních panneau do Německého divadla v New Yorku, provedenými stejnou technikou, a hlavně – s obdobnou manýrou. Spíše literární výklad než díla sama jsou tlumočníkem Muchou zamýšlených významů. Vždyť podtitul Zrušení nevolnictví na Rusi zní Svobodná práce – osnovou států.[28] Fotografické snímky si naproti tomu zachovaly svěžest, ba víc – osvědčily schopnost aktualizace. Stačí uvést záběr znázorňující jednu z instalací transkontinentálně stěhovaného ateliéru, k jehož vybavení patřily i těžké krabice plné negativů neustále narůstajícího skleněného archivu. Záběr pracovny zaplněné do posledního místečka ostatně zdárně rozmnožuje plejádu pestrých muchovských pohlednic. Chaotická prostora na rue du Val-de-Grâce – osazená květy, od stropu splývajícími rouchy, výstředním trůnem a otočným zrcadlem, lebečními kostmi i přepodivně odívanou modlou – vyznívá jako tekuté surrealistické zátiší: figurky atleta, slona a Krista, preparovaný lední medvěd, harmonium a postroj s koňskou hlavou, devocionálie a osvětlovadla, hřbety bibliotéky a krbová římsa s fotografickou galerií…

Za Muchova života disponoval fotografický snímek ještě neotřeseným puncem autentičnosti. Jeho nadlidská přesnost nebyla lhostejná zejména výtvarníkovi, soustředěnému k vysněnému ideálu krásy natolik, že dokázal ztrácet ze zřetele objektivní fakta. Muchův životní příběh oplývá překvapivými výstupy, občas až anekdotickými, do nichž se vrhal s chronickou přehlíživostí. „Otec," vypráví Jiří Mucha, „měl přímo fantastickou schopnost plést si lidi, nepoznávat je a zaměňovat jednu osobu s druhou. Byl na to tak zvyklý, že později v New Yorku místo na party pořádanou na jeho počest zabloudil do jiného domu, kde náhodou měli také hosty, zůstal dvě hodiny a vůbec mu nepřipadalo divné, že nezná jediného člověka."[29]

Byly to zejména ženy, jež Mucha „povznášel a přetvářel v neosobní nositelky veškeré krásy".[30] Modelkám, které skicoval „na živo", zakrýval prý rouškou tvář, pokud ho příliš rušila. Při fotografování to nedělal, naopak některé litografie těží uhrančivost pohledu zobrazených figur právě z pomocných snímků. Zorničky soustředěné původně na objektiv (a spoutané nehybností nezbytnou při druhdy delších ateliérových expozicích) vysílají pojednou signál zaměřený k pozorovateli plakátu, kalendáře či panneau – příkladně Růže (1897) nebo Smaragd (1900). Vyhlášené Muchovy krásky působí smyslně, ale nikoli v prvním plánu – třeba vyzývavým výrazem. Průraznost tu zaručuje prolnutí fantazijní vize s jejím anatomicky hodnověrným podáním. Má-li přihlížející pocit, jako by dávnou pin-up girl očima svlékal, dostal se do vleku kreslířova fotografického zření: vypjatá póza bývala předem fixována snímkem právě proto, aby se pod zákresem šatstva dala uhlídat pomyslná nahota. Zde je též zřídlo profánní roviny Muchových aktů coby sbírky erotických povyražení a kuriozit.[31]

Fotografie Alfonse Muchy znamenají přínos dějinám oboru nejen pro sugestivitu prosakování výtvarného myšlení do příbuzné disciplíny – jakkoli čerpají valný díl svého půvabu z původní umělecké intence. Ve změněném kulturním kontextu přijímáme snímky jako svéprávné miniatury. Jsou nabity sympatickou dynamikou, syrovostí a autenticitou, jež nemohl tvůrce v jiném médiu uplatnit stejně bezprostředně. Se samozřejmostí ducha fotografie, mnohdy protikladného uhlazenosti výtvarného díla, se Mucha dotýká okolnosti, že pro umění přelomu 19. a 20. století byla přednostním úkolem rozluka s minulostí a nalezení vztahu k budoucnosti. Pro to máme zostřenou citlivost, neboť zlom tisíciletí si také říká o zaujetí postoje... Alfons Mucha tvořil na pomezí dvou epoch a obě reprezentuje. Při hledání nové klasicity se jako výtvarník vztahoval k tradici; zájem o jeho fotografickou pozůstalost pak dokládá, že to není až malba, ale hned snímek, jenž zároveň se zobrazeným jevem vykazuje jemu přikládaný smysl.

Poznámky

1 Alfons Mucha: *Slovanská epopeje*, Praha, Česká grafická unie v Praze 1930, s. 3.

2 Jana Brabcová: *Alfons Mucha*, Praha, Panorama 1980, nestránkováno.

3 Srov. -rna.: Mucha Alfons, in: *Ottův slovník naučný nové doby. Dodatky k velikému Ottovu slovníku naučnému IV/1*, Praha, Novina 1936, s. 377.

4 Srov. Petr Wittlich: *Alfons Mucha. Pastely, plakáty, kresby a fotografie. Výstava v Císařské konírně Pražského hradu*, London, Nadace Mucha 1994, s. 18.

5 Jana Brabcová dává tuto etapu tvorby do souvislosti s faustovskými výjevy z časů mnichovského pobytu. Srov. Jana Brabcová: Hledání další cesty, in: Jiří Kotalík (ed.): *Alfons Mucha (1860–1939)*, Praha, Národní galerie 1980, s. 85.

6 Zde je na místě vzpomenout příkladu Brita Williama Morrise, jehož první veřejná přednáška roku 1877 měla název The Decorative Arts. Srov. Alfons Mucha: *Tři projevy o životě a díle*, Brno, Brněnský klub 1936, s. 9: „Umění je jedinou potravou hladovících a žíznících duší zde na zemi. Kdo je krmí odpadky, zasévá všechny možné choroby v duši lidu."

7 Jiří Mucha: strojopis bez nadpisu, s. 4–5. Studie je uvedena zmínkou o pětadevadesátiletém odstupu od mnichovských záběrů, z čehož lze usuzovat, že text vznikl v roce 1981. Kratší verze stati vyšla v úvodu katalogu *Alfons Mucha fotografem* v červnu 1982. Pořadatelem expozice v Chebském muzeu bylo Uměleckoprůmyslové museum v Praze, autorem koncepce výstavy i katalogu byl kurátor Jiří Řapek. Jeho zásluhou došlo k určení datací a motivů další velké části snímků (mimo jiné odhalil záludný fakt, že Mucha v různých letech převlékal modelky do stejných kostýmů vlastní garderoby). Patří mu rovněž dík za uchování citovaného spisu Jiřího Muchy, který je důležitý pro stanovení začátku fotografické tvorby Alfonse Muchy, neboť opravuje dříve publikovanou chybu. Podle monografie Grahama Ovendena vznikly první Muchovy záběry při pracovním pobytu v rakouském hlavním městě na negativy čtvercového formátu 7 x 7 cm – viz Tržní náměstí ve Vídni (1880), převzaté Vladimírem Remešem jako obrazový doprovod k referátu o britské monografii Alfons Mucha jako fotograf, in: *Revue Fotografie* 21, 1977, č. 4, s. 23; tento údaj pronikl i do další literatury – Daniela Mrázková & Vladimír Remeš: *Tschechoslowakische Fotografen 1900–1940*, Leipzig, VEB Fotokinoverlag 1983, s. 10; Daniela Mrázková: *Příběh fotografie*, Praha, Mladá fronta 1985, s. 28; Daniela Mrázková & Vladimír Remeš: *Cesty československé fotografie*, Praha, Mladá fronta 1989, s. 34–35; Pavel Scheufler: Mucha Alfons, in: *Encyklopedie českých a slovenských fotografů*, Praha, ASCO 1993, s. 244–245; jiný snímek stejné série s popisem Mnichov (1880) vyšel k článku Jiřího Muchy Alfons Mucha, *Fotografie* 23, 1979, č. 3, s. 54. Teprve v chebském katalogu *Alfons Mucha fotografem*, vydaném za spoluautorství Jiřího Muchy, nacházíme záběr identického prostředí, určený jako Pohled z okna pokoje Alfonse Muchy v Mnichově v sousedství Amalienstrasse (1886). Jiří Mucha k tomu v uvedeném strojopisu poznamenal: „První fotografie mého otce vznikly před devadesáti pěti roky v Mnichově. Nevíme, jakého tehdy používal aparátu – soudíme, že vypůjčeného – a fotografoval z okna svého pokoje v Amalienstrasse život v ulici. [...] Čtvercový aparát se asi vrátil majiteli, protože z let 1887 až 1892, kdy studoval na akademii Julian a později Colarossi, se žádné fotografie nedochovaly."

8 Anna Fárová: *Osobnosti české fotografie I/ ze sbírek Uměleckoprůmyslového musea v Praze*, katalogy Galerie výtvarného umění v Roudnici nad Labem 1973 a Uměleckoprůmyslového musea v Praze 1974.

9 Srov. Jan Mlčoch: tisková zpráva k výstavě *Alfons Mucha: Fotografické studie*, Galerie Josefa Sudka v Praze, 3. VI. 1998. Při této výstavě jedenadvaceti originálů došlo péčí kurátorů Jana Mlčocha a Petra Štembery k určení několika dříve neidentifikovaných záběrů. Nejspíše není správná informace uvedená v komuniké, že se akce stává „vůbec první samostatnou výstavou původních fotografií tohoto světového umělce"; *Československá fotografie* referovala roku 1978 o expozici 40 snímků v Italském kulturním institutu; název výstavy sice zůstává nezjištěn, fotografie však pocházely z majetku architekta Paola Porthoghesiho, který je přivezl z Itálie a vystavil u příležitosti svých pražských přednášek.

10 Cit. dle Jiří Kotalík: Alfons Mucha a české umění, in: Jiří Kotalík (ed.): *Alfons Mucha (1860–1939)*, Praha, Národní galerie 1980, s. 38.

11 Jiří Mucha: *Alfons Mucha*, Praha, Mladá fronta 1982, s. 228.

12 Tamtéž. Pronikavost postřehu vynikne při srovnání formulace problému s tezemi ve stati Vlastimila Jiříka Vztah výtvarných oborů k prostoru a času. Několik poznámek k umělecko-historickému pojmu prostoru a času, in: *Filosofický časopis* 30, 1982, č. 3, s. 490–495. K režírování živých obrazů se později Alfons Mucha skutečně dostal. Srov. Jiří Mucha: *Alfons Mucha*, Praha, Mladá fronta 1982, s. 416–421.

13 Jiří Mucha: *Alfons Mucha*, Praha, Mladá fronta 1982, s. 87. Srov. Antonín Dufek: Společnost před kamerou I. Žánr a reportáž v XIX. století, *Československá fotografie* 27, 1976, č. 6, s. 269.

14 Vydavatel a redaktor Lumíra, básník Josef Václav Sládek, byl rovněž vášnivým fotografem. S Muchou ho pojil i mezinárodní rozhled, v posledku navíc domicil ve Zbiroze. Srov. J. V. Sládek: Fotografie momentní, *Lumír* 14, 1886, září, s. 431–432: „Fotografické aparáty začínají se v poslední době také u nás šířiti, kasta dilettantův se vzmáhá. Bohužel jest většinou výzbroj jejich tak bídný, že na obraz dobrého zrna téměř ani pomysliti nelze."

15 To neznamená, že nemá následníky. Srov. Antonín Nový: Mucha Girls (1974) – viz *Encyklopedie českých a slovenských fotografů*, Praha, ASCO 1993, s. 259–260. Zde jsou i odkazy na další literaturu.

16 Cit. dle Jan Neruda: Umění není fotografie, in: Vladimír Dostál (ed.): *Čítanka z dějin české a slovenské estetiky XIX. století*, Praha, Československý spisovatel 1972, s. 104. Srov. Pavel Scheufler: *Pražské fotografické ateliéry 1839–1918. II/ 1889–1918*, Praha, Muzeum hlavního města Prahy 1989, s. 29: „Ve fotografii ovšem přímost obrazového sdělení u aktu působila nadmíru dráždivě a podle soudobých představ nebyla schopna vzhledem k povaze fotografie umělecké stylizace. [...] Teprve práce v duchu piktorialismu přinesly obecné zhodnocení této tvorby a možnost prezentace fotografických aktů na veřejnosti." Kontinuitu nerudovského postoje reprezentují V. V. Štech, Josef Čapek a Karel Teige. Srov. Antonín Dufek: Fotografie dvacátých let, in: *Dějiny českého výtvarného umění 1890–1938 (IV/2)*, Praha, Academia 1998, s. 213–214.

17 Srov. Anna Fárová: *Osobnosti české fotografie I/ ze sbírek Uměleckoprůmyslového musea v Praze*, Praha, Uměleckoprůmyslové museum 1974.

18 Srov. Antonín Dufek: Fotografie 1890–1918, in: *Dějiny českého výtvarného umění 1890–1938 (IV/1)*, Praha, Academia 1998, s. 195 a násl. Jak složitá vedla cesta z této druhé vlny piktorialismu k dalšímu pokroku, ukazuje příběh Edwarda Steichena, jenž se s Muchou seznámil hned při

příchodu do Paříže roku 1900. Srov. Jiří Mucha: *Alfons Mucha*, Praha, Mladá fronta 1982, s. 252. Viz též René d'Harnoncourt: *Steichen Fotograf*, Praha, Galerie „d" 1969. K vymezení pojmu secesní piktorialismus viz Antonín Dufek: Piktorialismus a jeho prehistorie v českých zemích, *Československá fotografie* 27, 1976, č. 4, s. 173; Vladimír Birgus: Piktorialismus, čili zmatek nad zmatek, *Československá fotografie* 31, 1980, č. 10, s. 446; Antonín Dufek: Z historie české fotografie (od r. 1890 do r. 1918), *Fotografie* 28, 1984, č. 4, s. 36; Pavel Scheufler: *Pražské fotografické ateliéry 1839–1918. II/ 1889–1918*, Praha 1989, s. 15.

19 Srov. Michel Frizot: *Historie de voir. Le médium des temps modernes (1880–1939)*, Paris, Centre National de la Photographie 1989, s. 26; Elvire Perego: Privatsphäre und geheime Gärten. Der Künstler als Amateurfotograf, in: Michel Frizot (ed.): *Neue Geschichte der Fotografie*, Köln, Könemann 1998, s. 336. Poměry na české scéně popisuje Pavel Scheufler: *Přehled vývoje fotografie v Praze v letech 1839–1918. II/ 1889–1918*, Praha, Státní pedagogické nakladatelství 1991, s. 62–64.

20 Albert de Rochas d'Aiglun: *Les sentiments, la musique et le geste*, Grenoble, H. Falque et F. Perrin 1900. Tuto stránku Muchova působení dobře vysvětluje již citovaný katalog – Petr Wittlich: *Alfons Mucha. Pastely, plakáty, kresby a fotografie. Výstava v Císařské konírně Pražského hradu*, London, Nadace Mucha 1994, s. 18–19.

21 Jana Brabcová: Cesta ke slávě, in: Jiří Kotalík (ed.): *Alfons Mucha (1860–1939)*, Praha, Národní galerie 1980, s. 42. Pozoruhodná je i dokreslená fotografie fasády Fouquetova klenotnictví v tomtéž svazku.

22 Srovnáním fotografické a grafické pozůstalosti se zabývá publikace trojice editorů: Jiří Mucha, Marina Henderson, Aaron Scharf: *Alphonse Mucha: Posters and Photographs*, London, Academy Editions 1971.

23 Jiří Mucha: strojopis bez názvu, s. 4–5.

24 Jiří Mucha: *Alfons Mucha*, Praha, Mladá fronta 1982, s. 108–109.

25 Anna Fárová: *Osobnosti české fotografie I / ze sbírek Uměleckoprůmyslového musea v Praze*, Galerie výtvarného umění v Roudnici nad Labem 1973, nestránkováno.

26 Jana Brabcová: *Alfons Mucha*, Praha, Svoboda 1996, s. 72.

27 Alfons Mucha: *Katalog výstavy obrazů Alfonse M. Muchy z cyklu Slovanská epopeje*, Praha, Klementinum 1919, nestránkováno.

28 Alfons Mucha: *Slovanská epopeje*, Praha, Česká grafická unie v Praze 1930, s. 43.

29 Jiří Mucha: *Alfons Mucha*, Praha, Mladá fronta 1982, s. 84.

30 Tamtéž, s. 187.

31 Jak dlouho zůstávaly v české fotografii Muchovy snímky obnažených modelů ojedinělé, vyplývá z článku začínajícího větou: „Fotografický akt je popelkou, o českém původním ani nemluvě." Srov. Viktor R.: O fotografickém aktu u nás, *Fotografický obzor* 42, 1934, č. 7, s. 101–103. Publikace prvního aktu dosáhl ve jmenovaném časopisu František Drtikol roku 1911. Mucha o generaci předcházel umělce *České fotografické moderny*. Srov. katalog děl Vladimíra Jindřicha Bufky, Františka Drtikola, Karla (Carola) Nováka a Josefa Antona Trčky, připravený kurátory Zdeňkem Kirschnerem a Josefem Kroutvorem v Uměleckoprůmyslovém museu v Praze roku 1989.

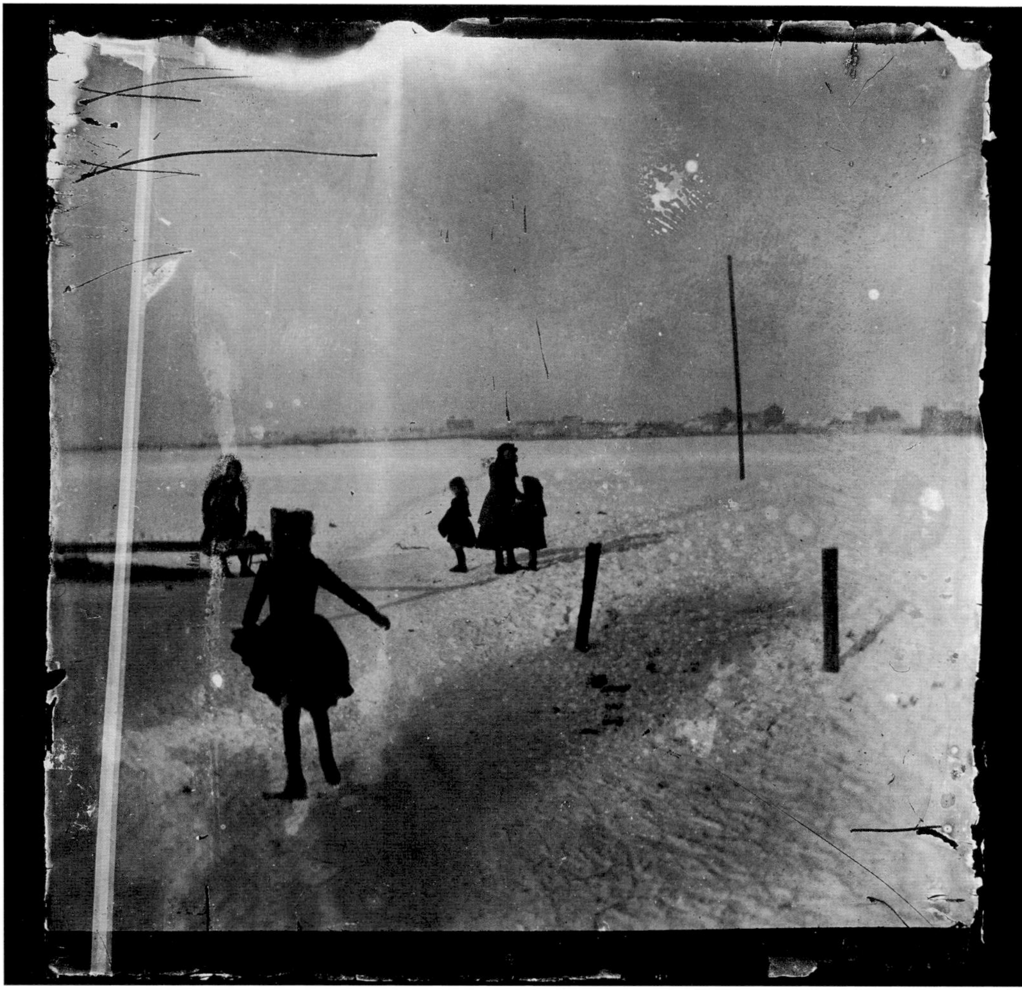

1 **Skating in Austria / Bruslení v Rakousku** 1887

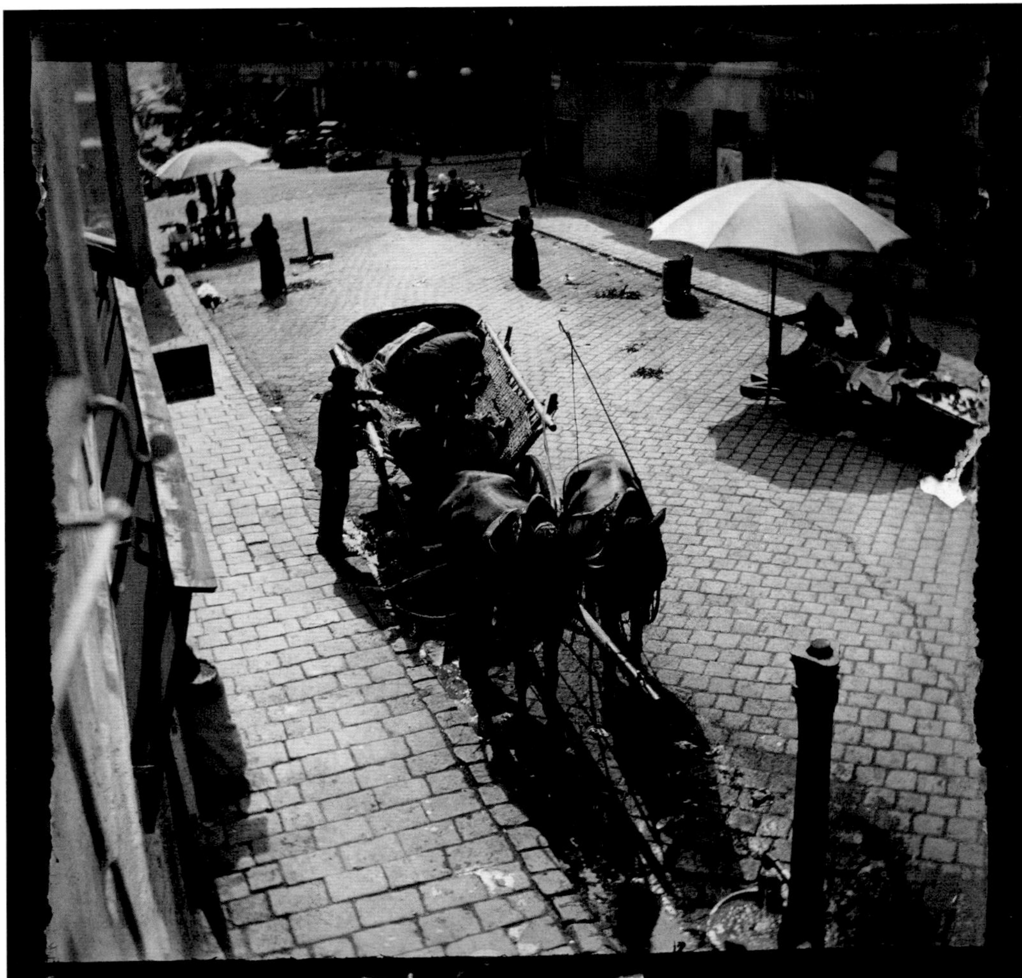

2 **München** 1886

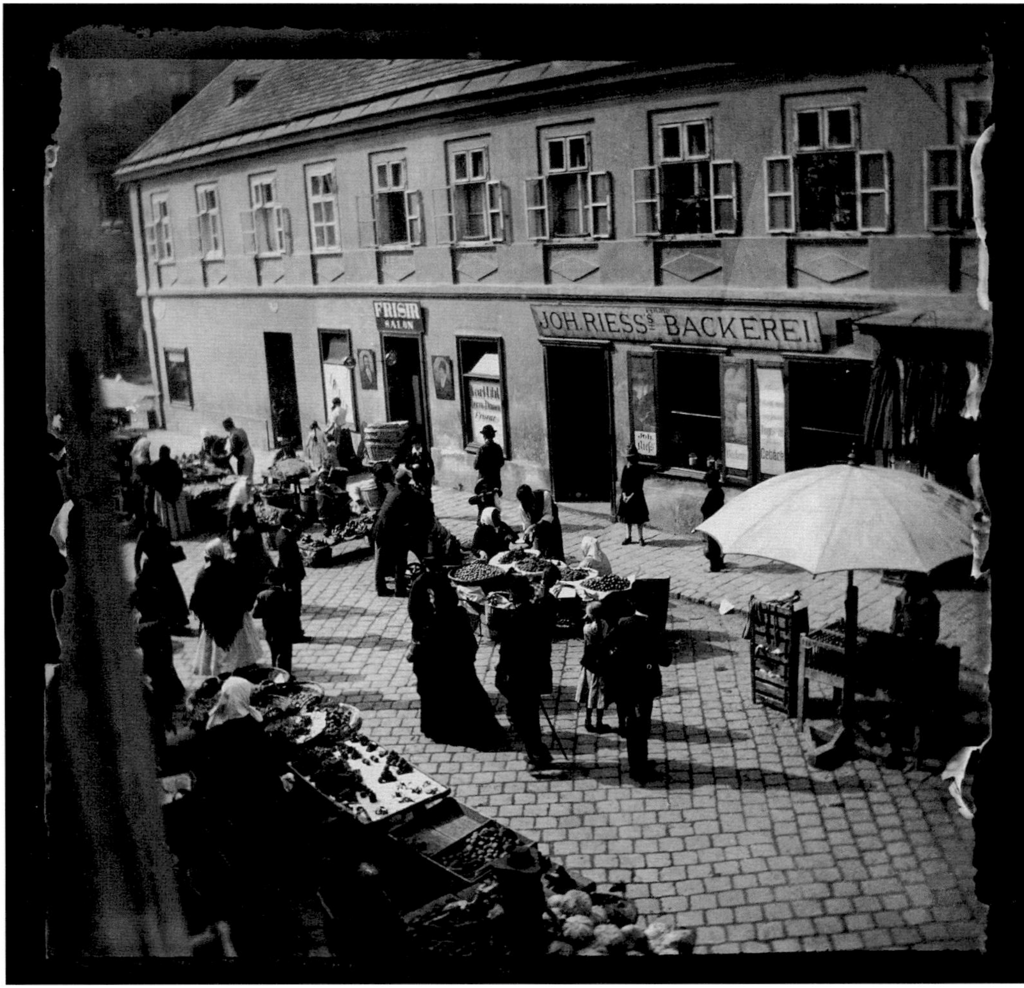

3 **München** 1886

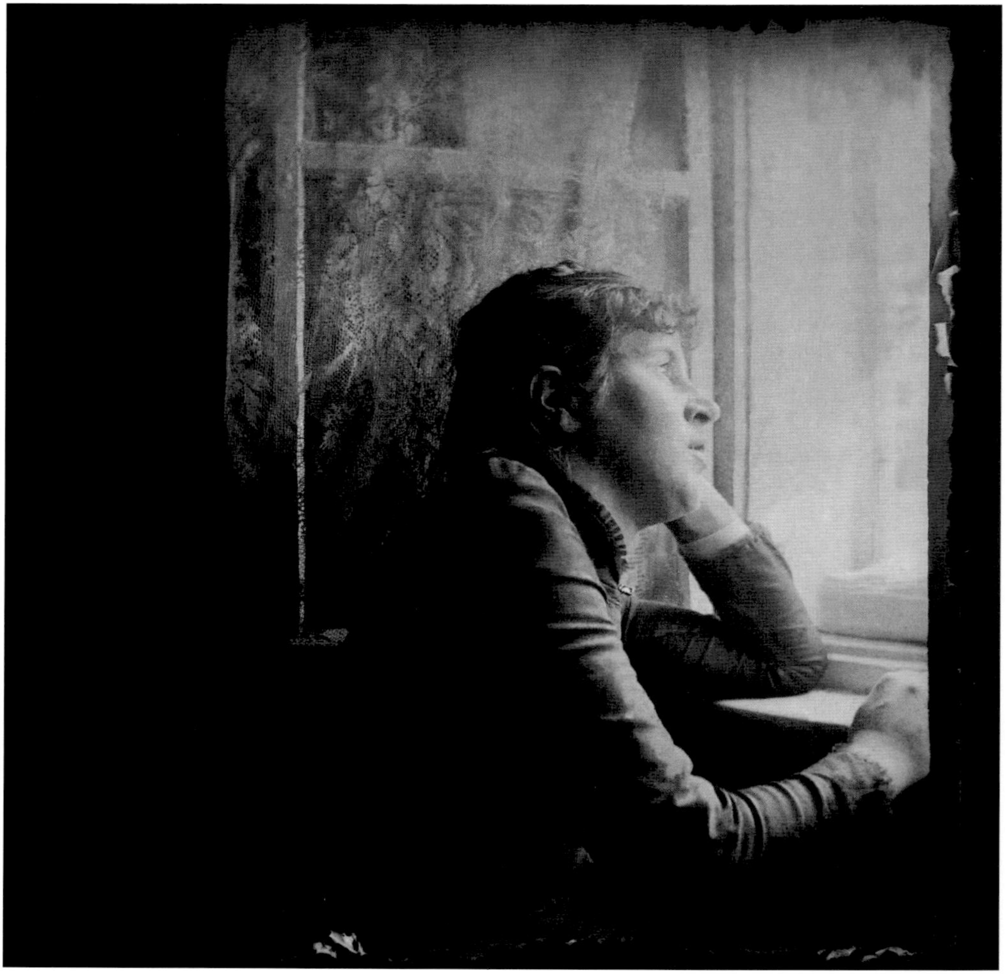

4 **München** 1886

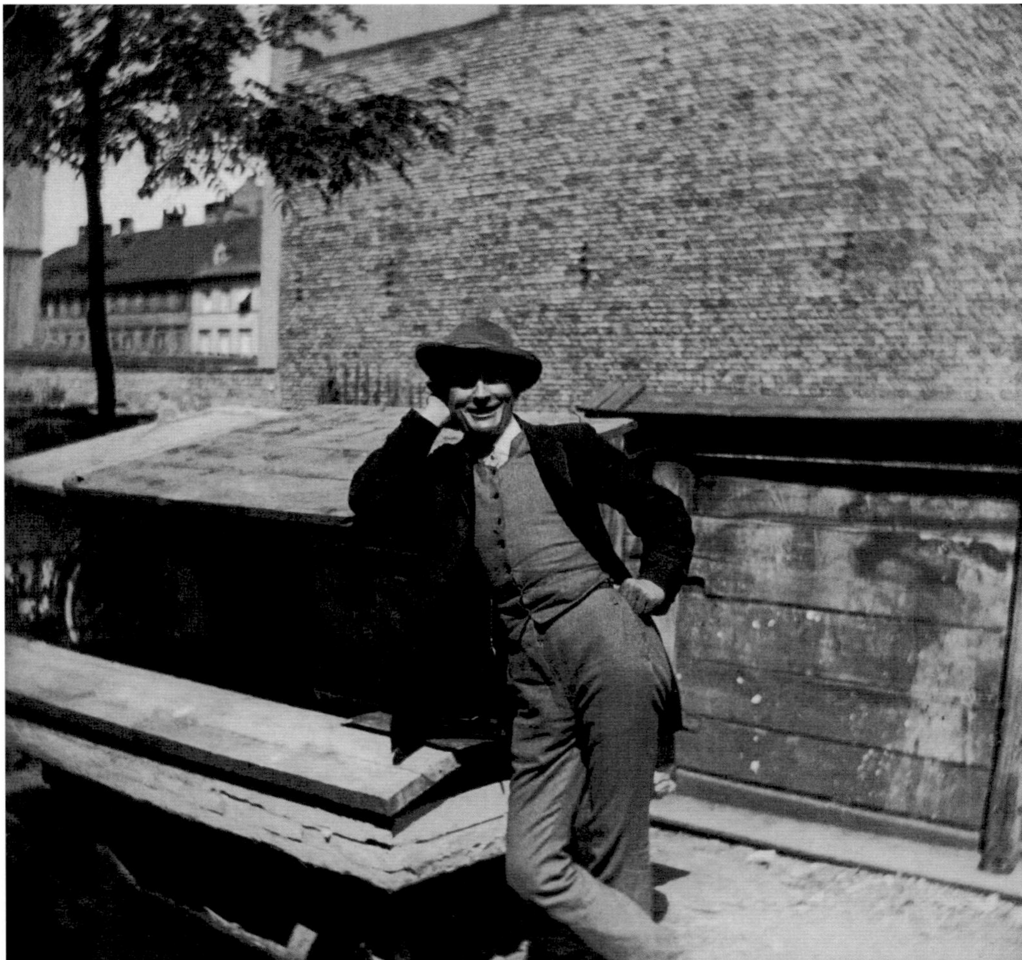

5 **The Painter K. V. Mašek / Malíř K. V. Mašek** c. 1887

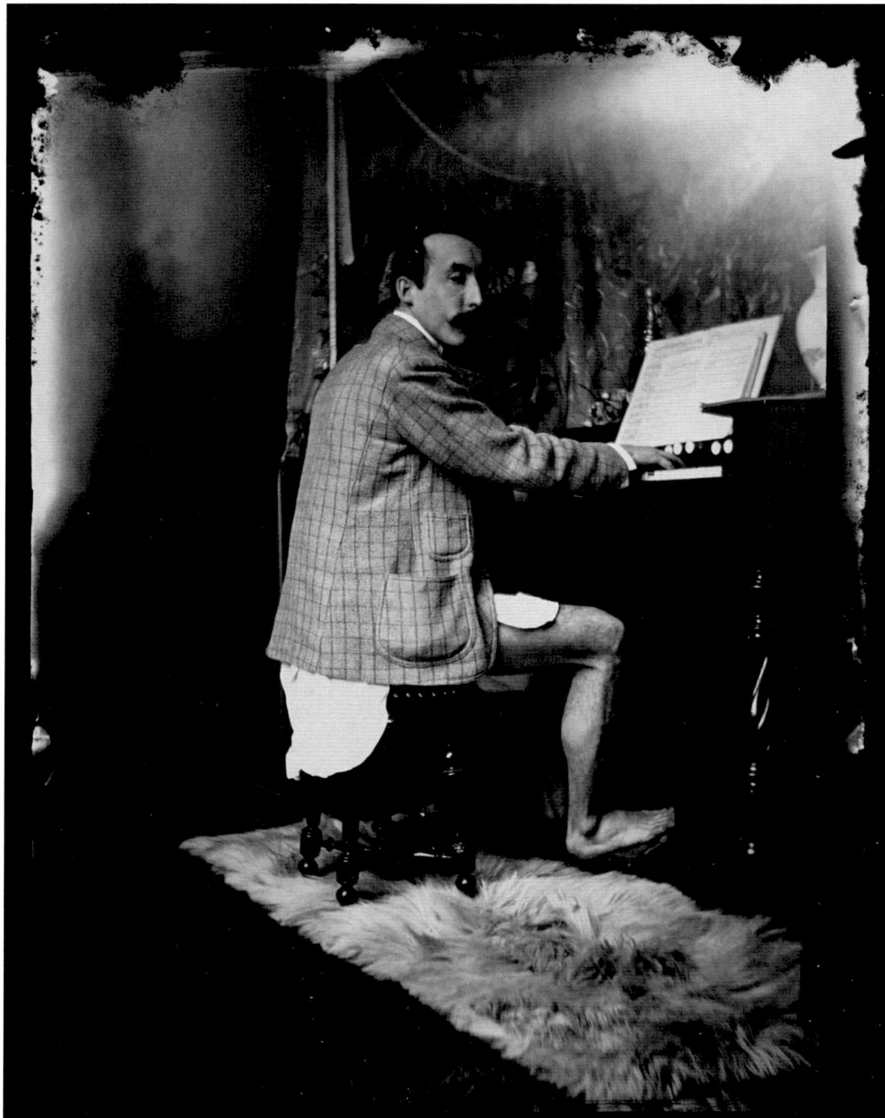

6 **Paul Gauguin** c. 1895

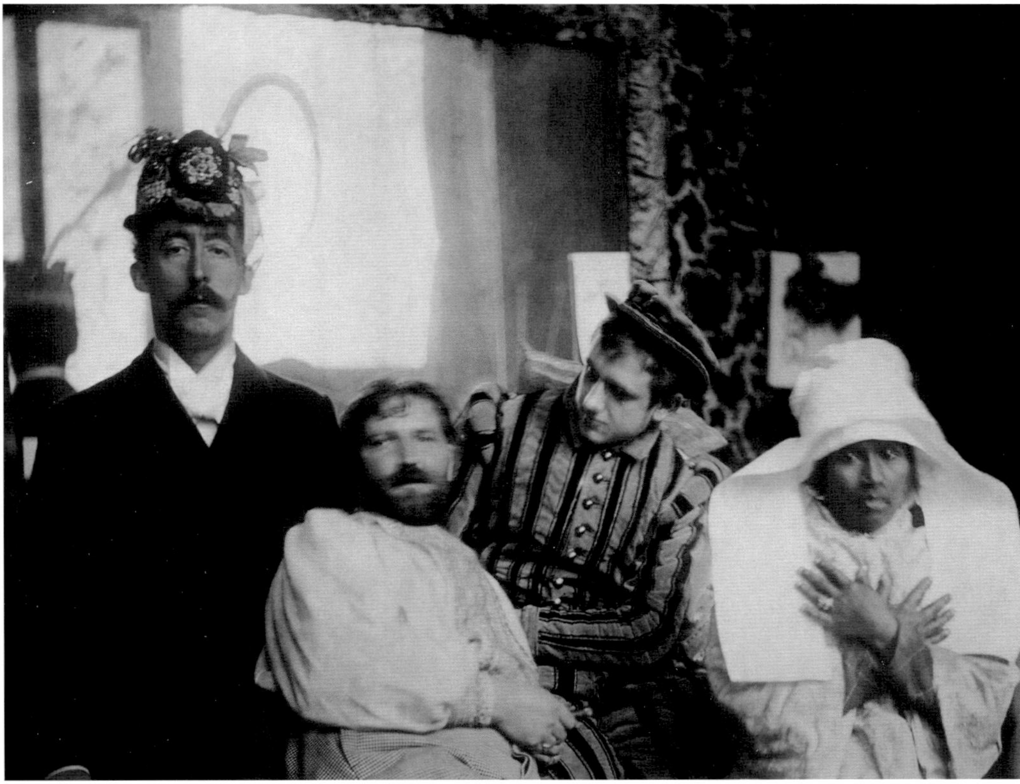

7 **Paul Gauguin, Alfons Mucha, Luděk Marold, Annah la Javanaise, Paris** 1896

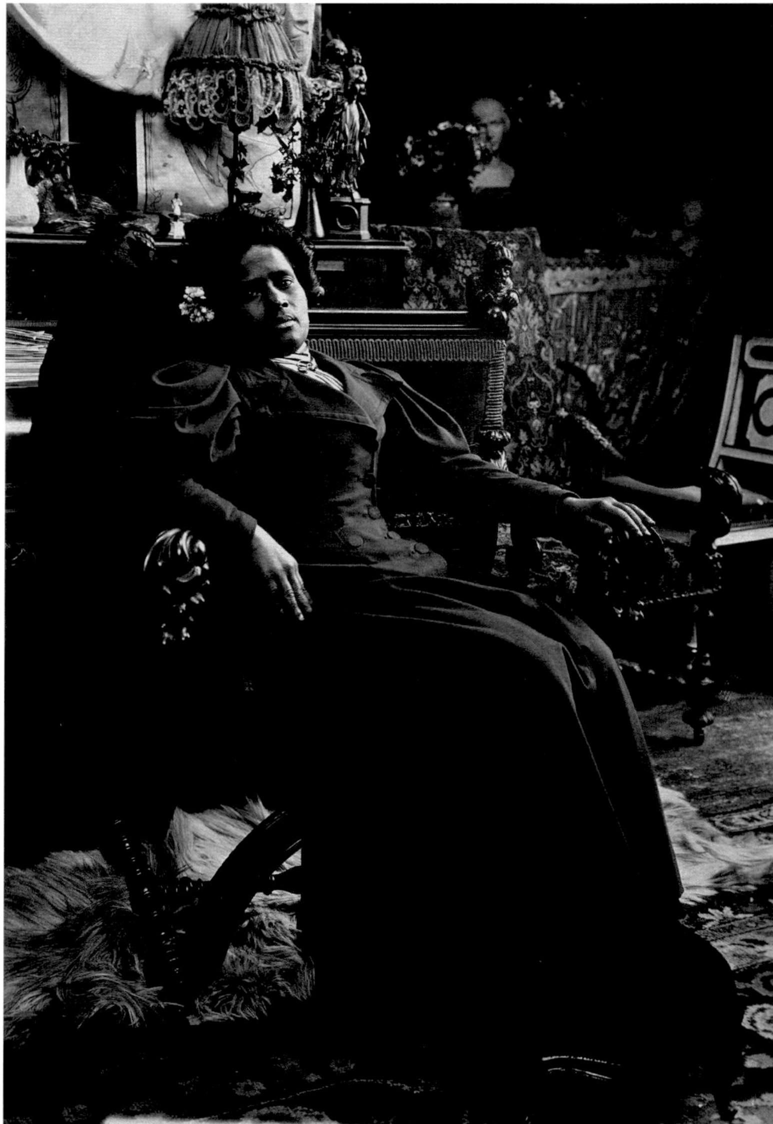

8 **Annah la Javanaise** c.1896

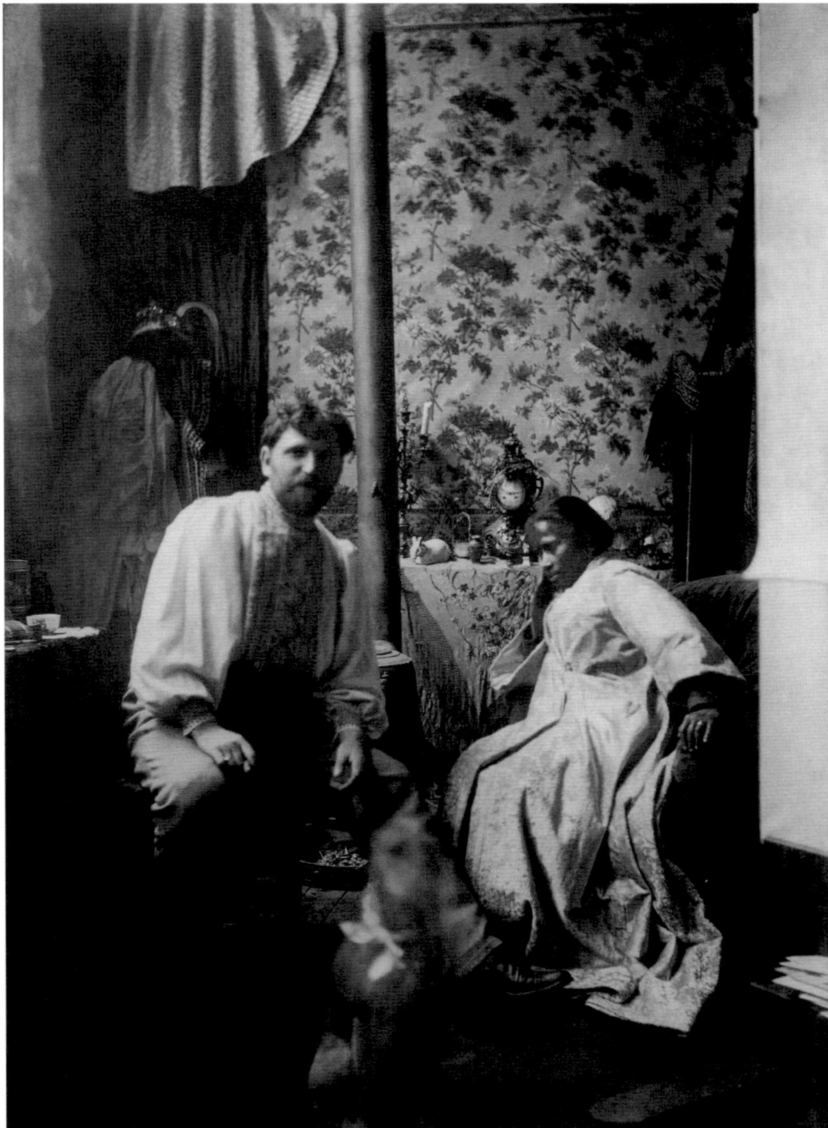

9 **Alfons Mucha, Annah la Javanaise** c. 1896

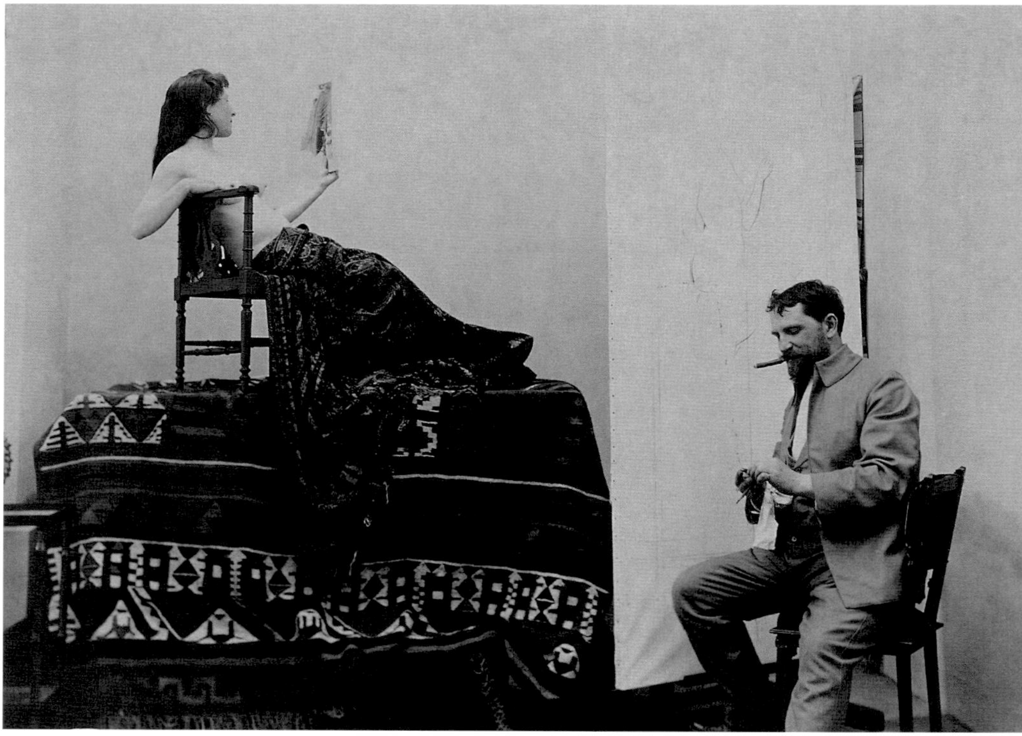

10 **Alfons Mucha in the Studio, Paris / Alfons Mucha v ateliéru, Paříž** 1897

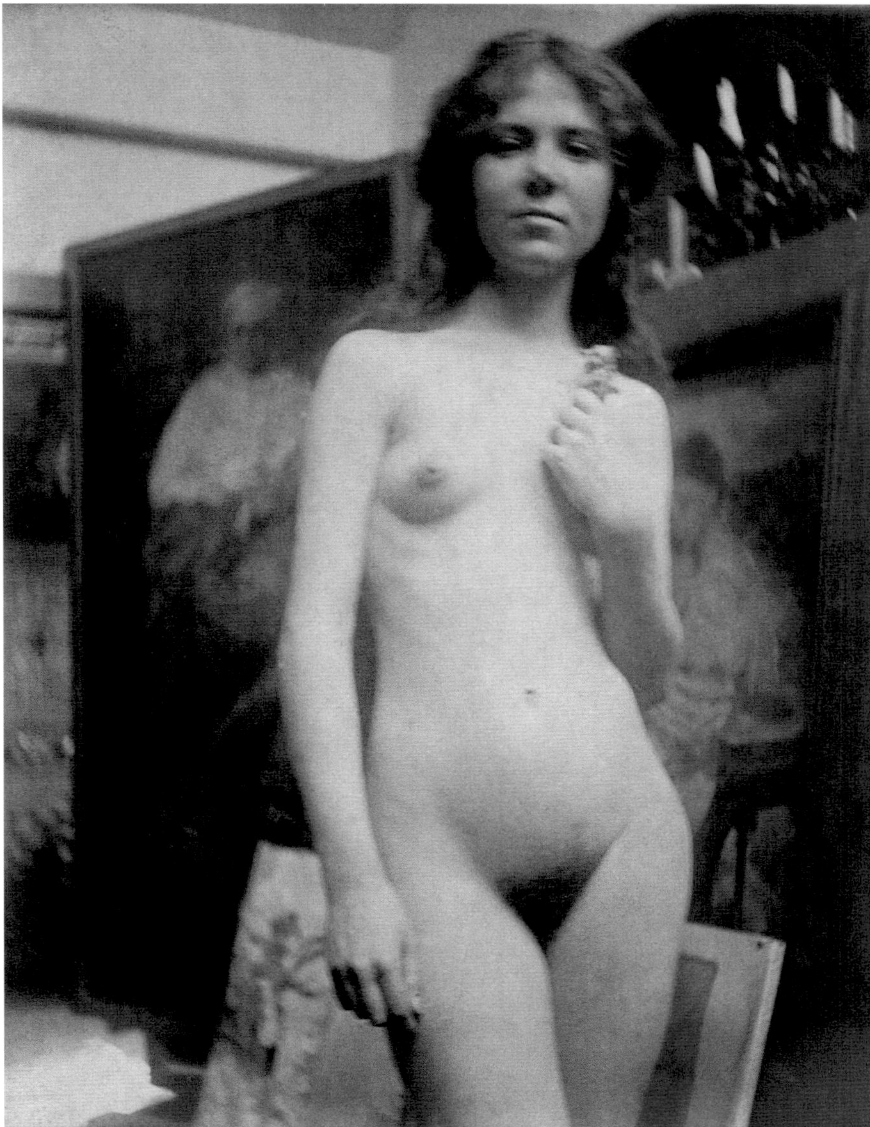

11 **Paris** 1897

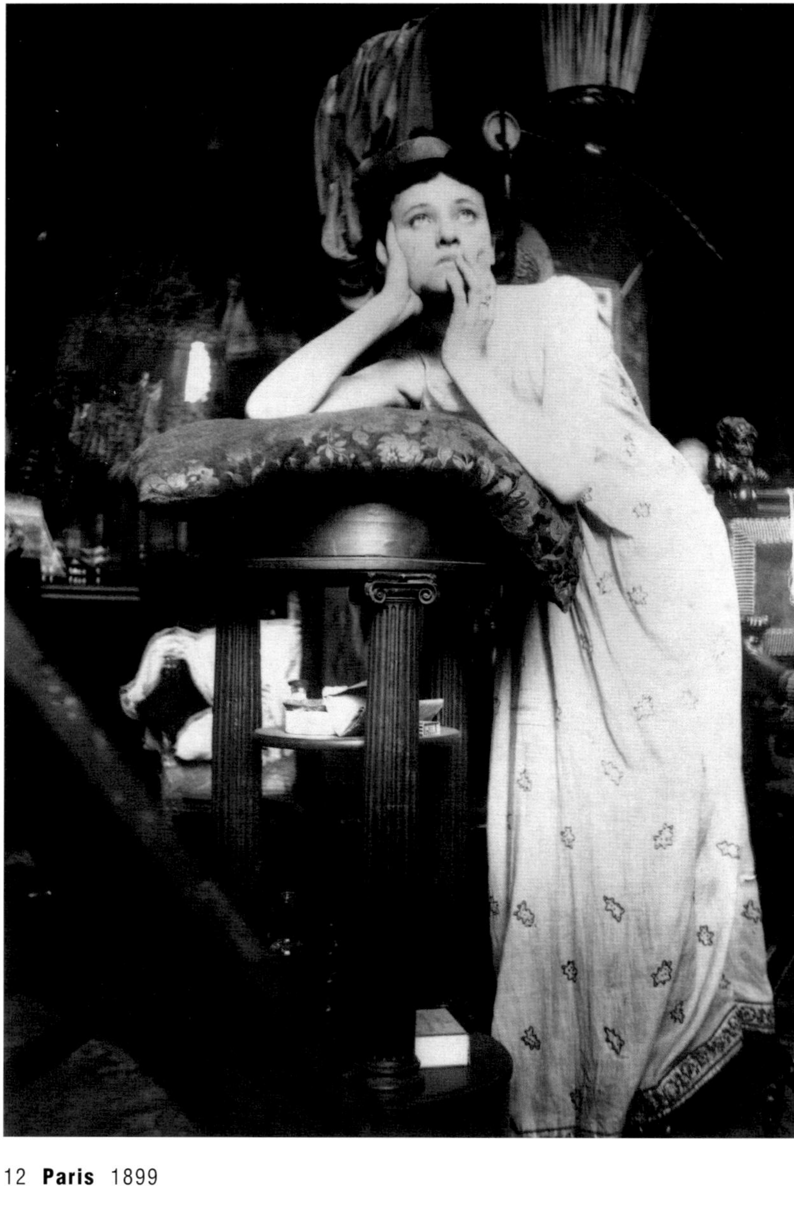

12 **Paris** 1899

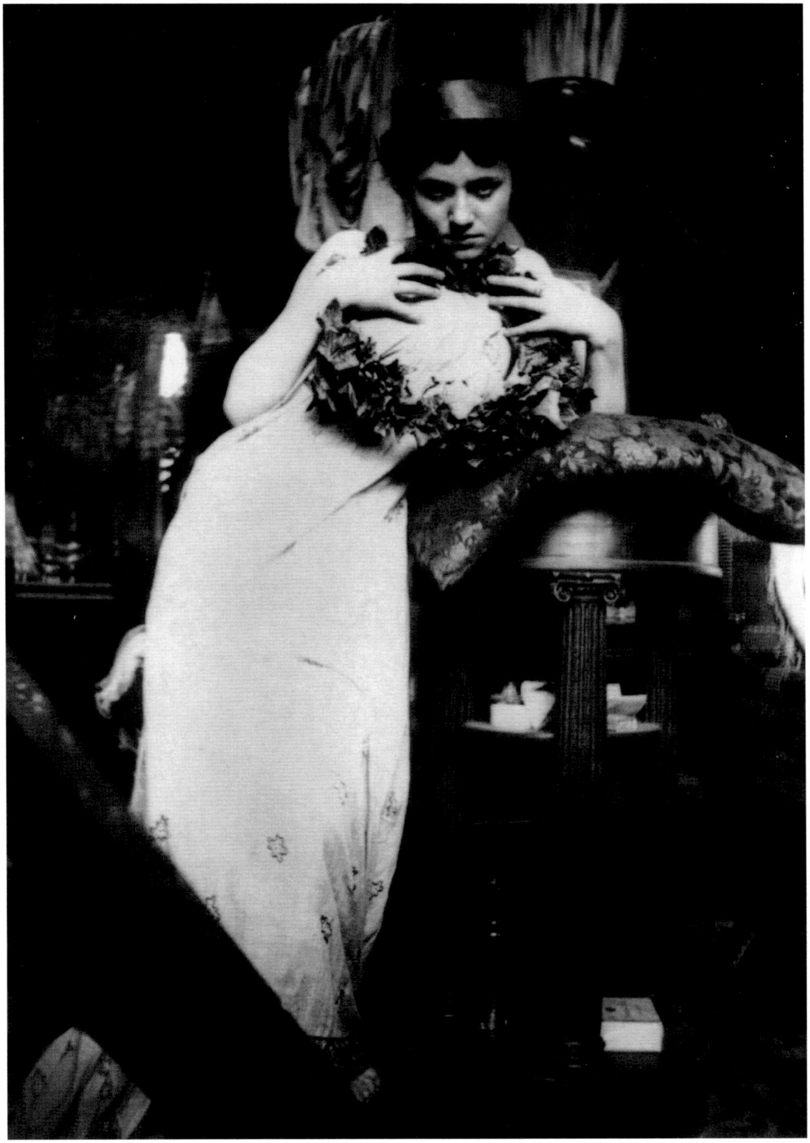

13 **Paris** 1899

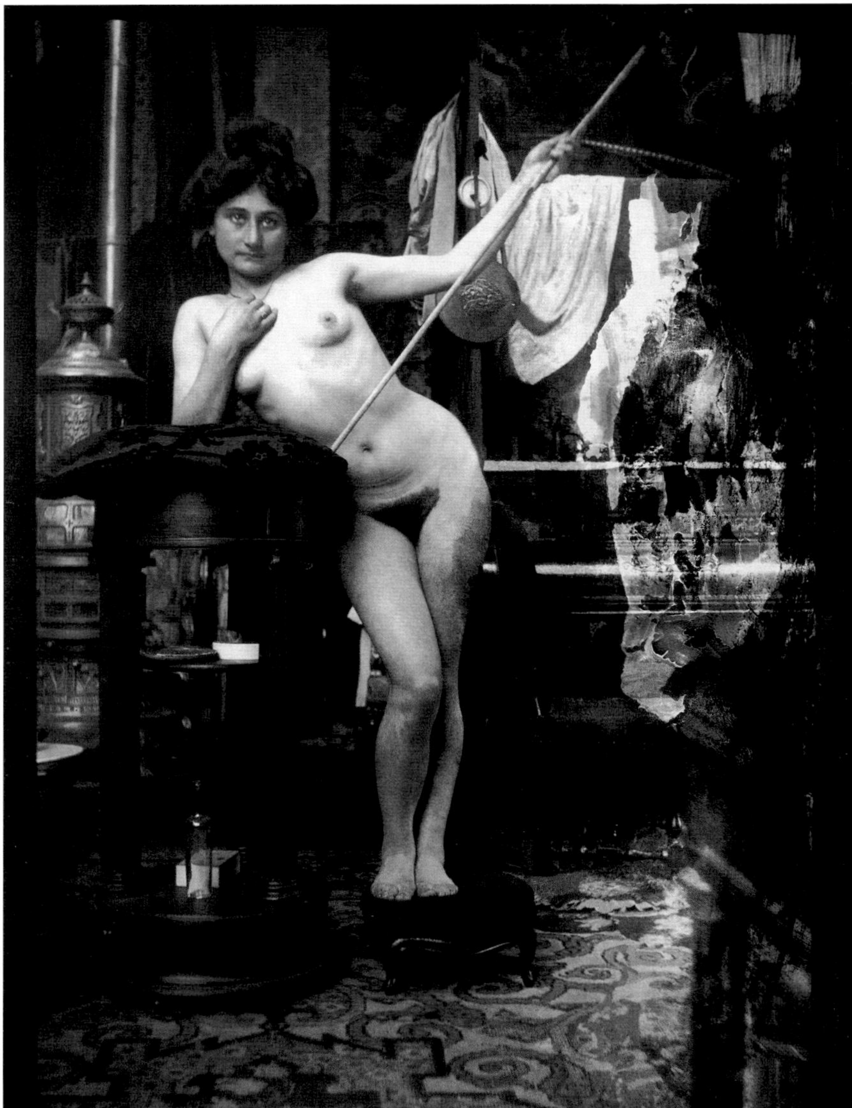

14 **Paris** 1899

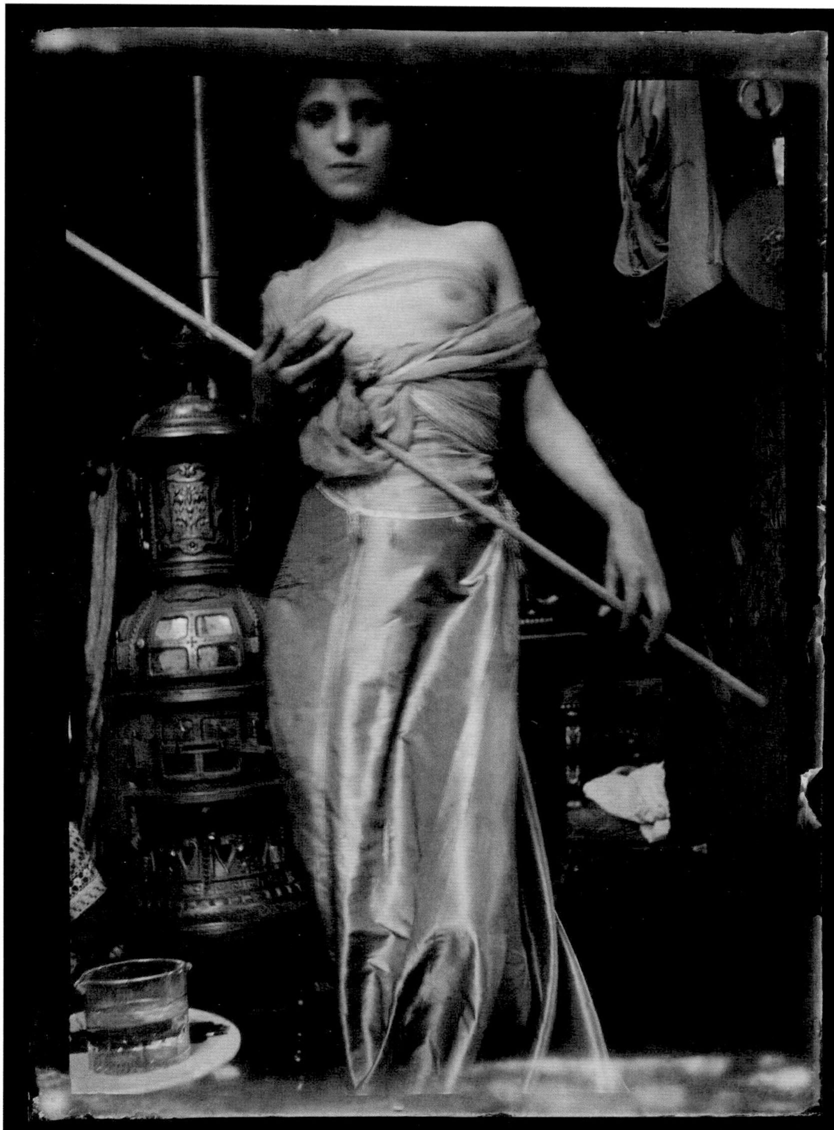

15 **Paris** 1899

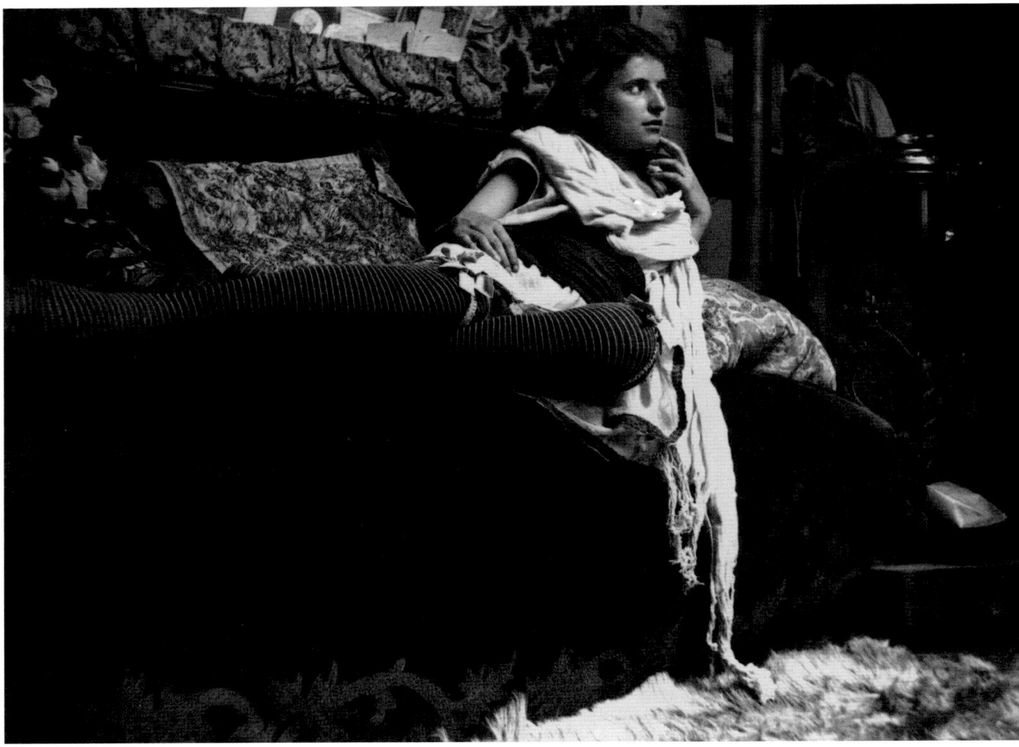

16 **Paris** 1899

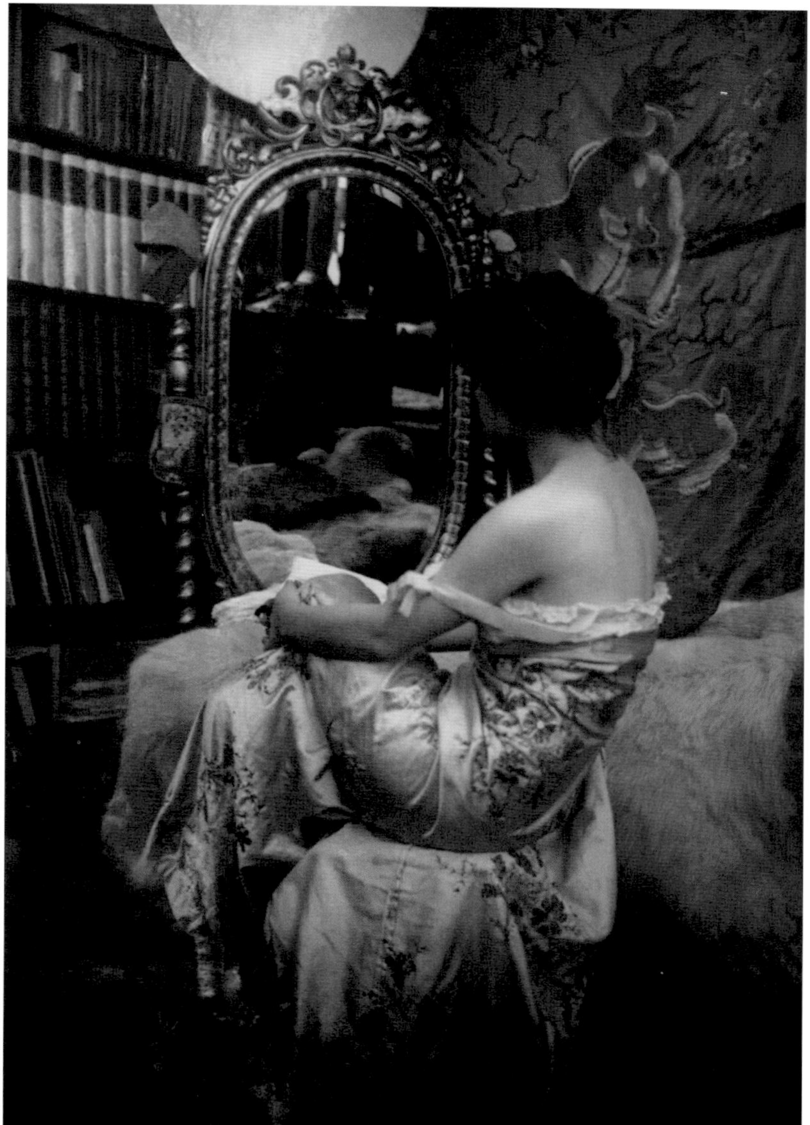

17 **Paris** 1899

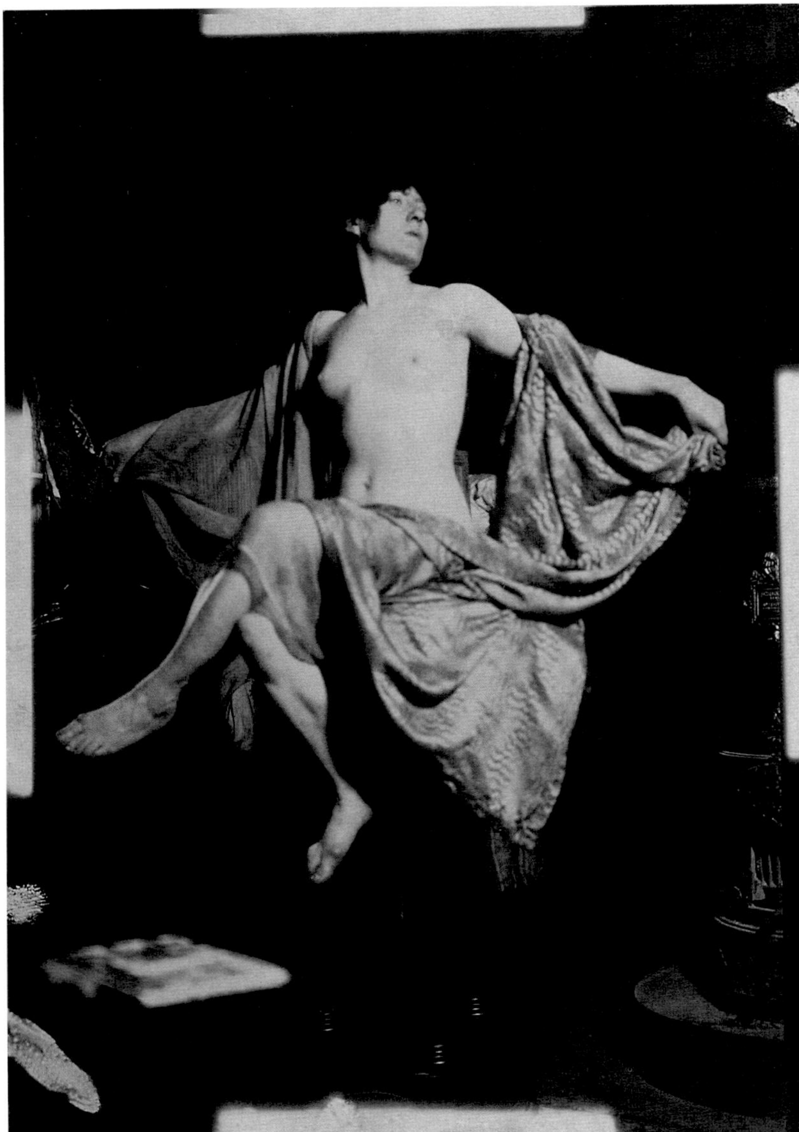

18 **Paris** 1899

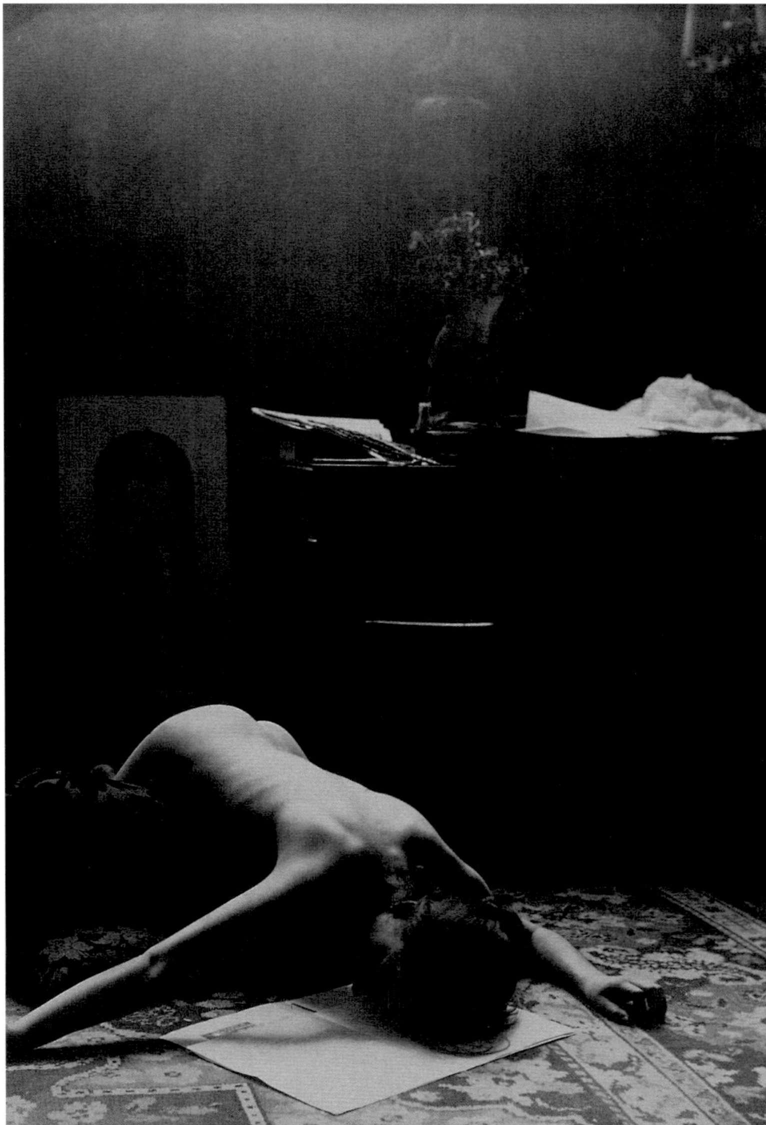

19 **Paris** 1898

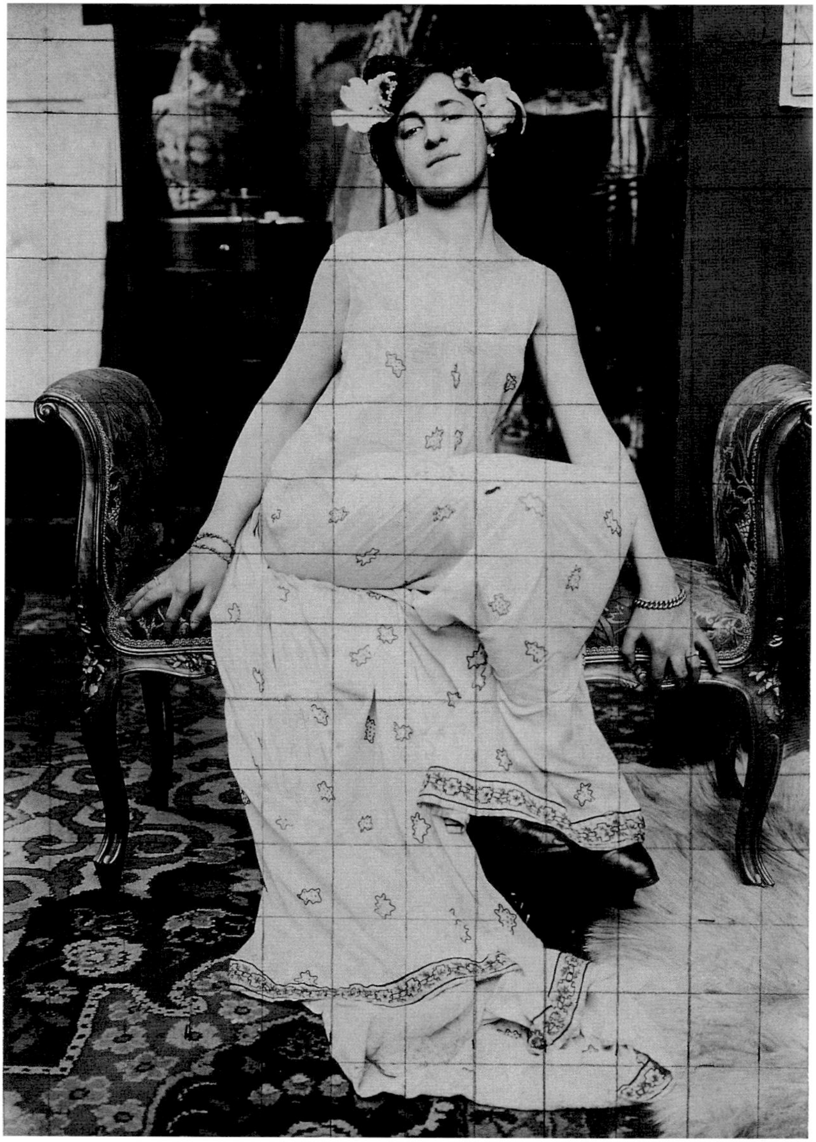

20 **Paris** 1899

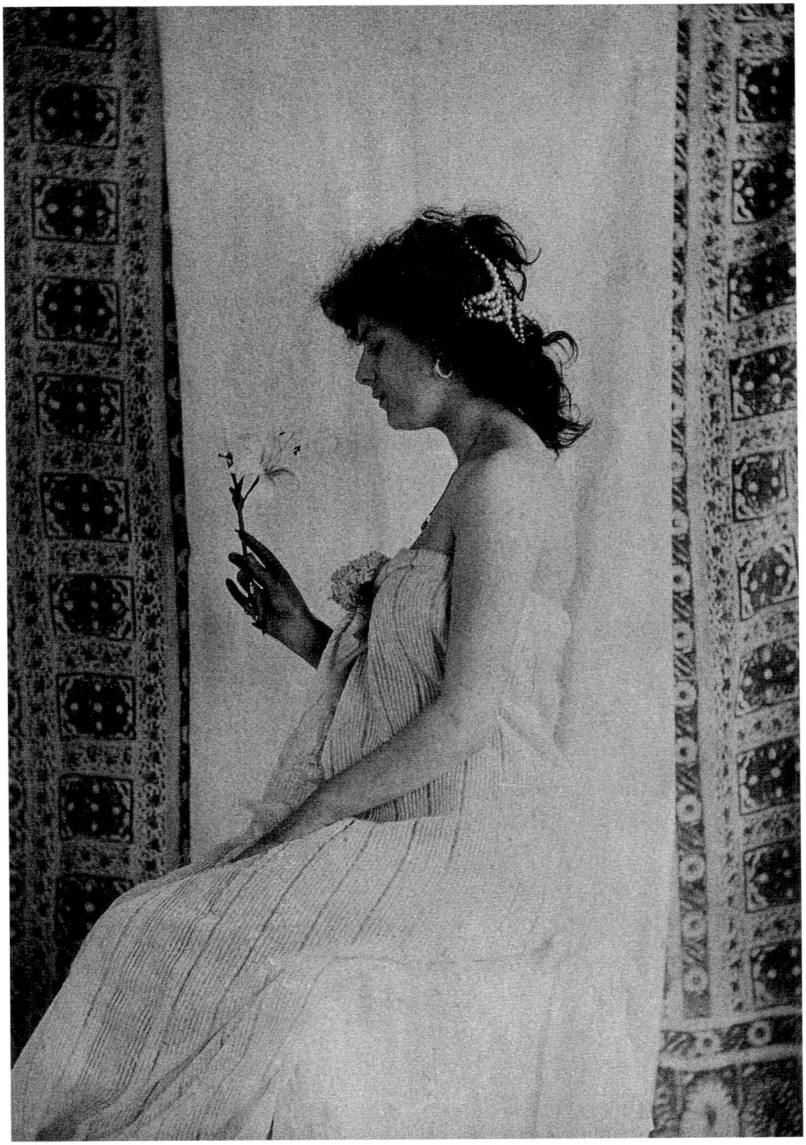

21 **Paris** 1899

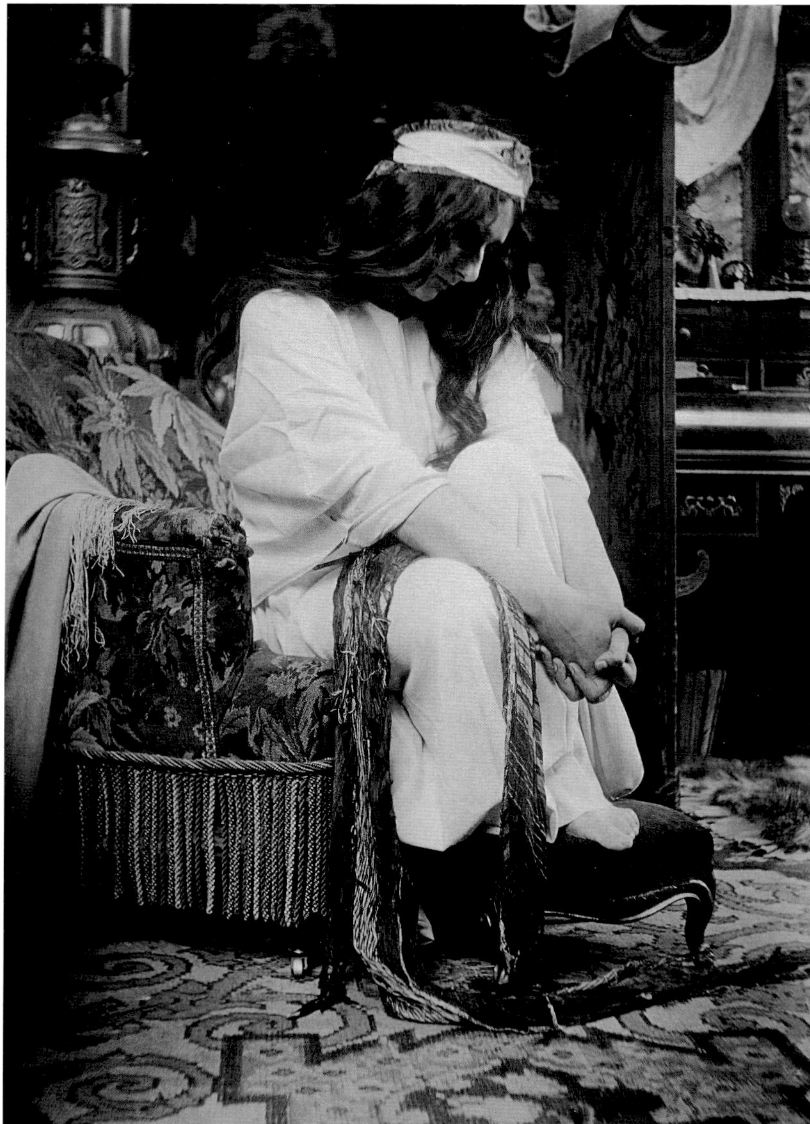

22 **Paris** 1900

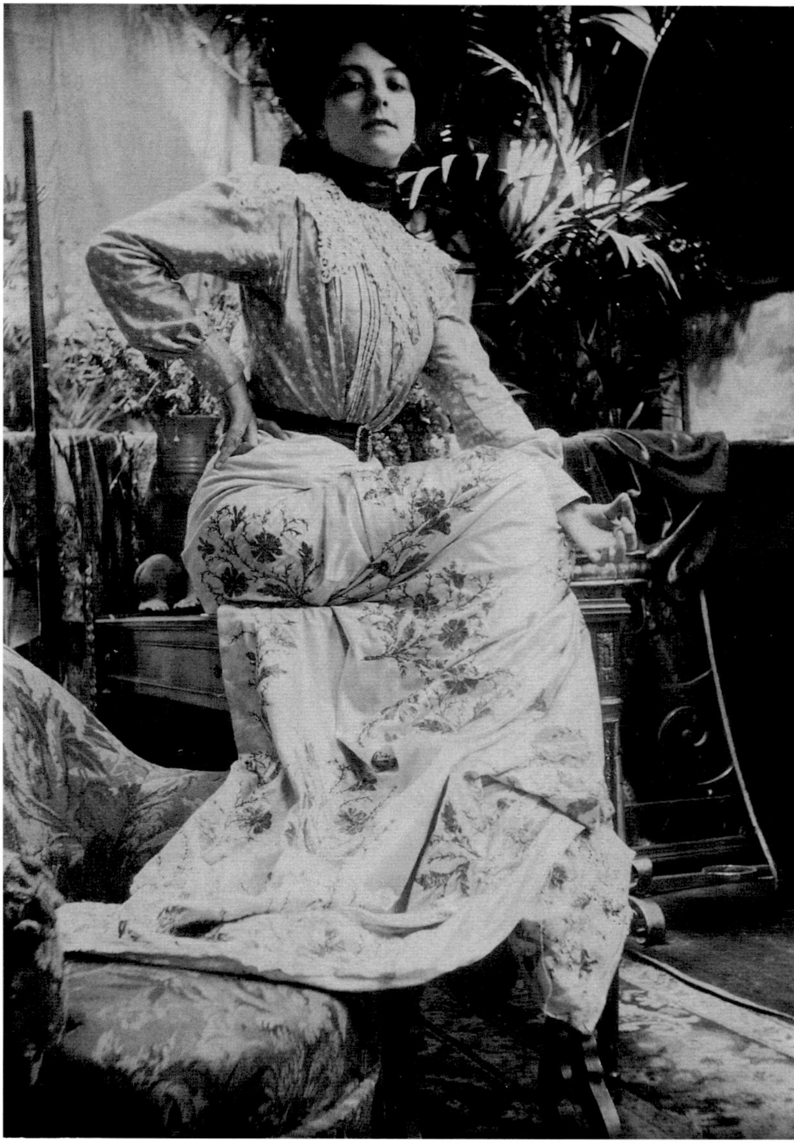

23 **Paris** 1898

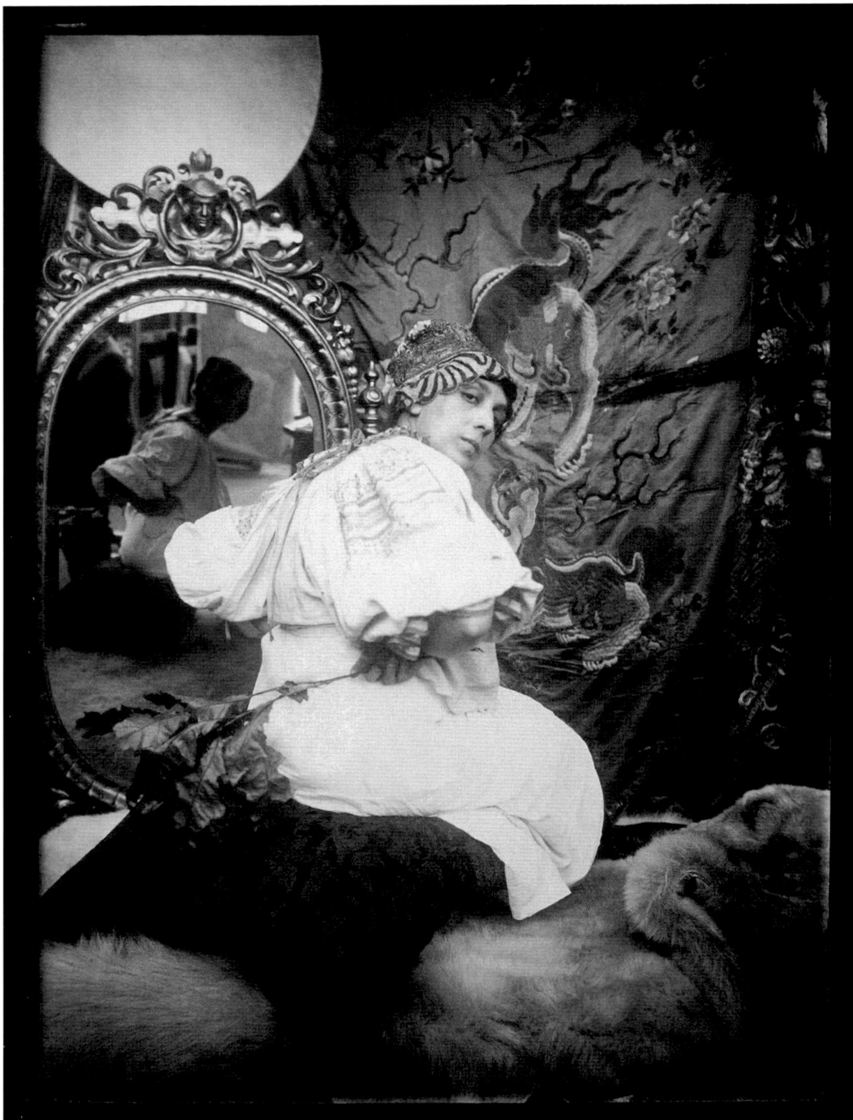

24 **Paris** 1899

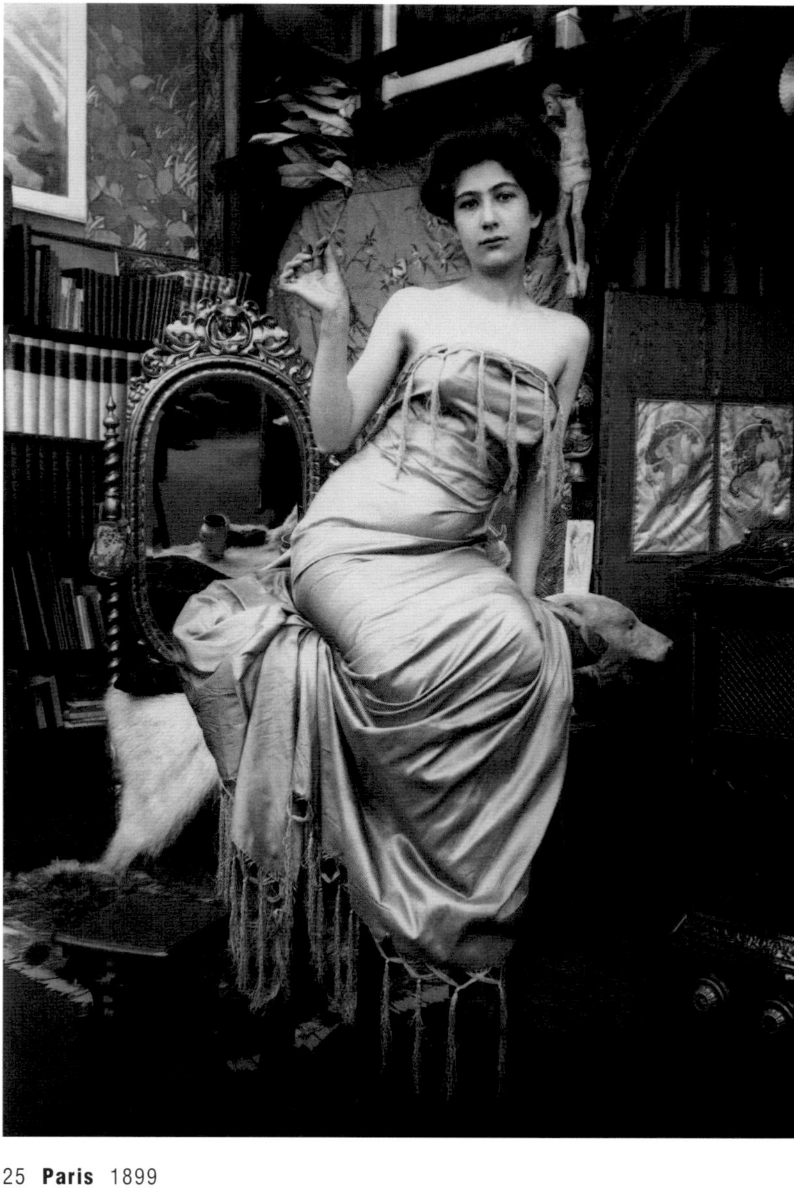

25 **Paris** 1899

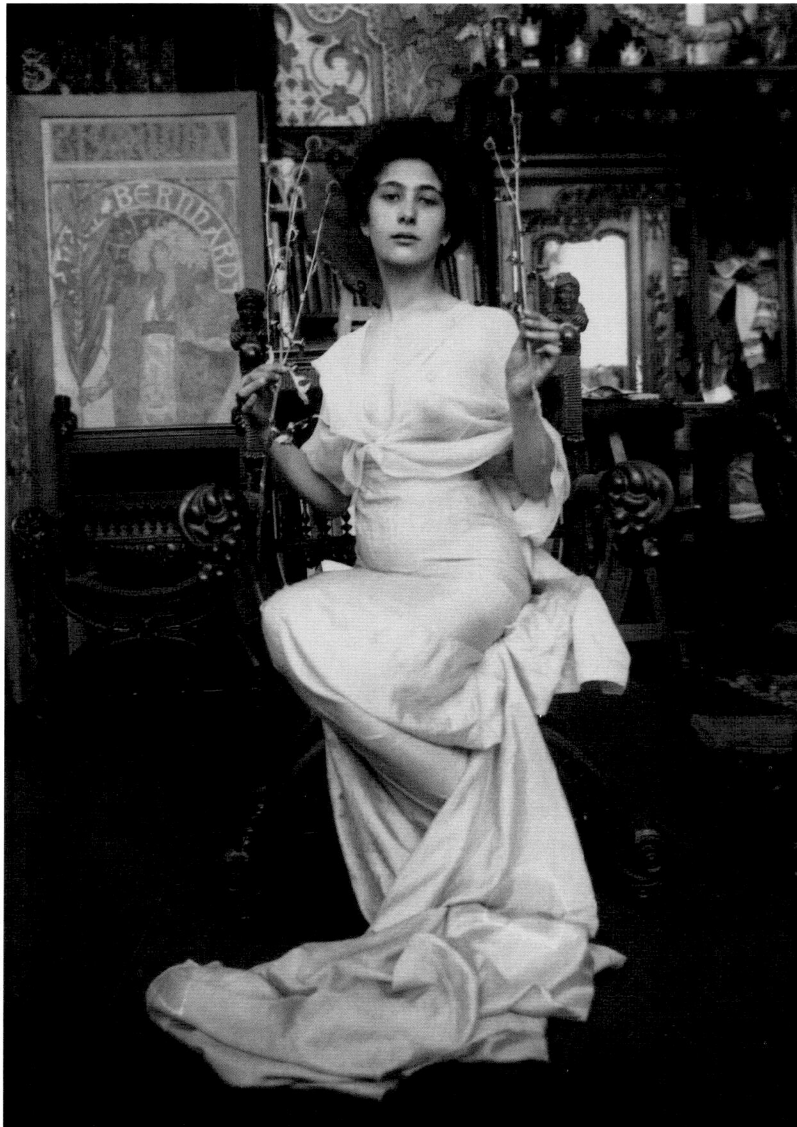

26 **Paris** c. 1899

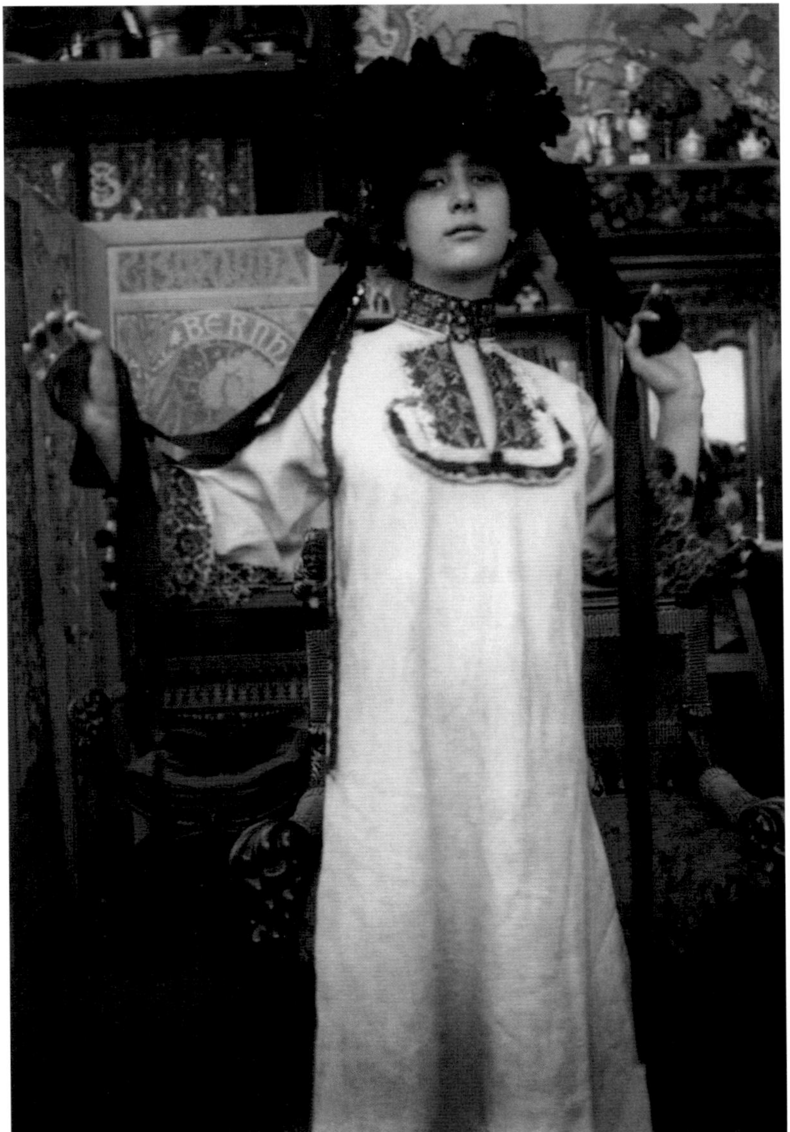

27 **Paris** 1899

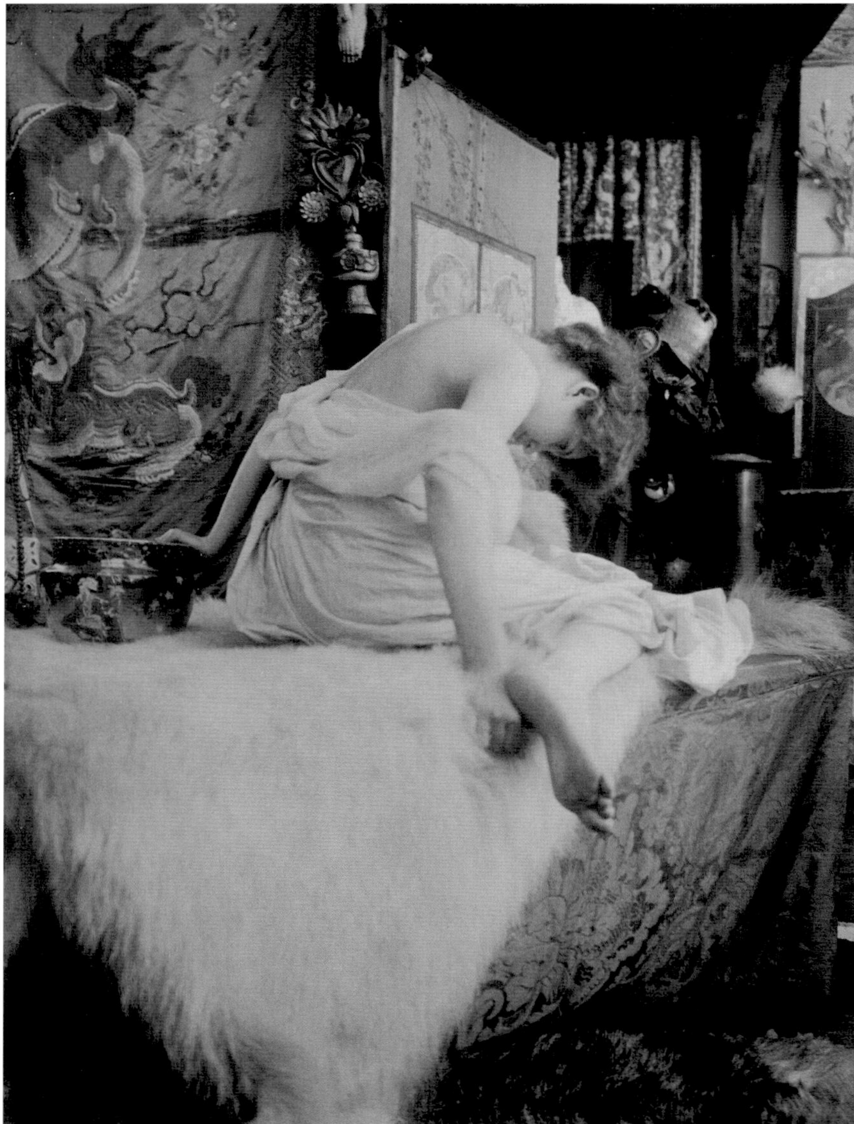

28 **Paris** 1899

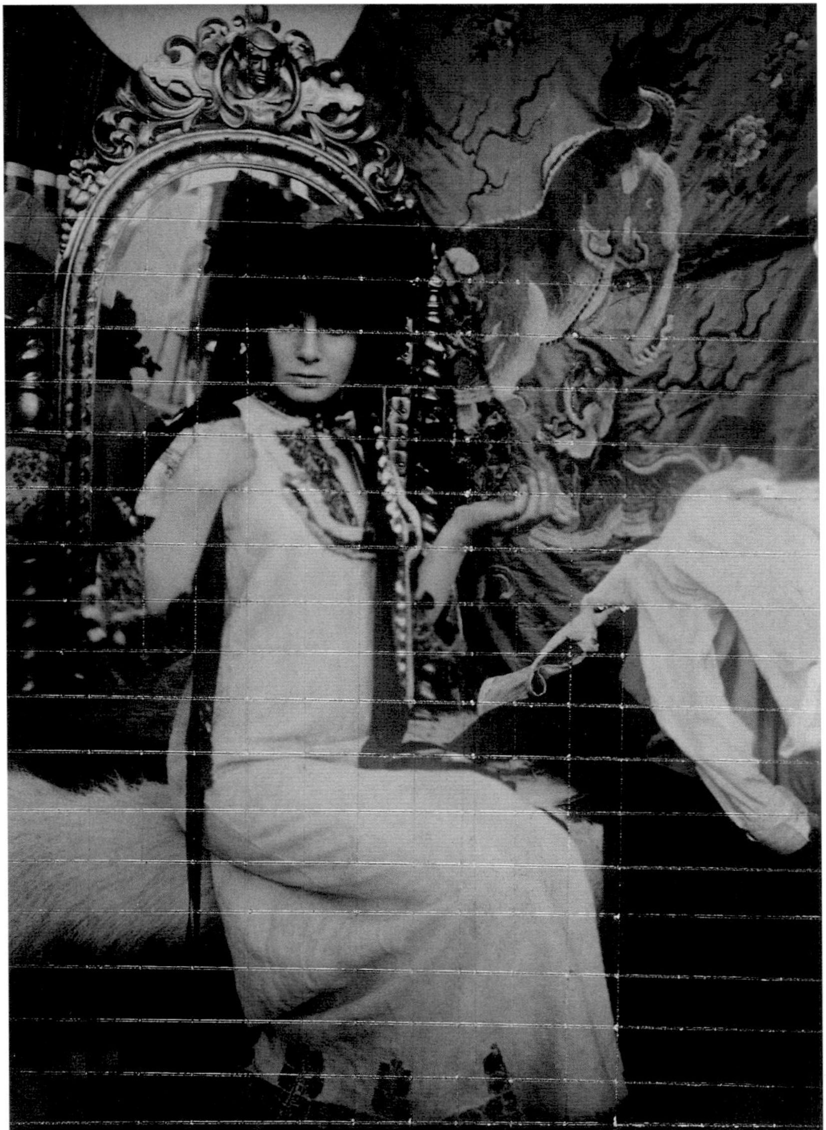

29 **Paris** 1899

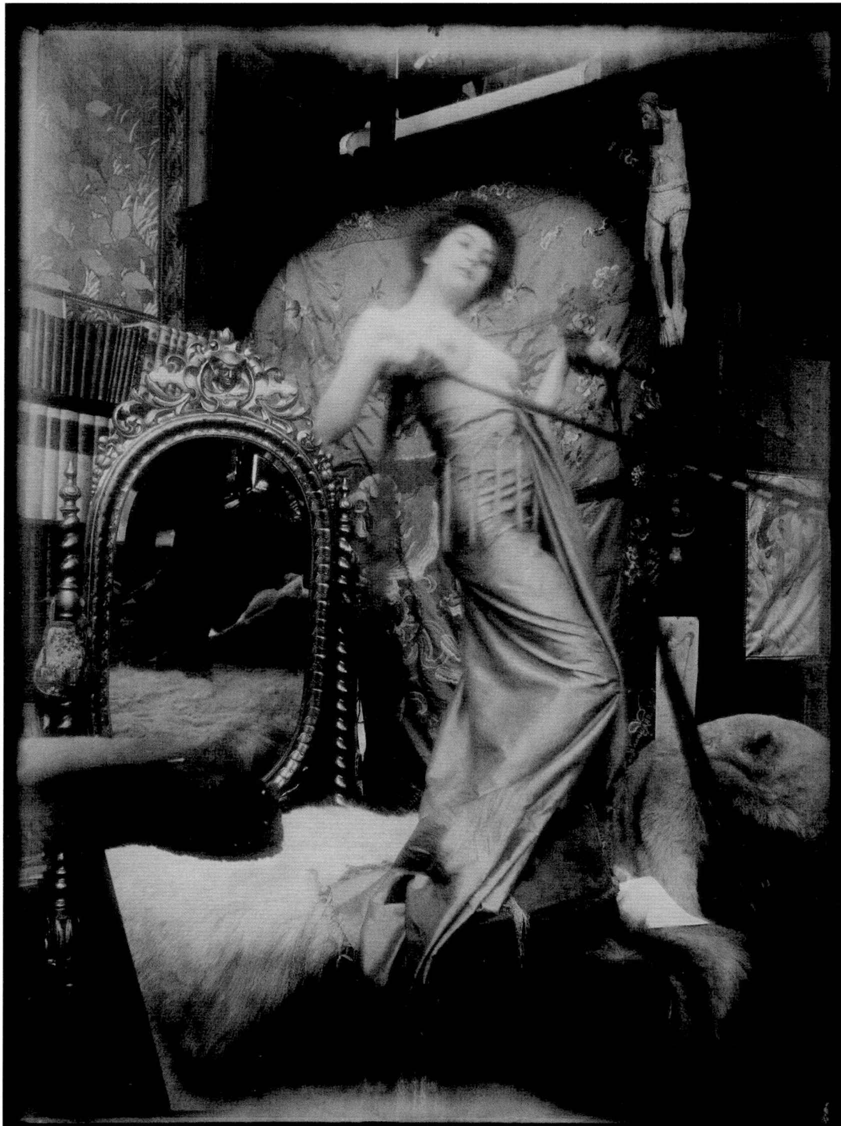

30 **Paris** 1899

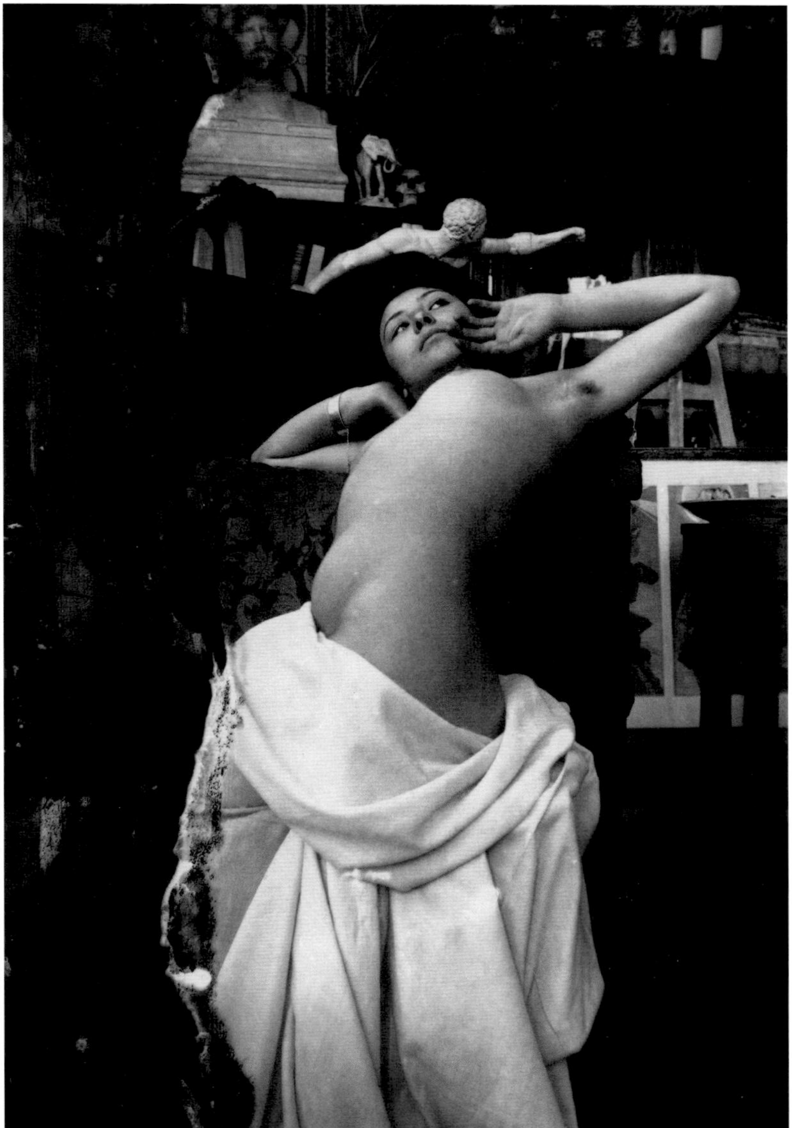

31 **Paris** 1899

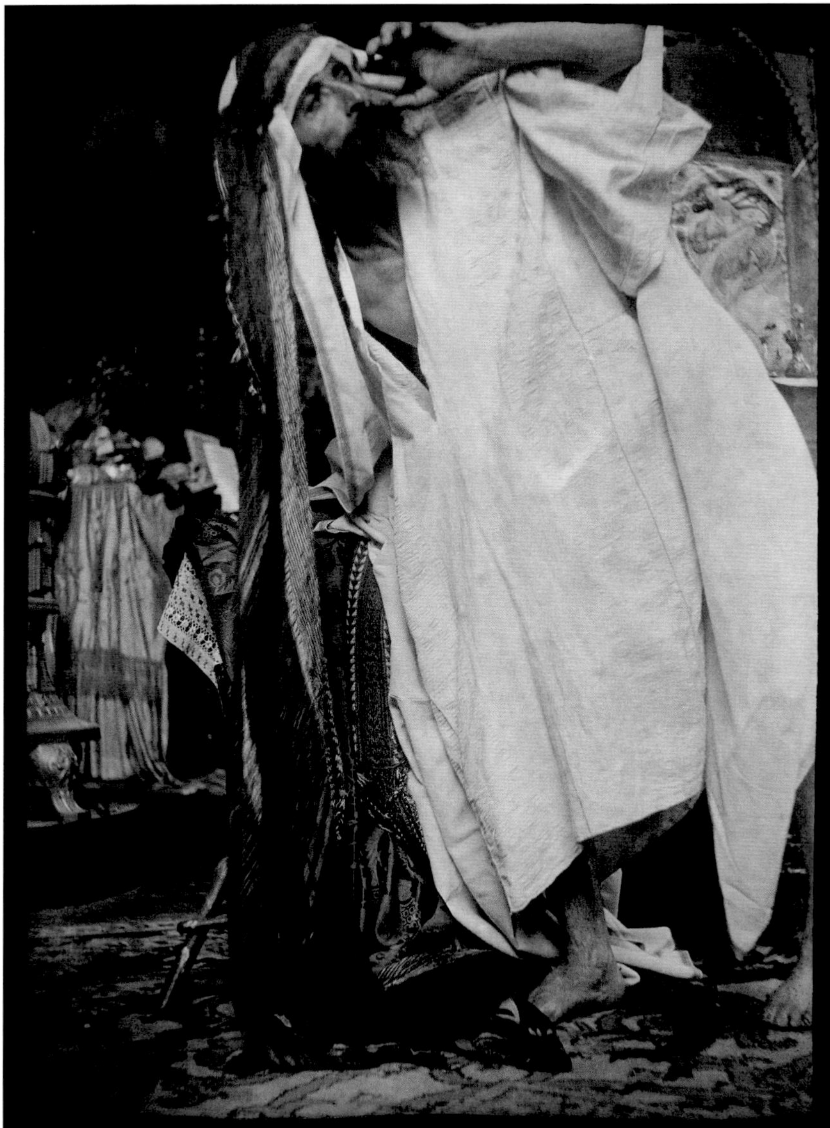

32 **Paris** 1900

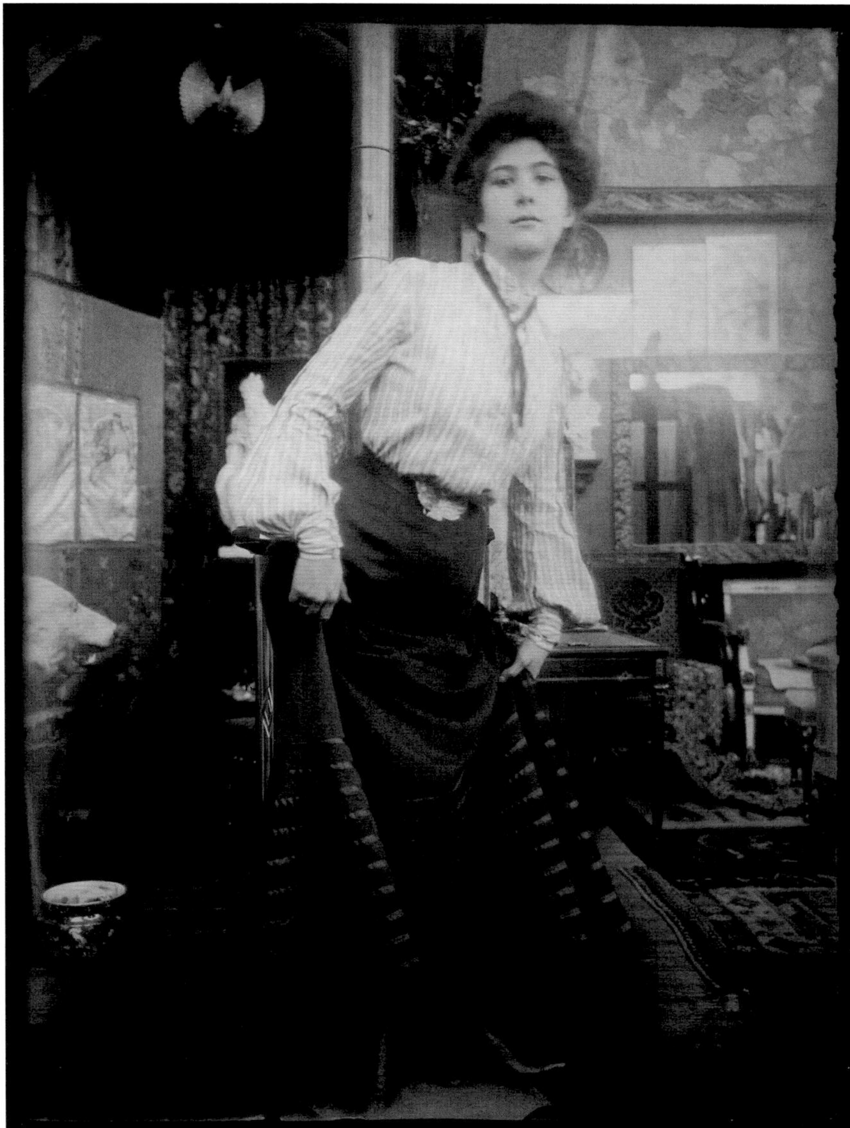

33 **Paris** 1899

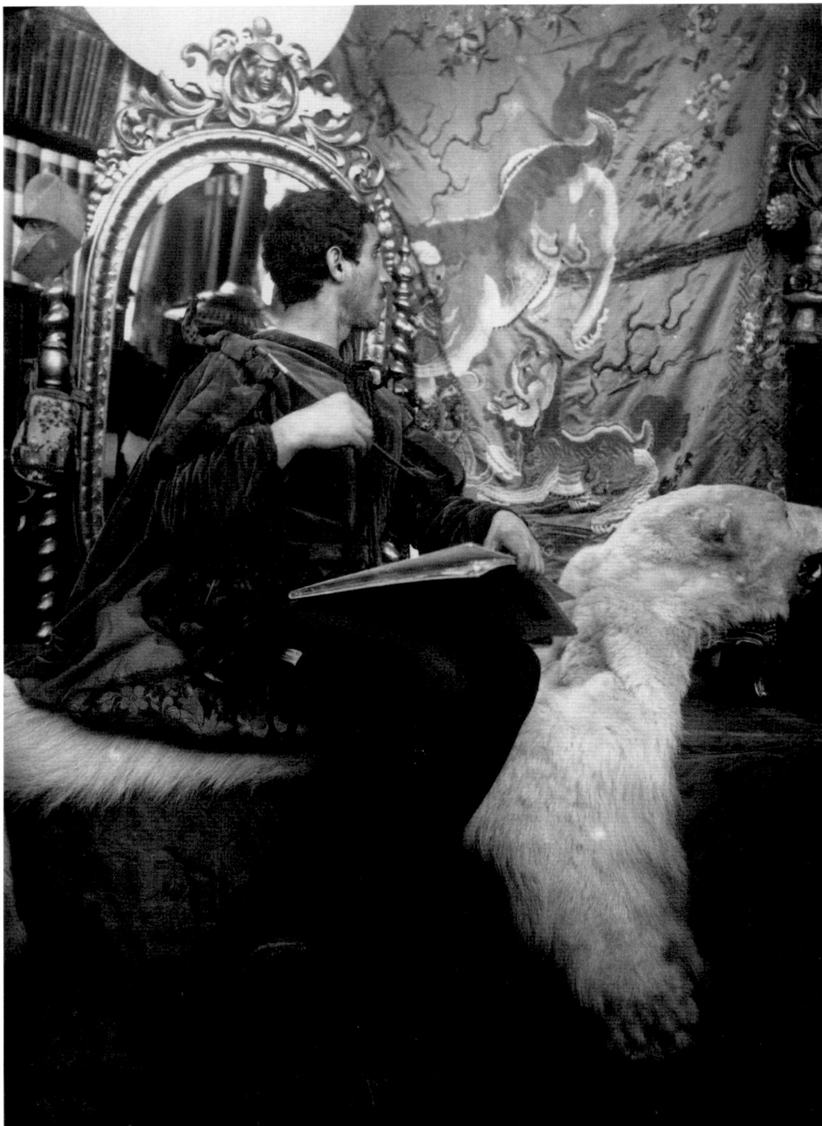

34 **Paris** 1899

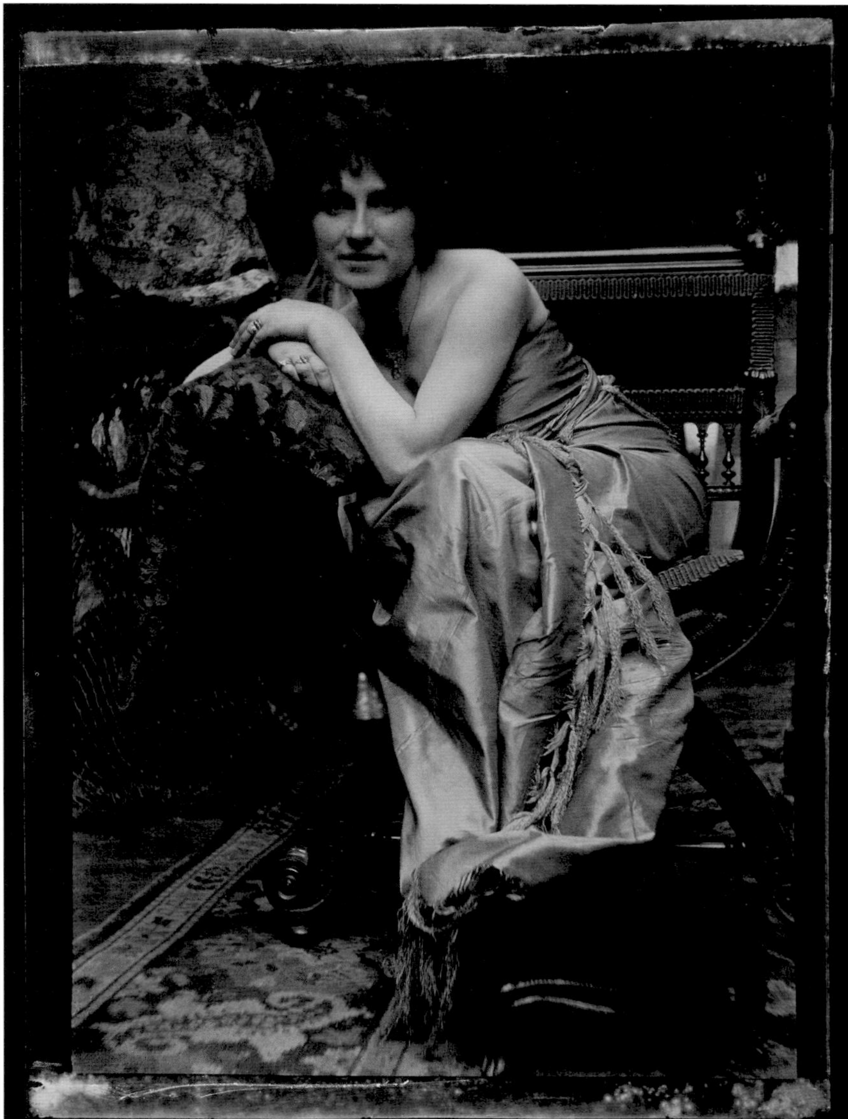

35 **Paris** 1900

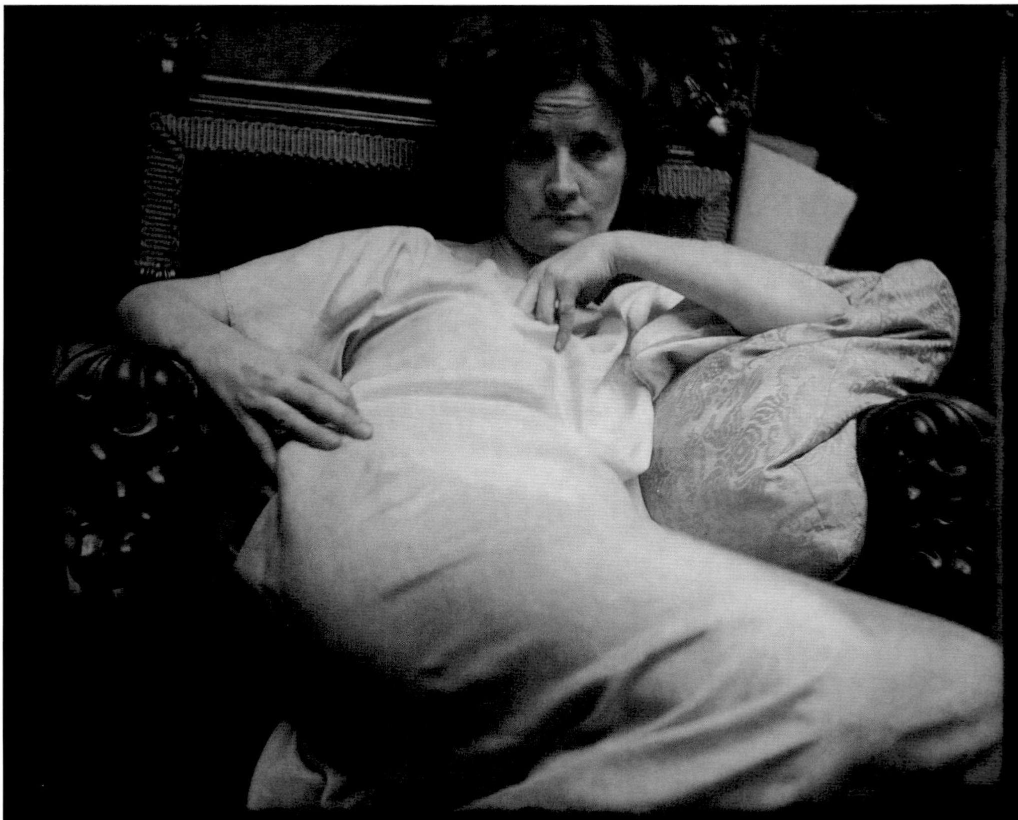

36 **Paris** 1903

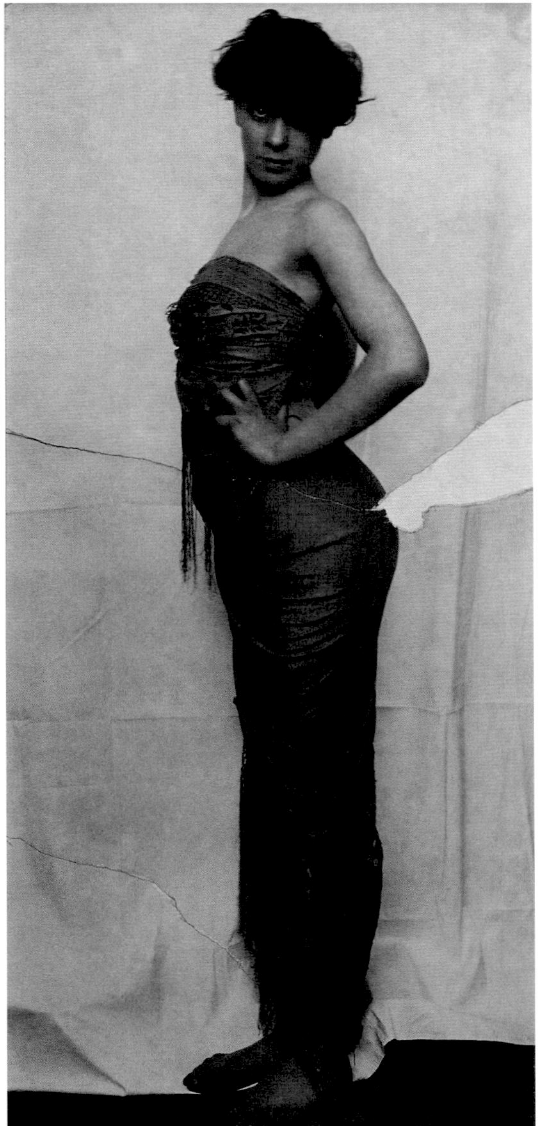

37 **Paris** 1901

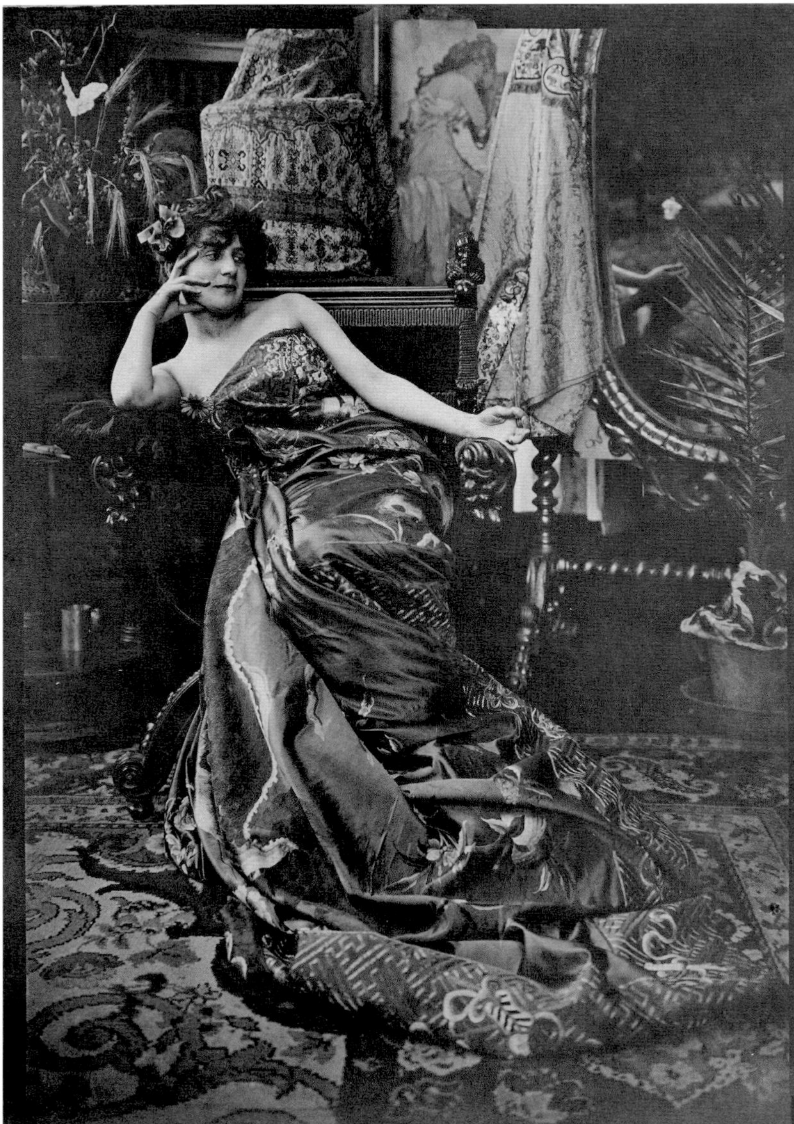

38 **Paris** 1897

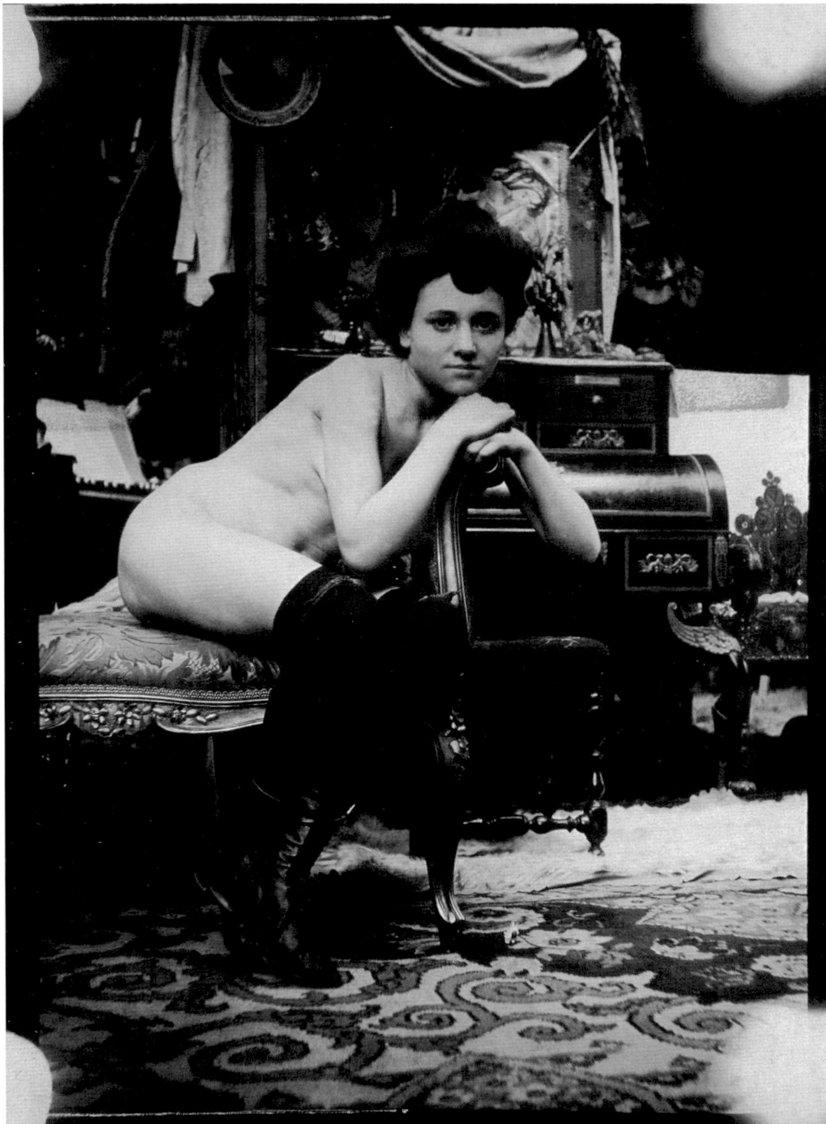

39 **Paris** 1897

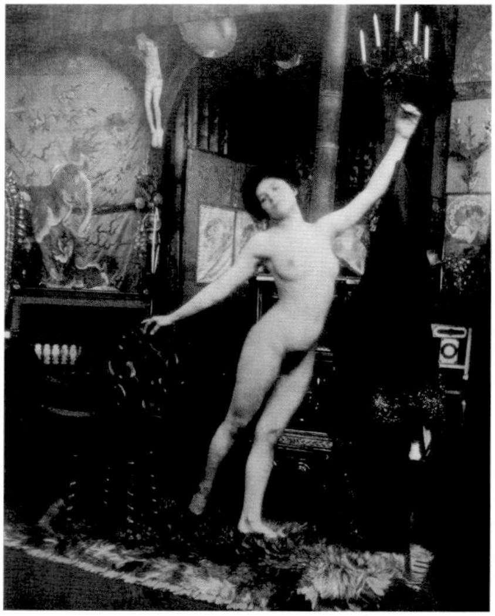

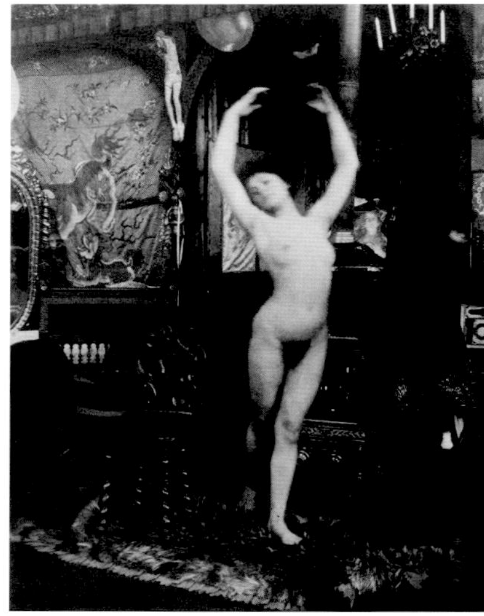

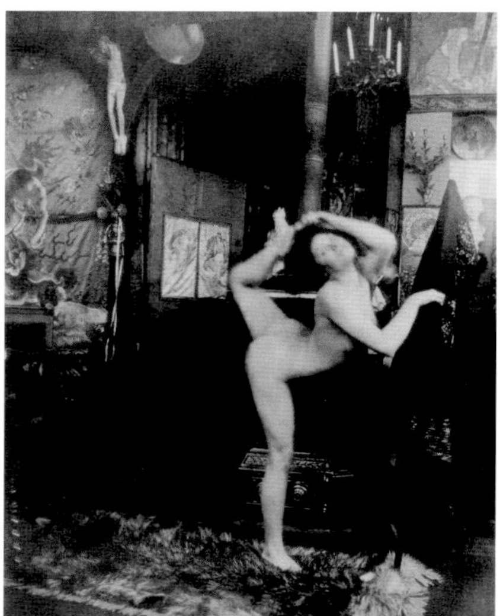

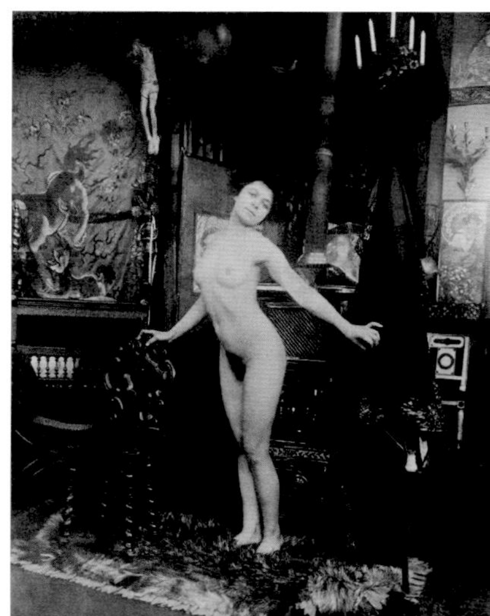

40 – 43 **Paris** 1901

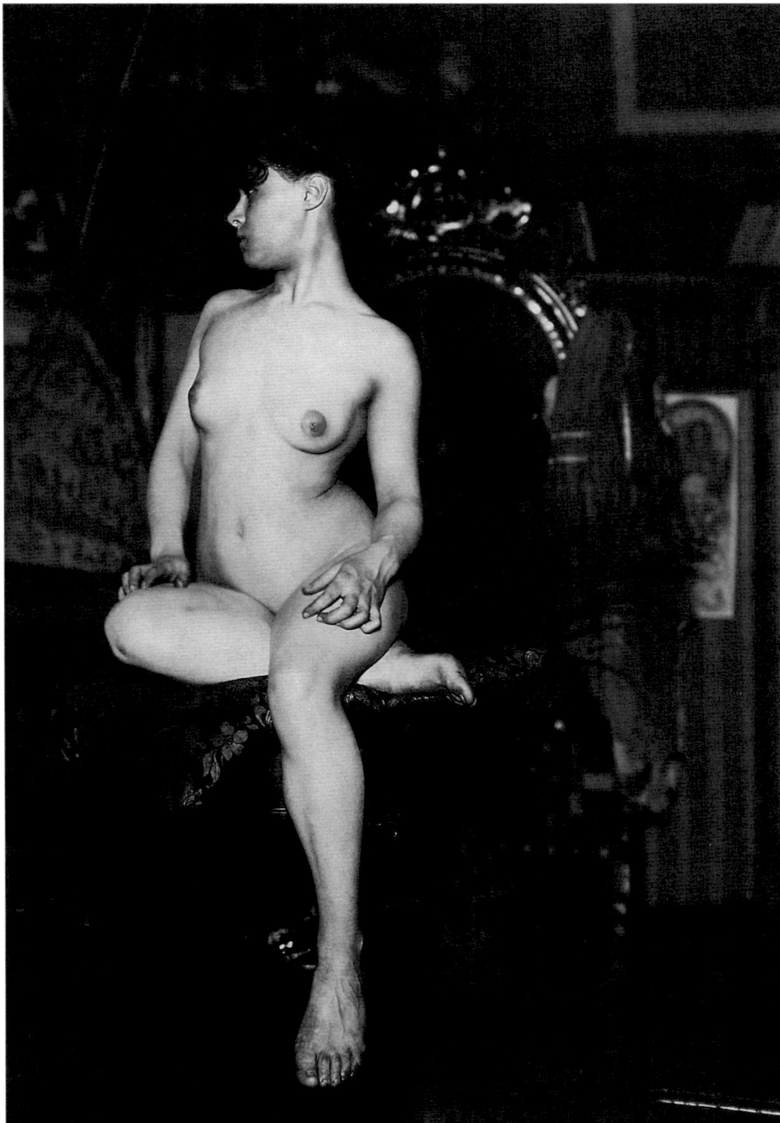

44 **Paris** 1899

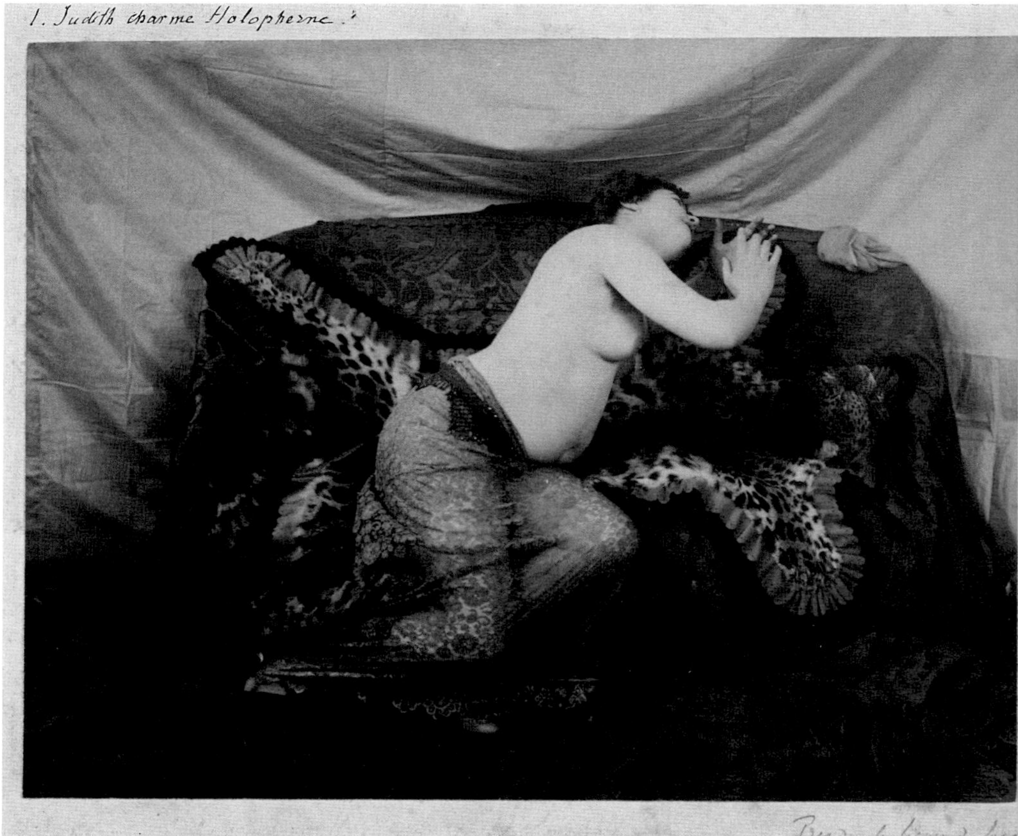

45 **Paris** 1899

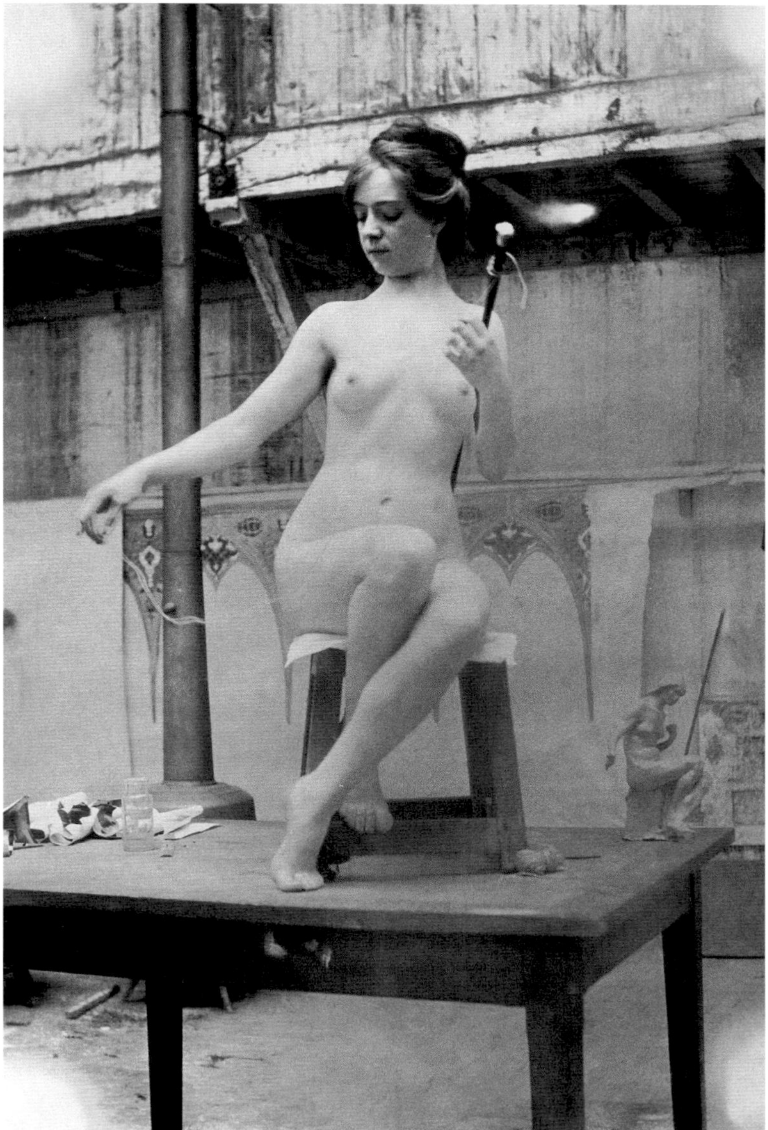

46 **Paris** 1899

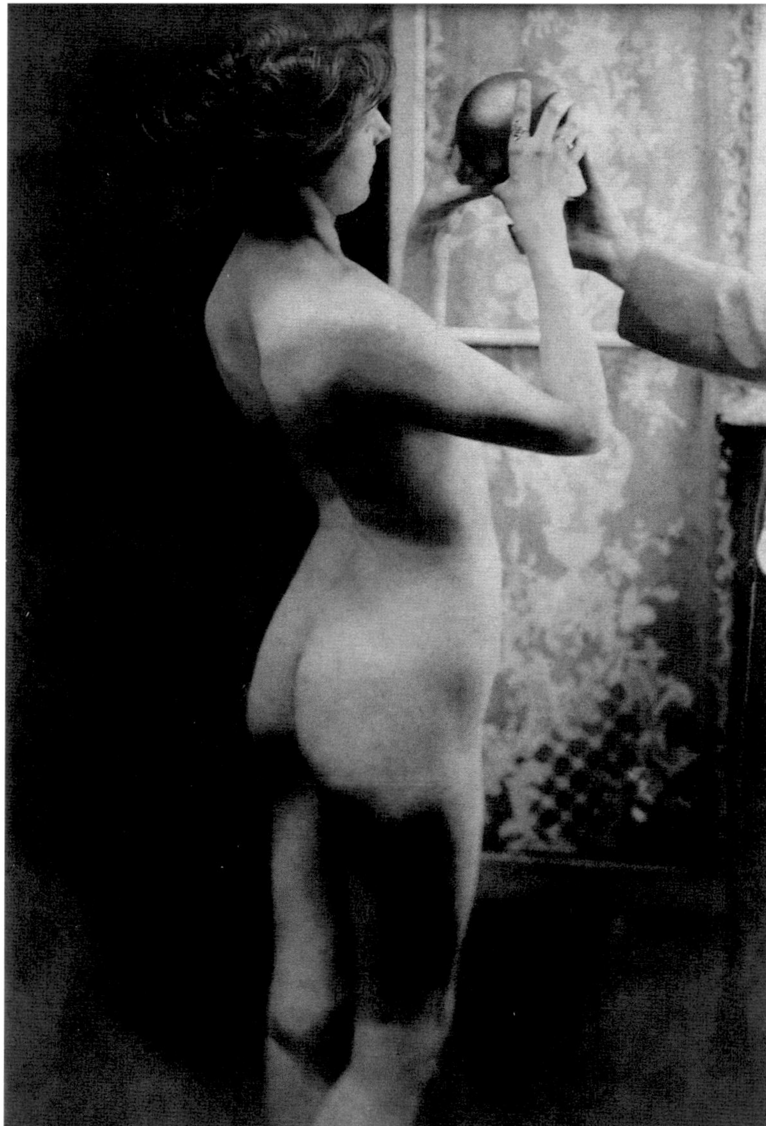

47 **Paris** 1902

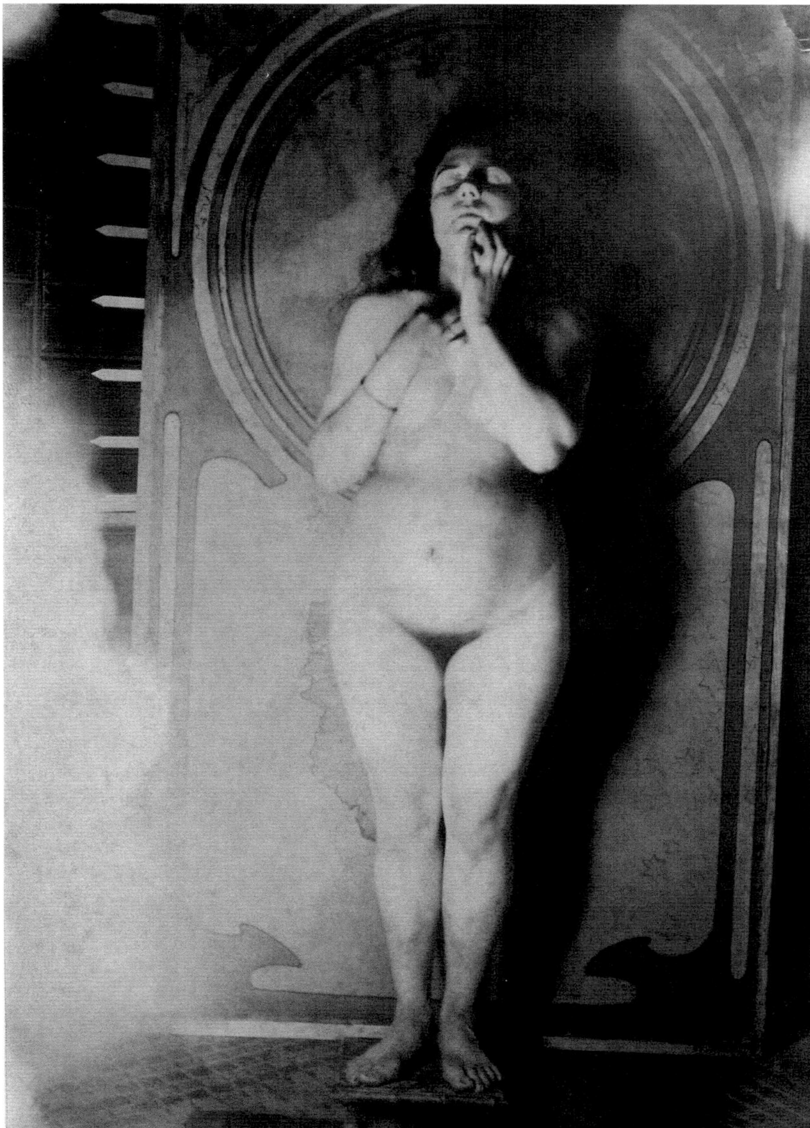

48 **Paris** 1902

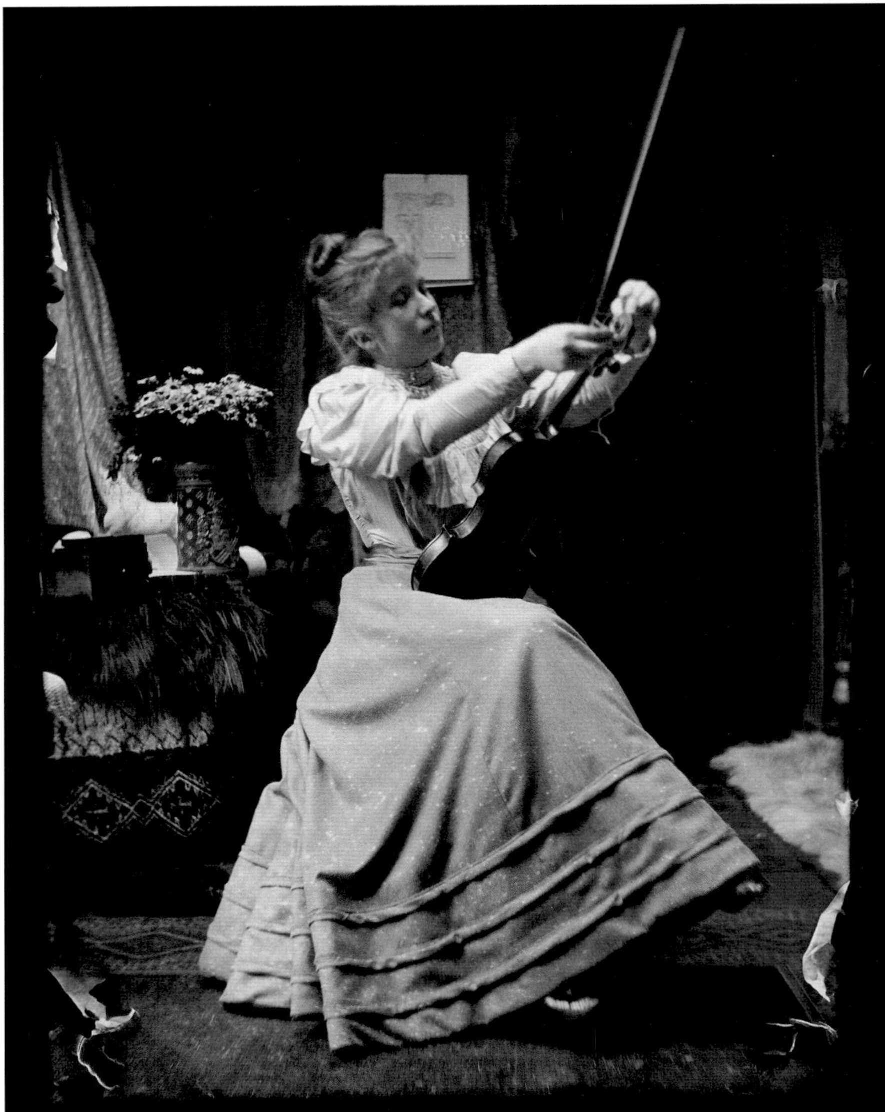

49 **Paris** c. 1900

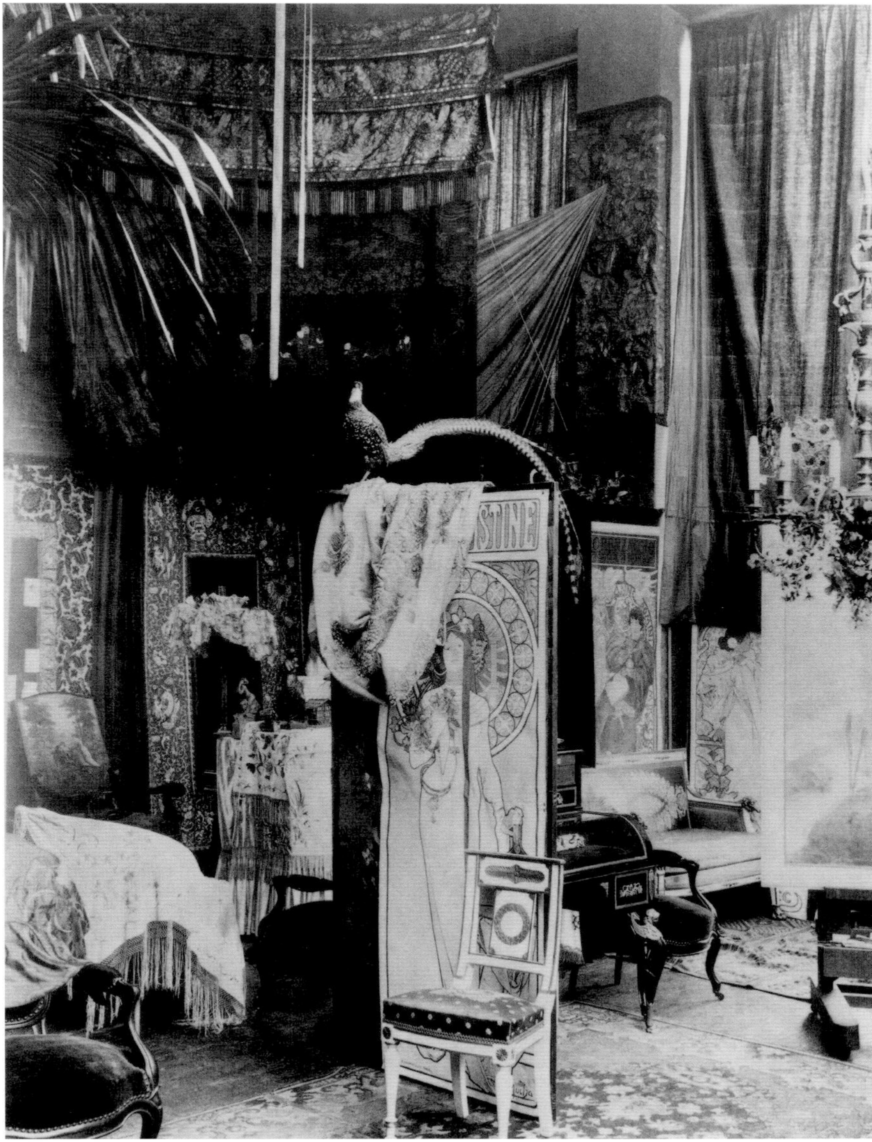

50 **Mucha's Studio in the rue Val de Grâce, Paris / Ateliér v ulici Val de Grâce** 1900

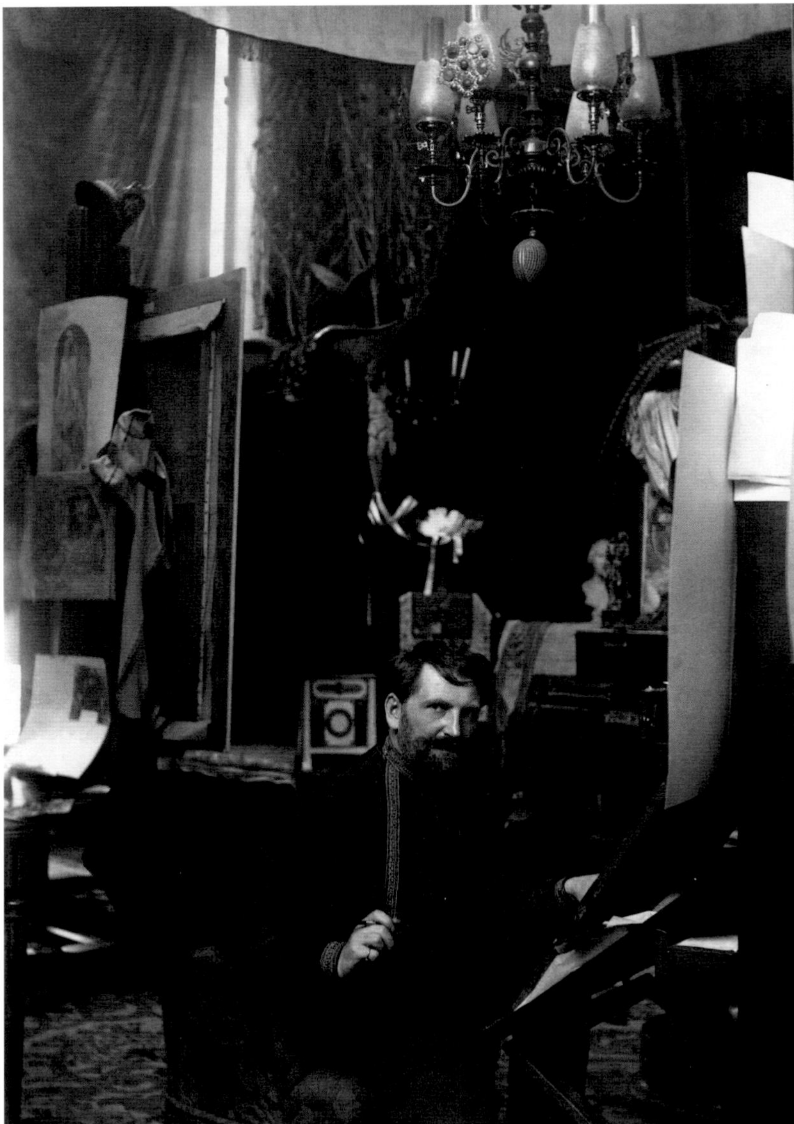

51 **Alfons Mucha, Paris** 1899

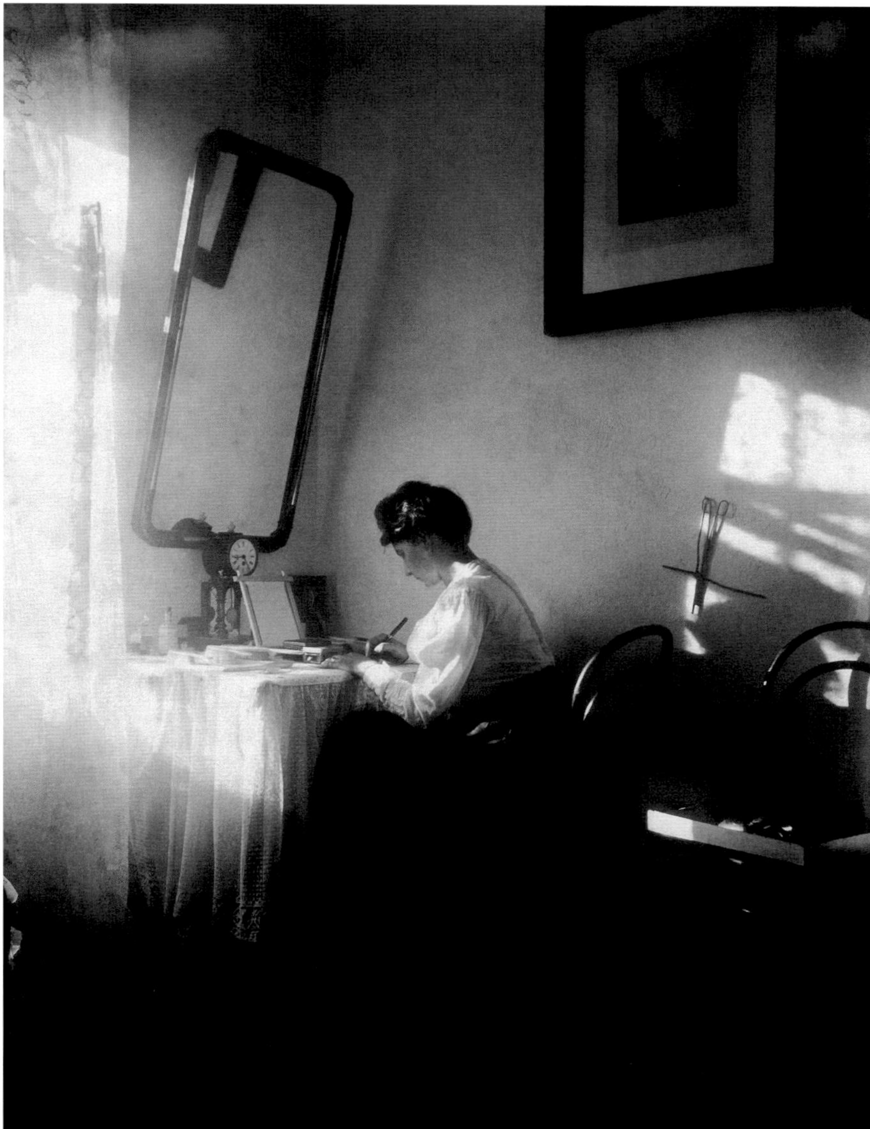

52 **Marie Chytilová, Chrudim, Bohemia** 1905

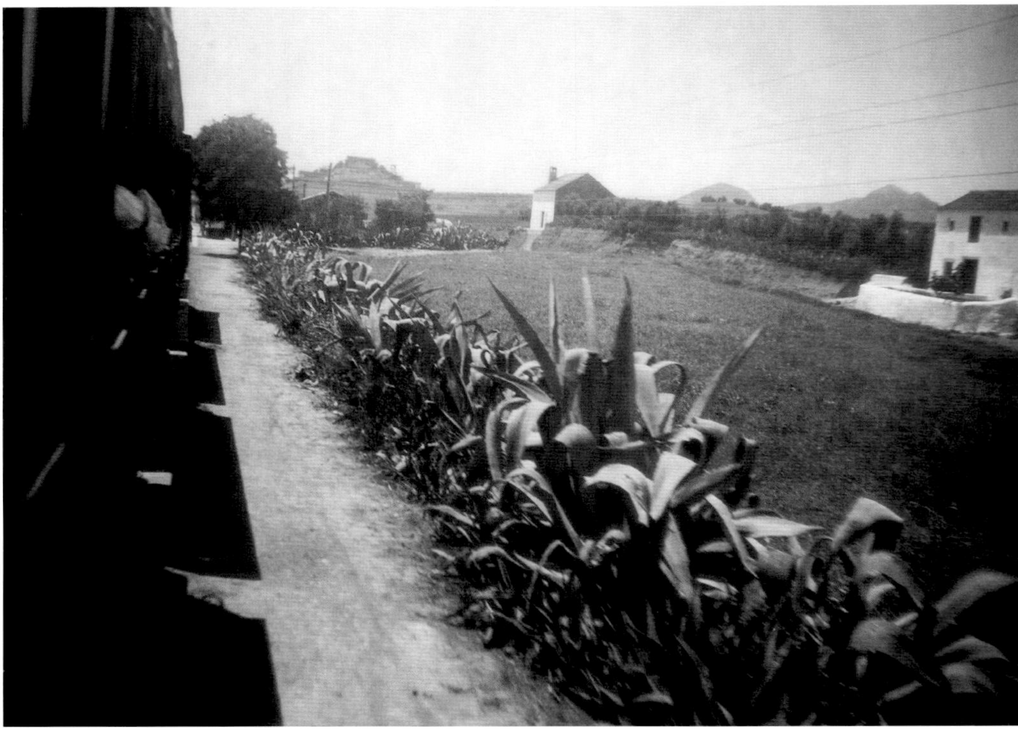

53 **The South of France, Landscape from a Train / Jihofrancouzská krajina z vlaku** c. 1900

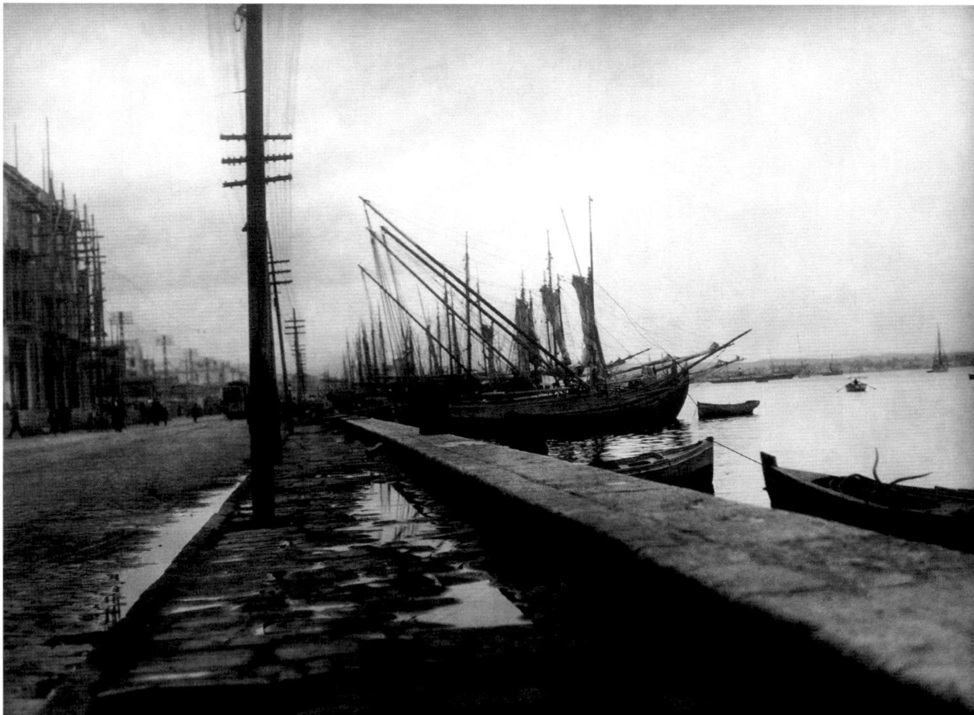

54 **Harbor / Přístav** c. 1900

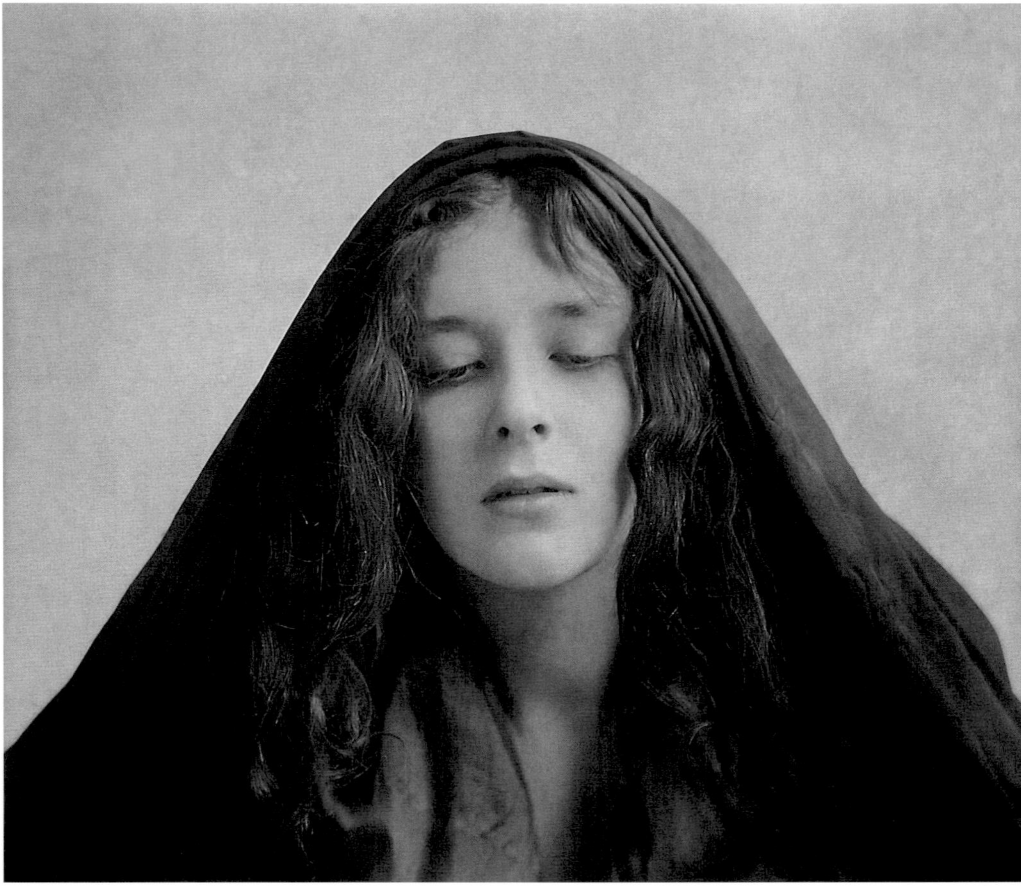

55 **New York** 1904

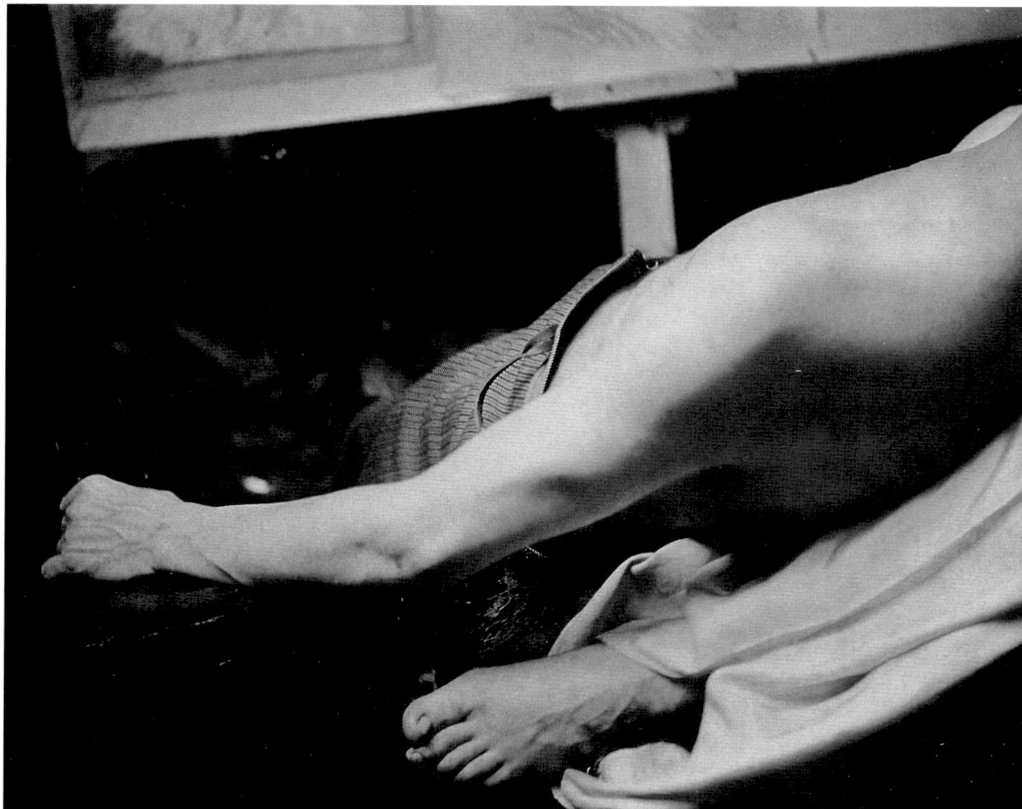

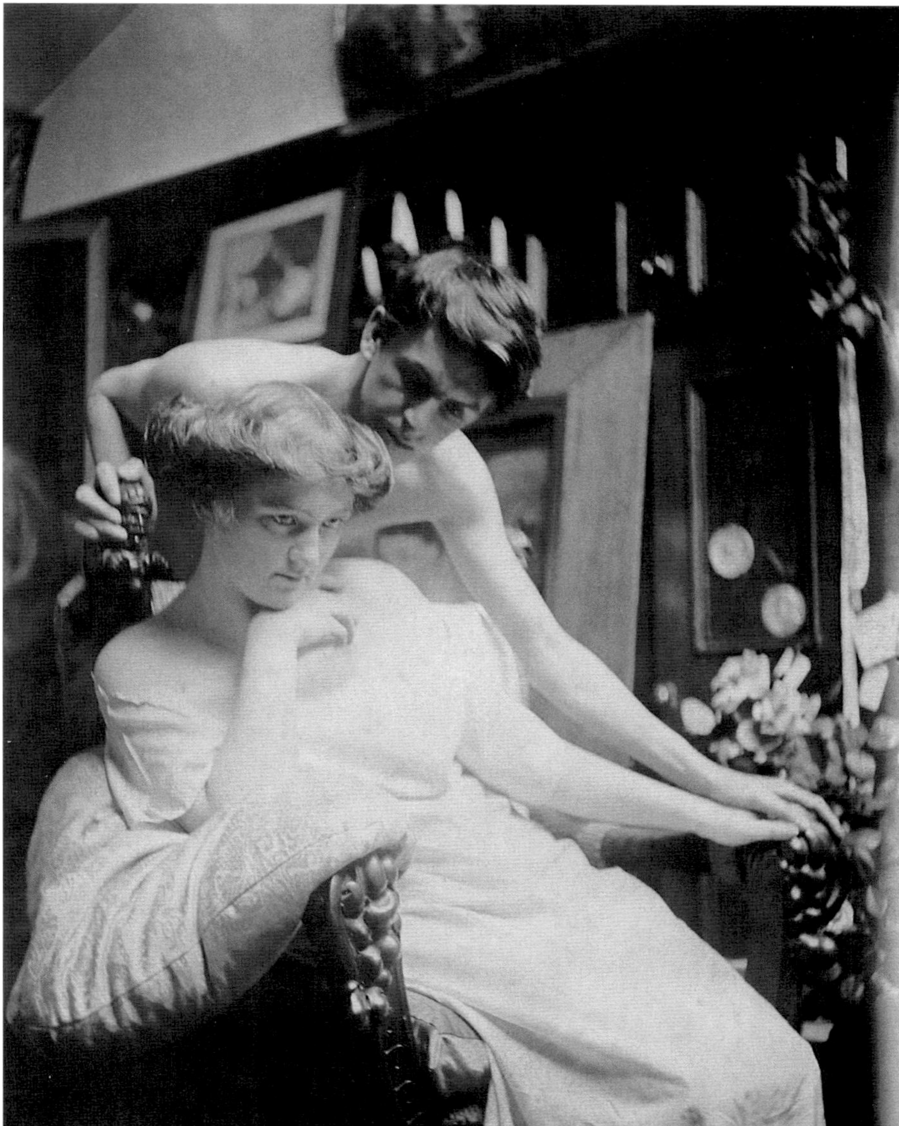

57 **New York** 1908

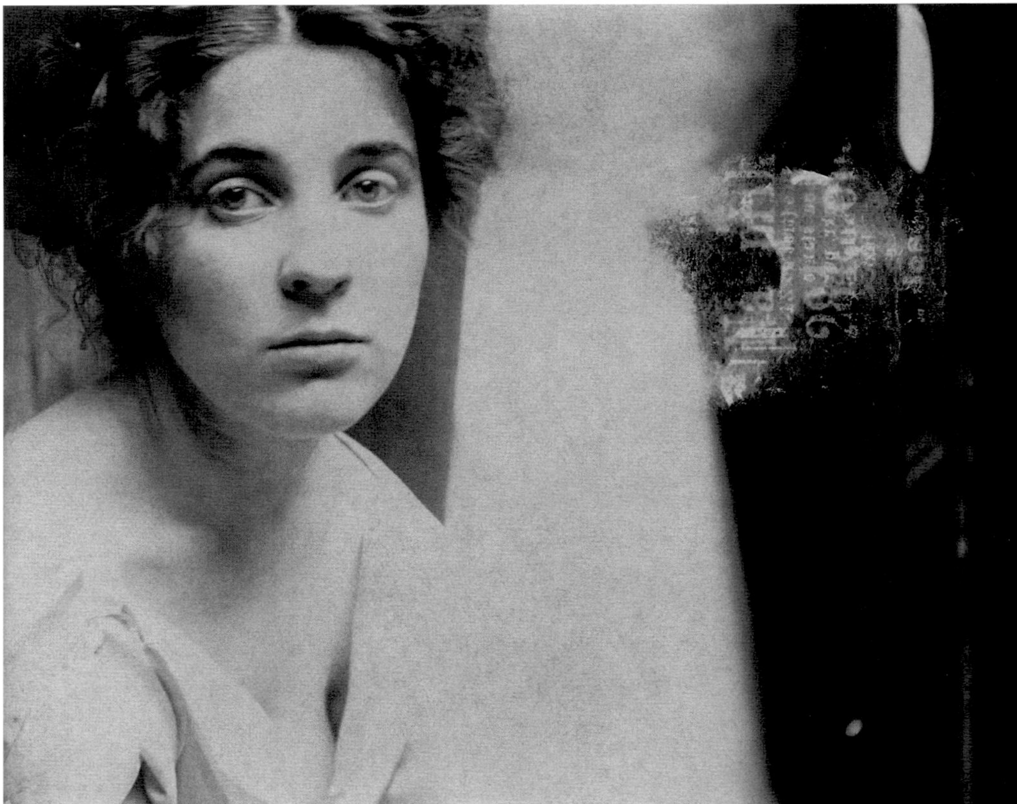

58 **New York** 1908

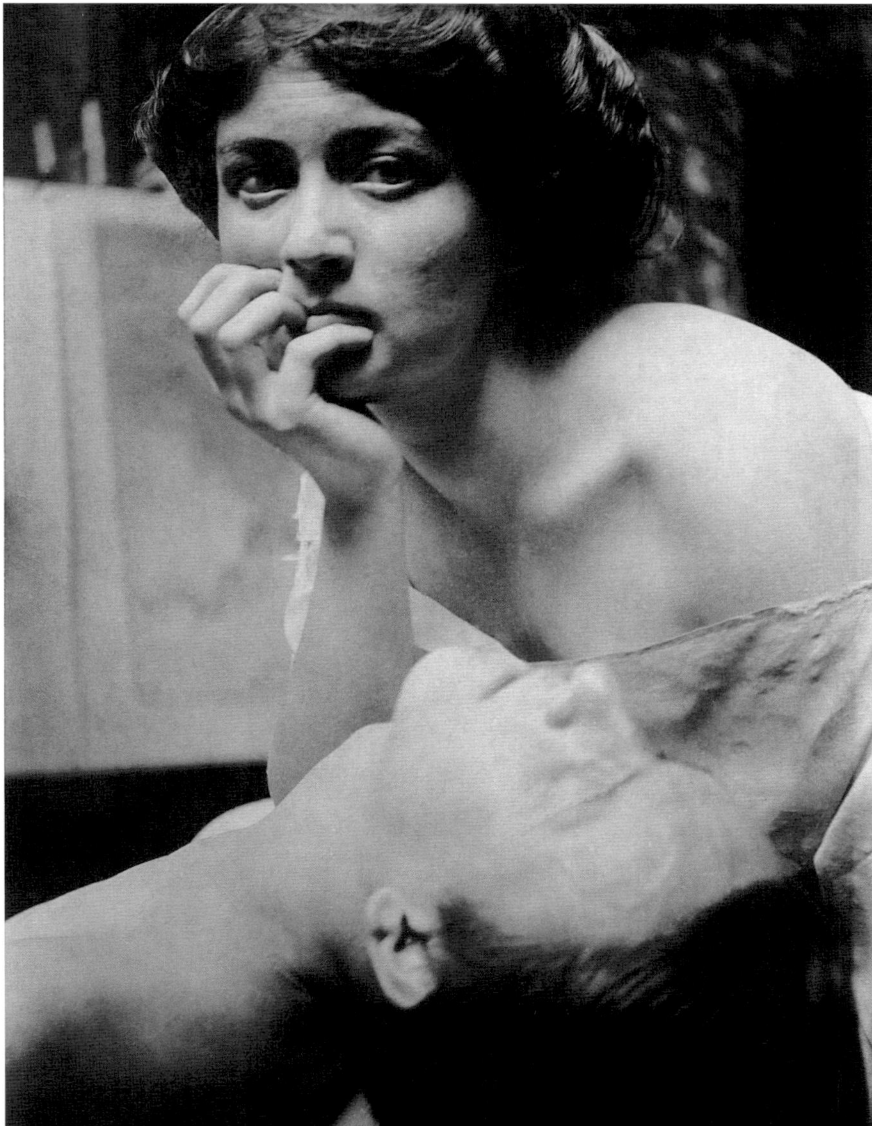

59 **New York** 1908

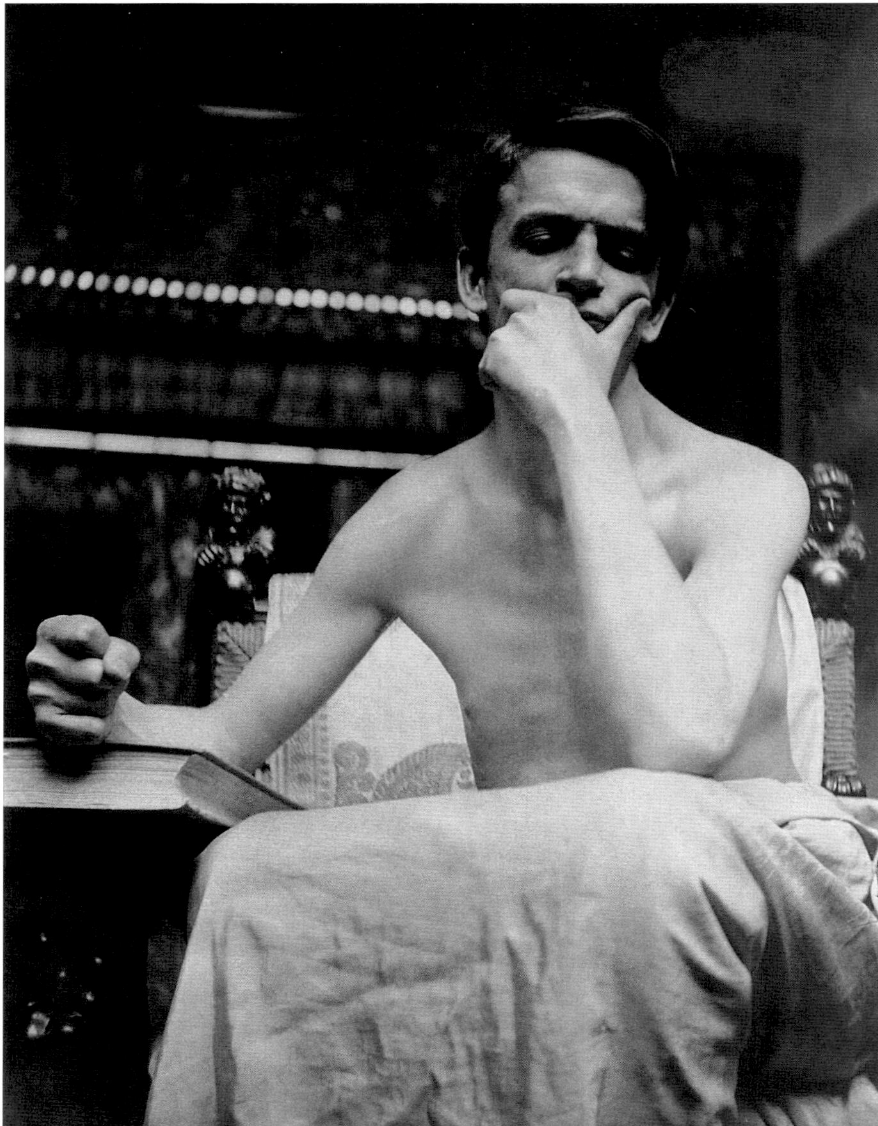

60 **New York** 1908

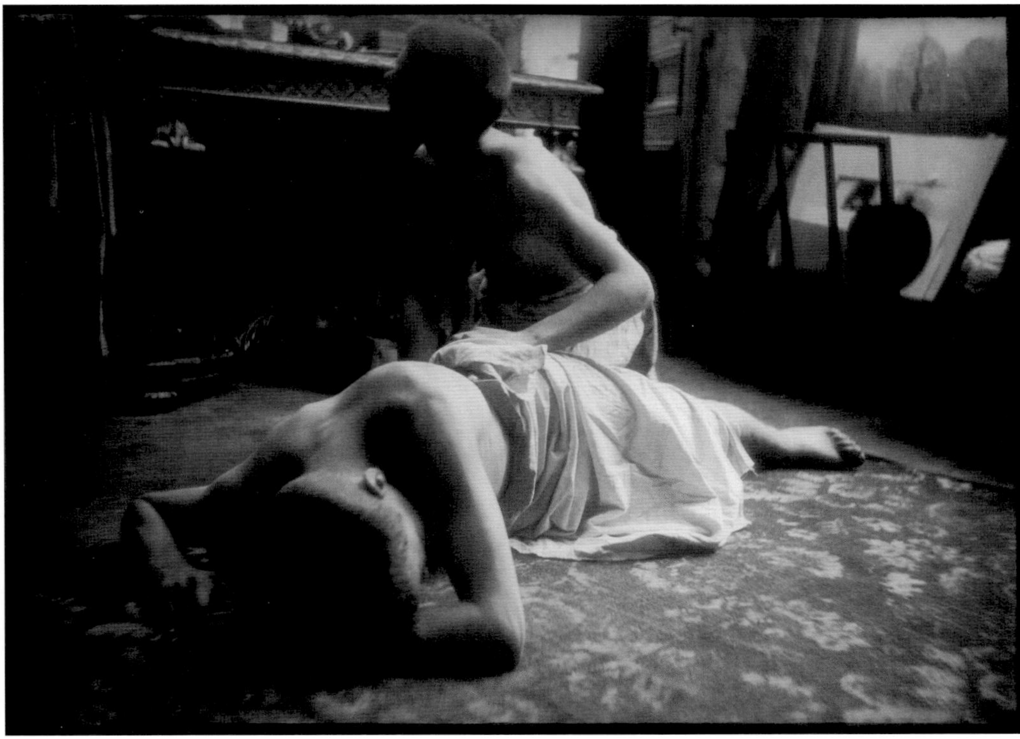

61 **New York** 1908

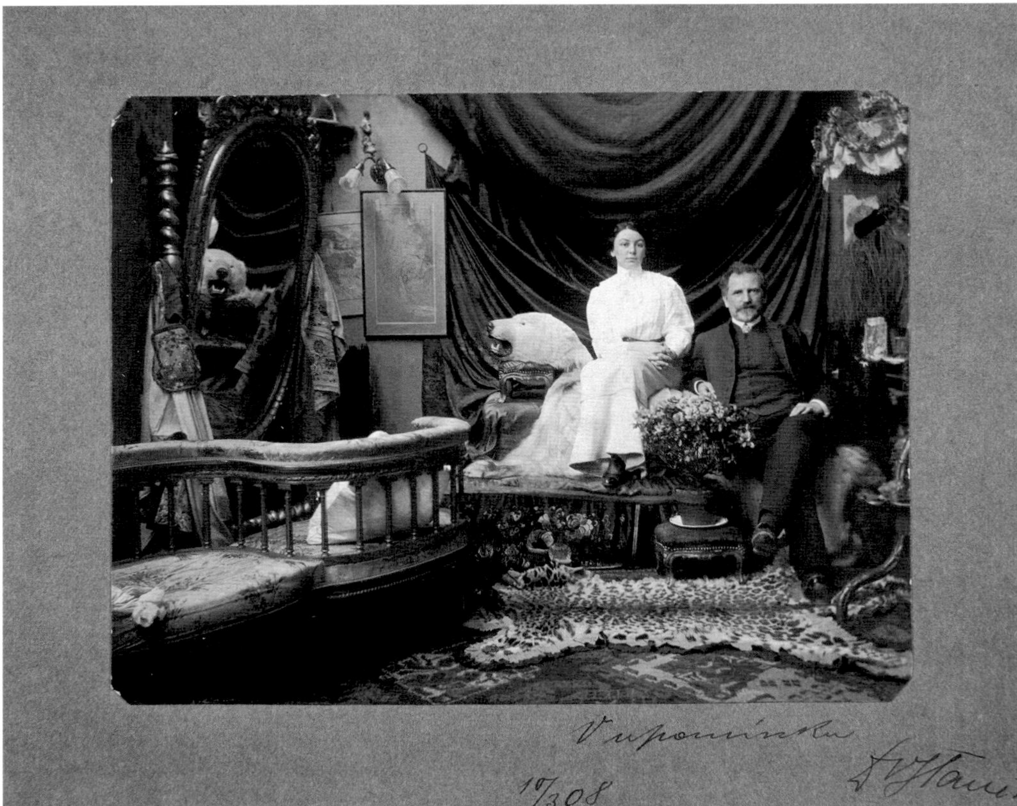
V upomínku
10/3 08.

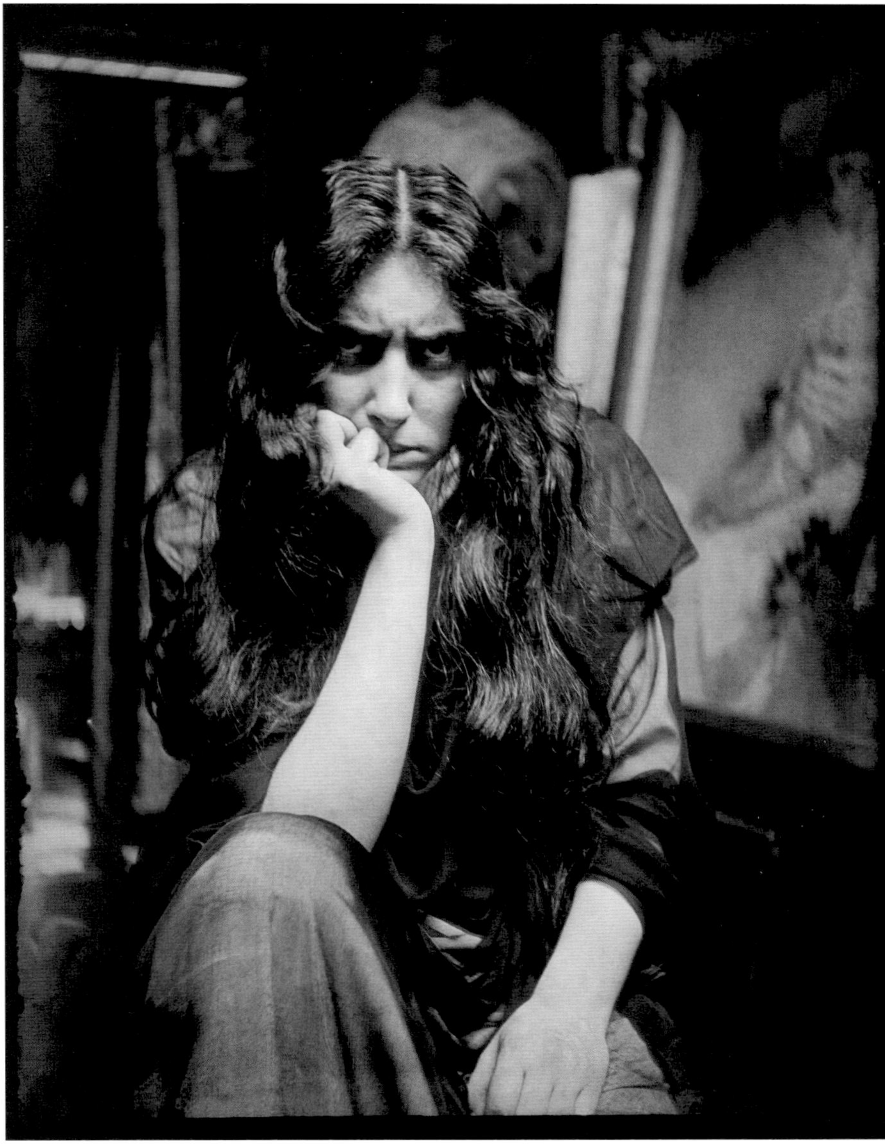

63 **New York** 1908

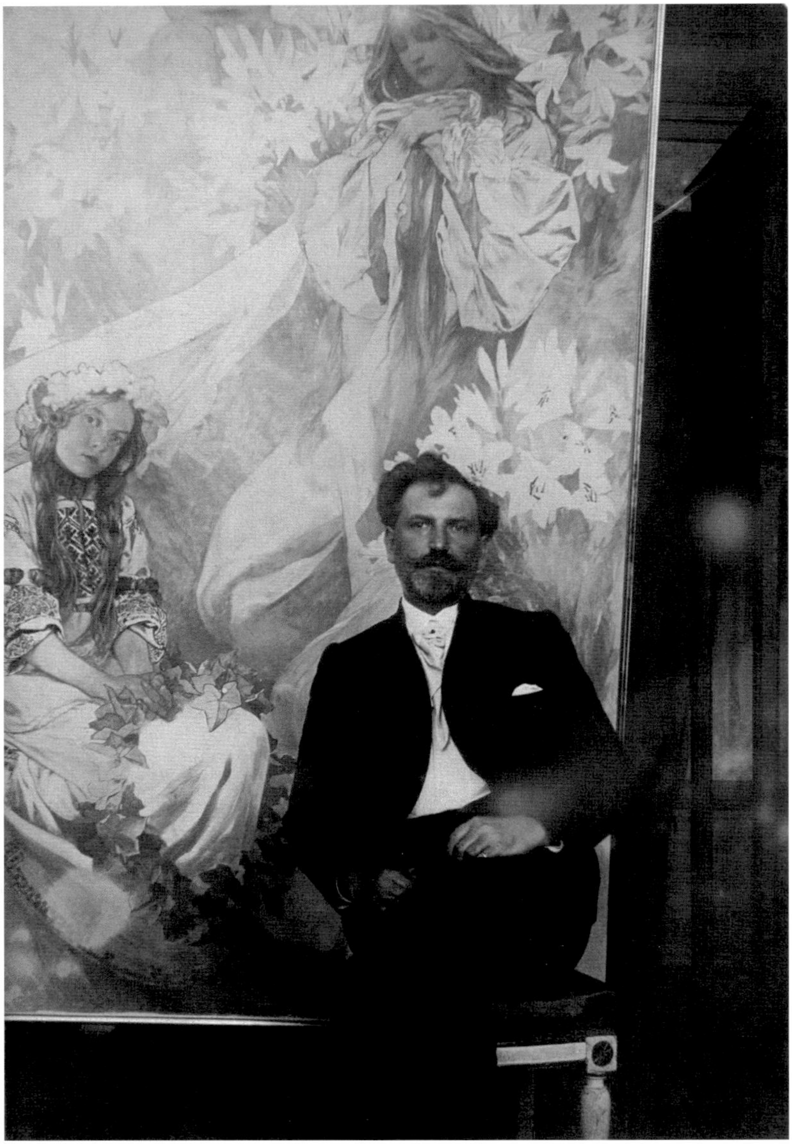

64 **New York** c. 1905

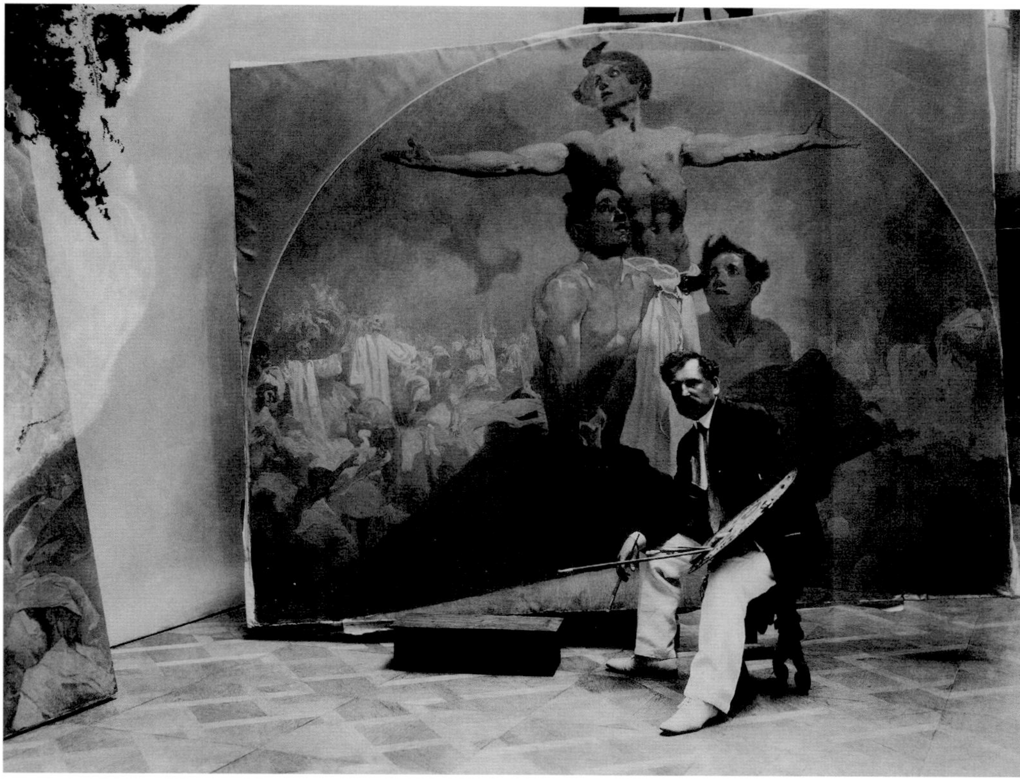

65 **Prague / Praha** 1911

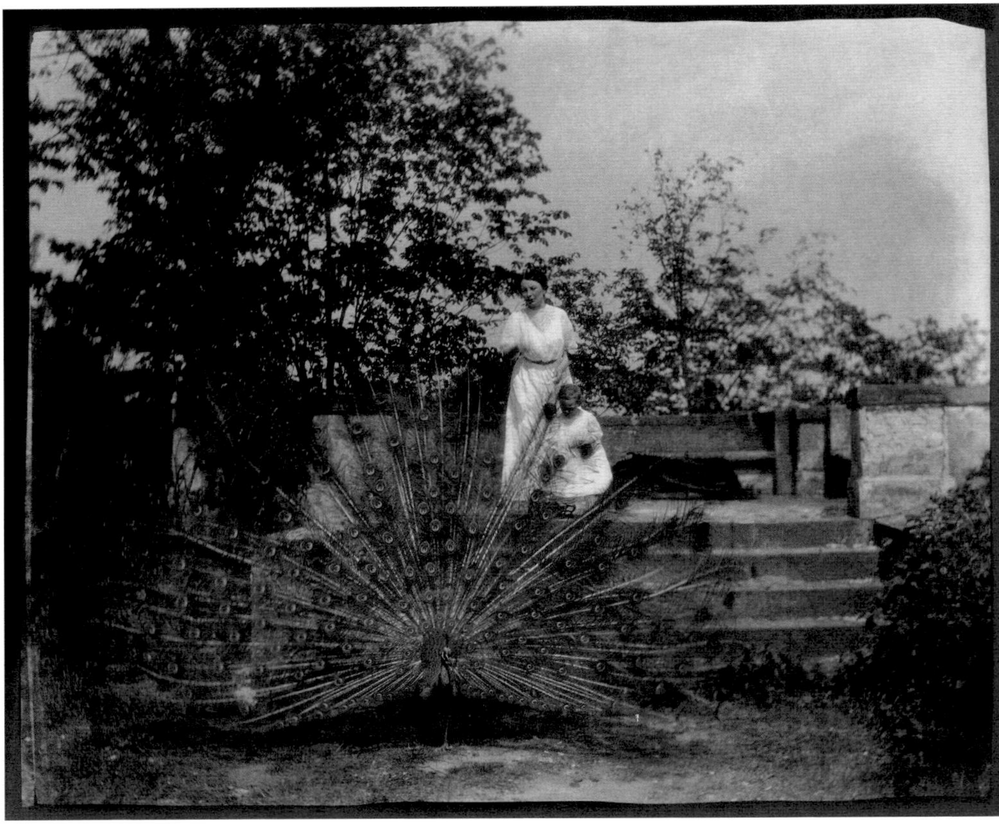

66 **Zbiroh, Bohemia** 1913

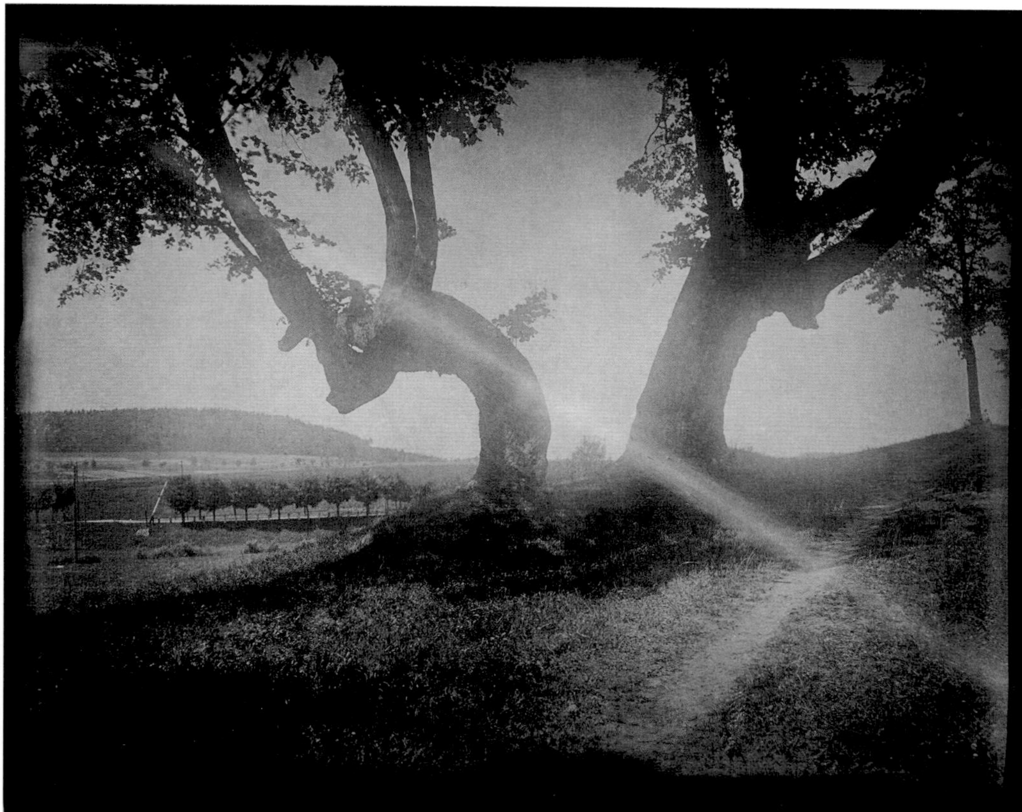

67 **Žamberk, Bohemia** 1925

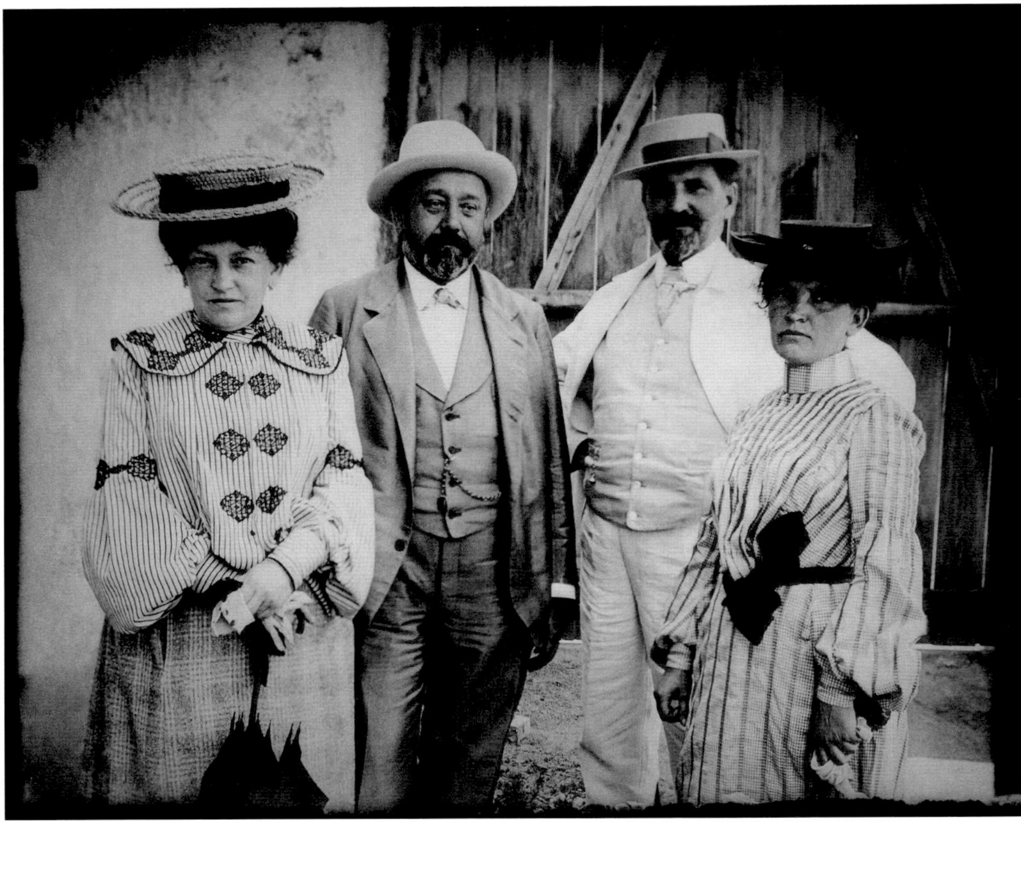

68 **Rosice, Moravia** c. 1911

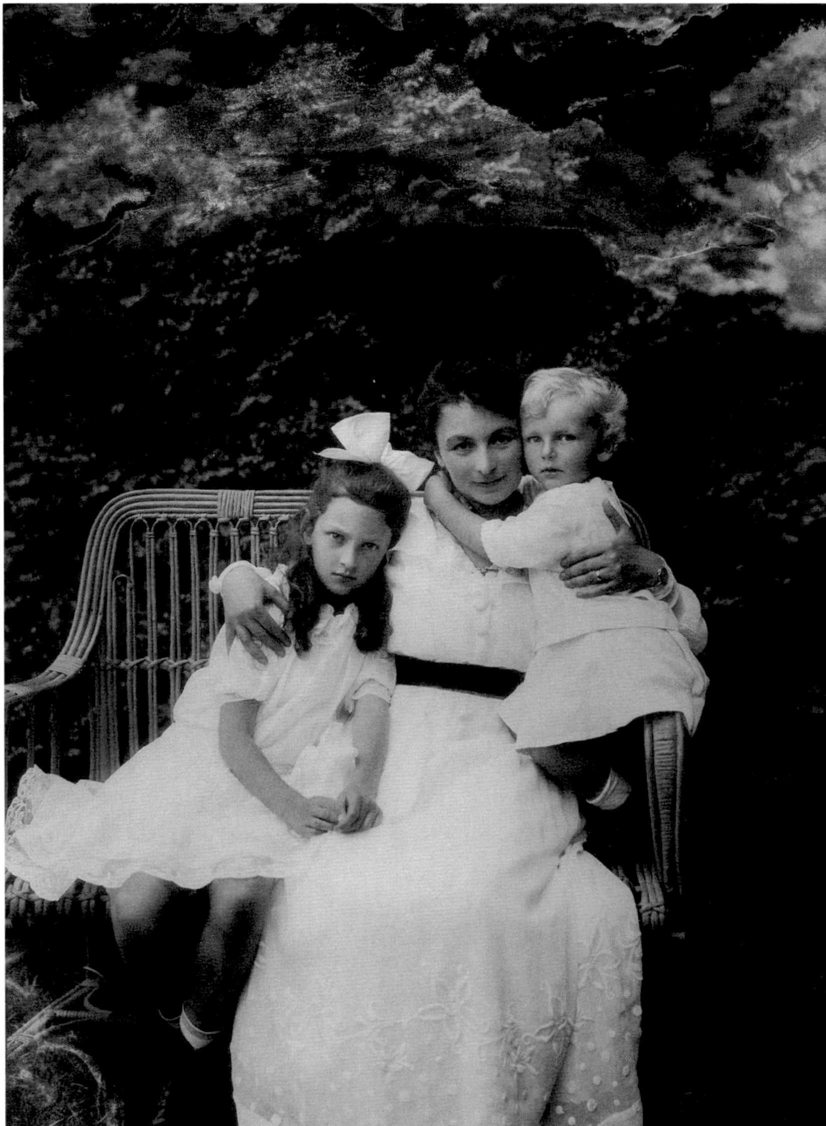

69 **Zbiroh, Bohemia** 1919

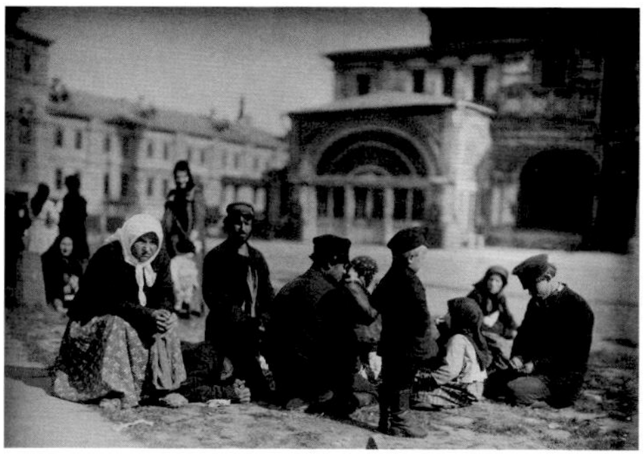

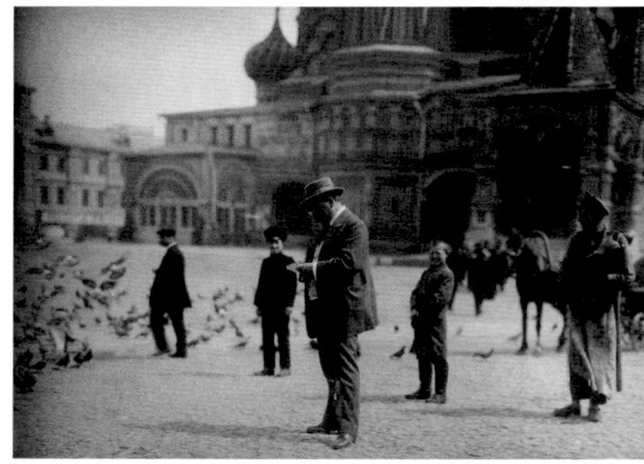

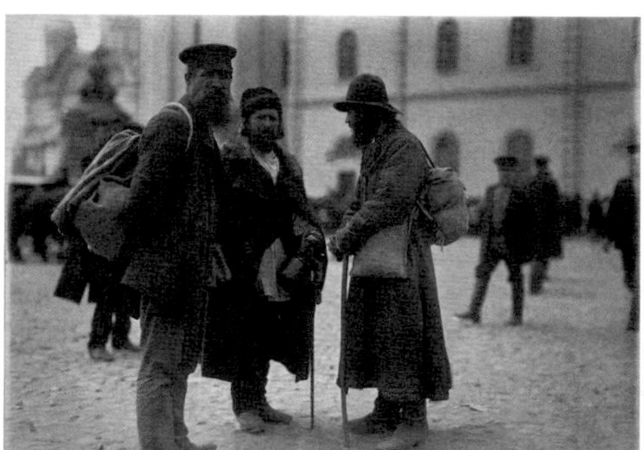

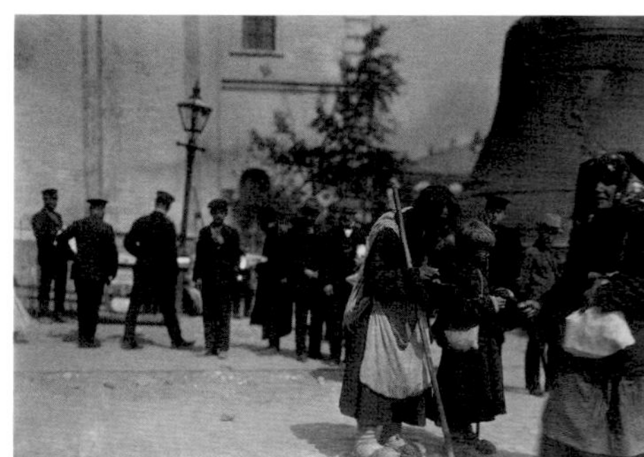

70 – 73 **Moscow / Moskva** 1913

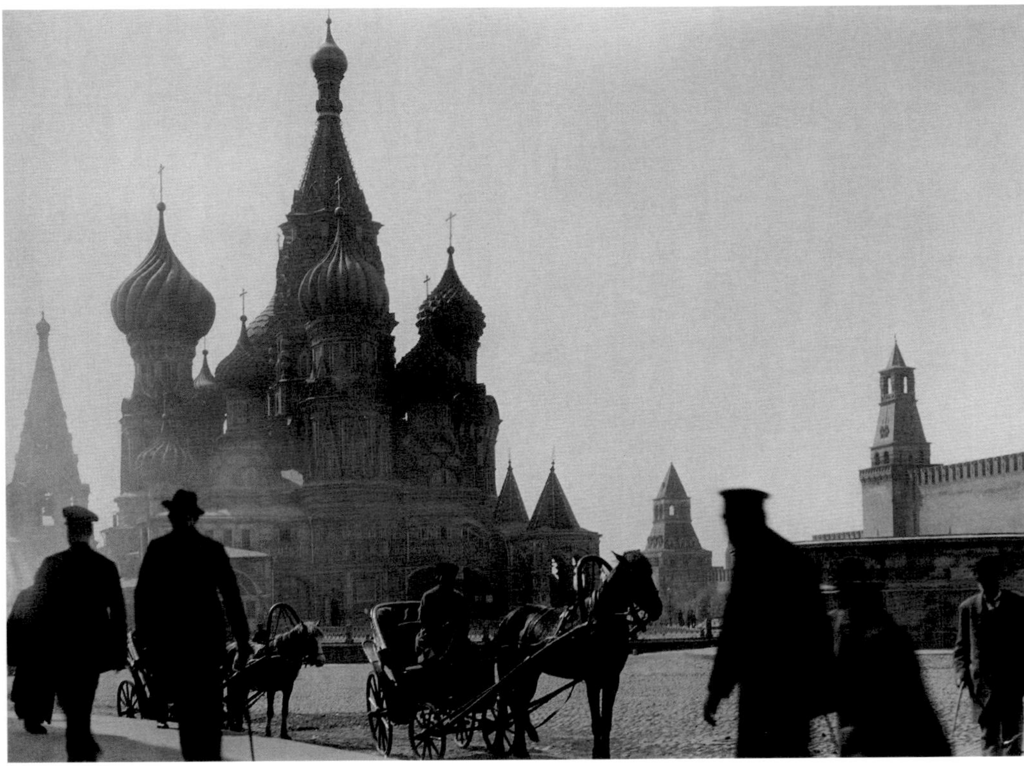

 Moscow / Moskva 1913

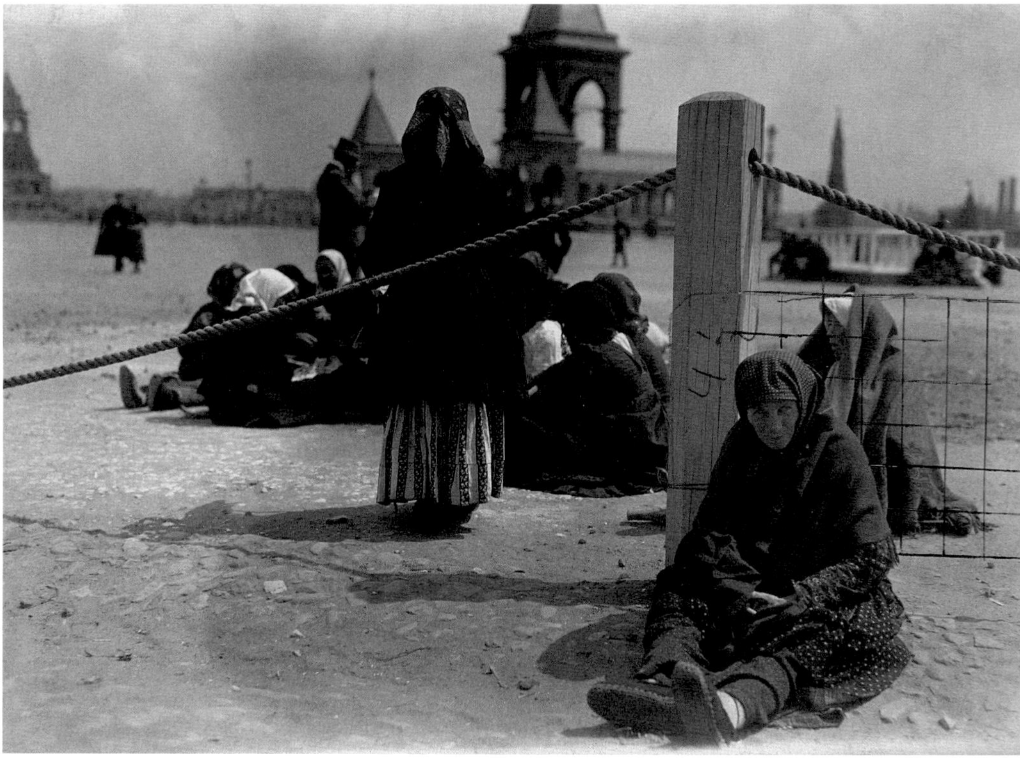

75 **Moscow / Moskva** 1913

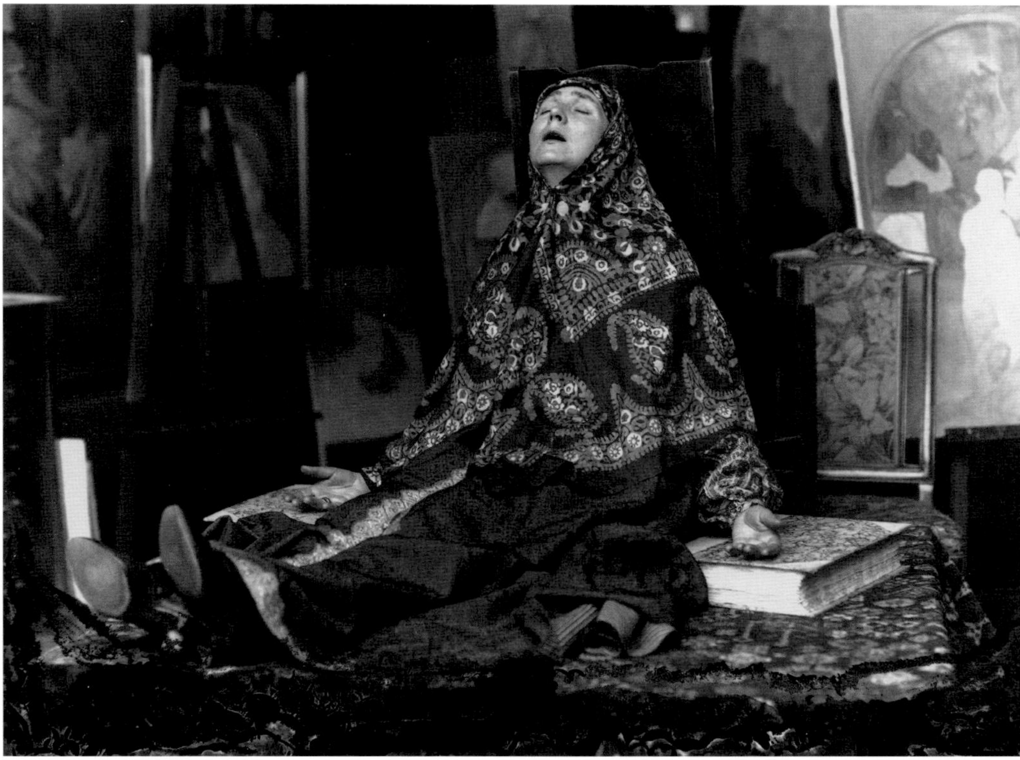

76 **Prague / Praha** c. 1920

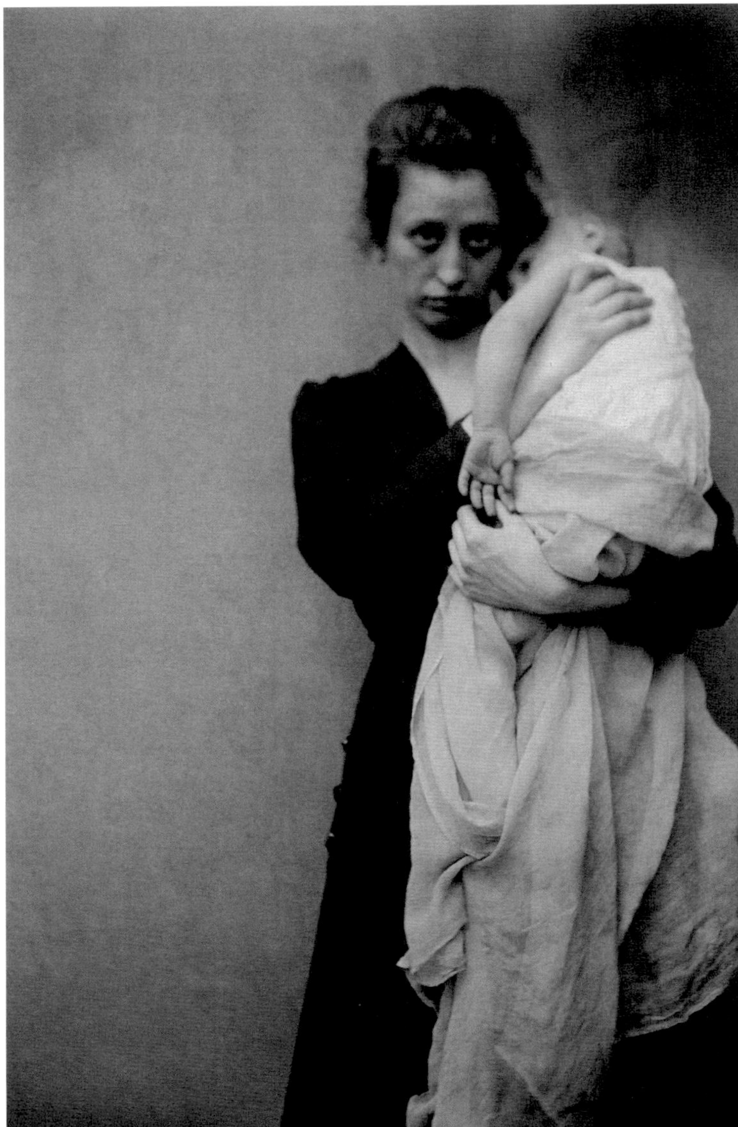

77 **Prague / Praha** c. 1921

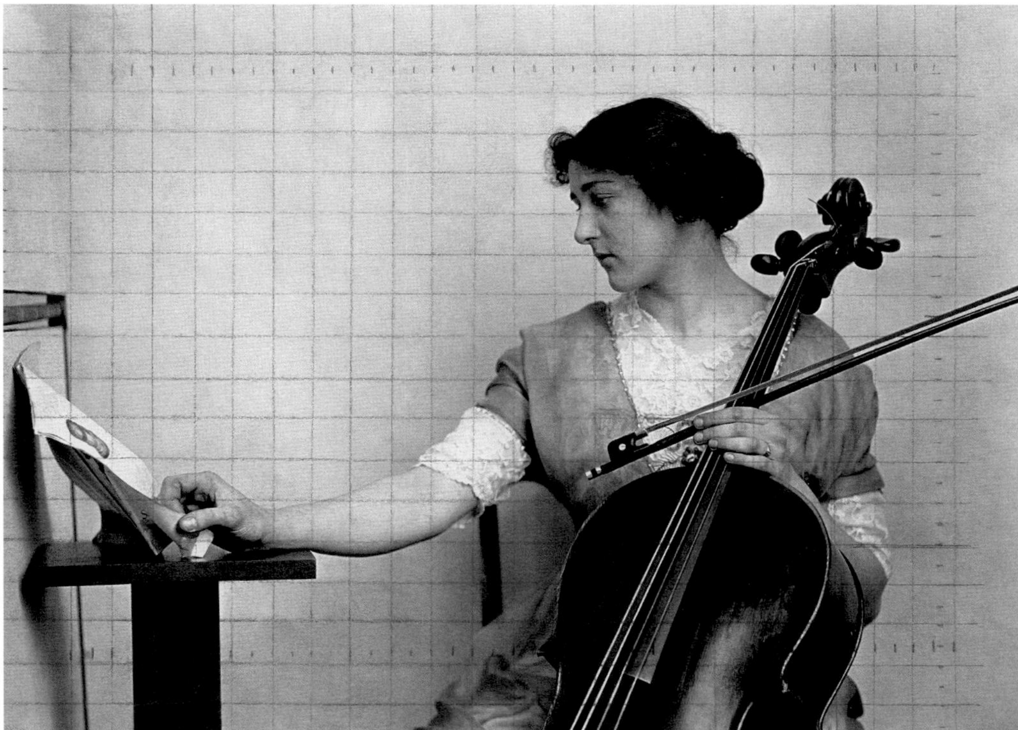

78 **Chicago** 1913

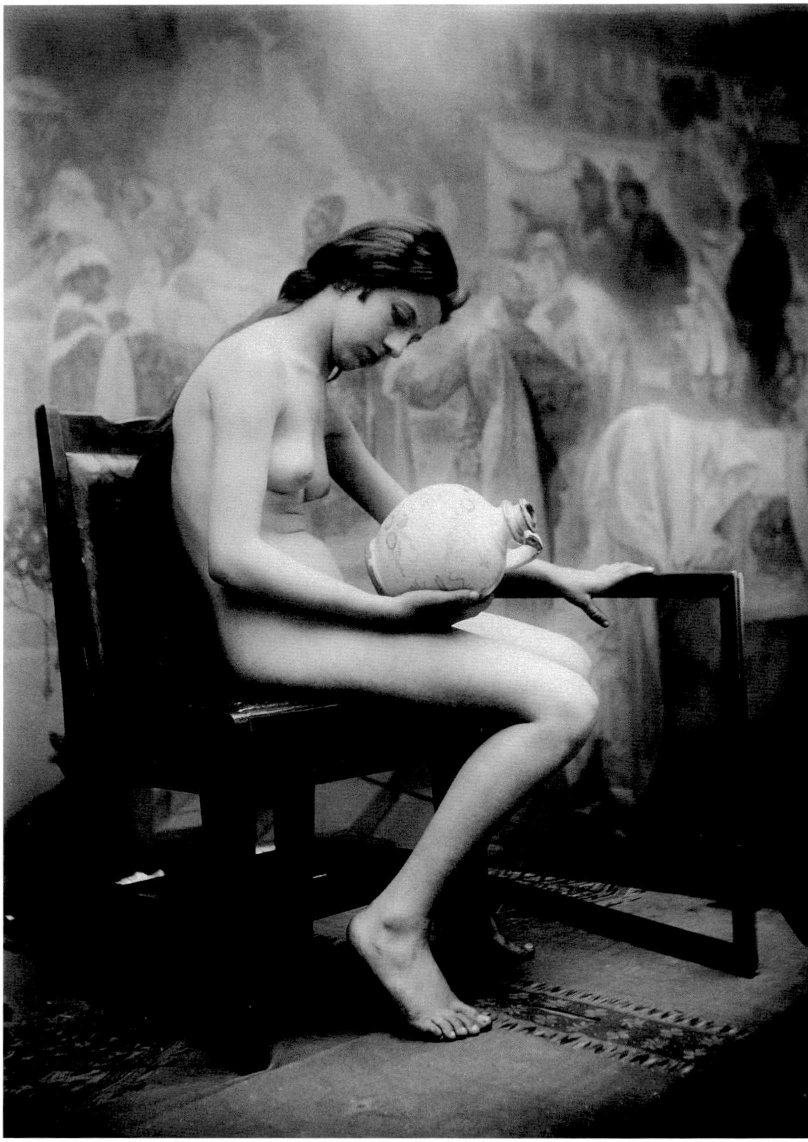

79 1927

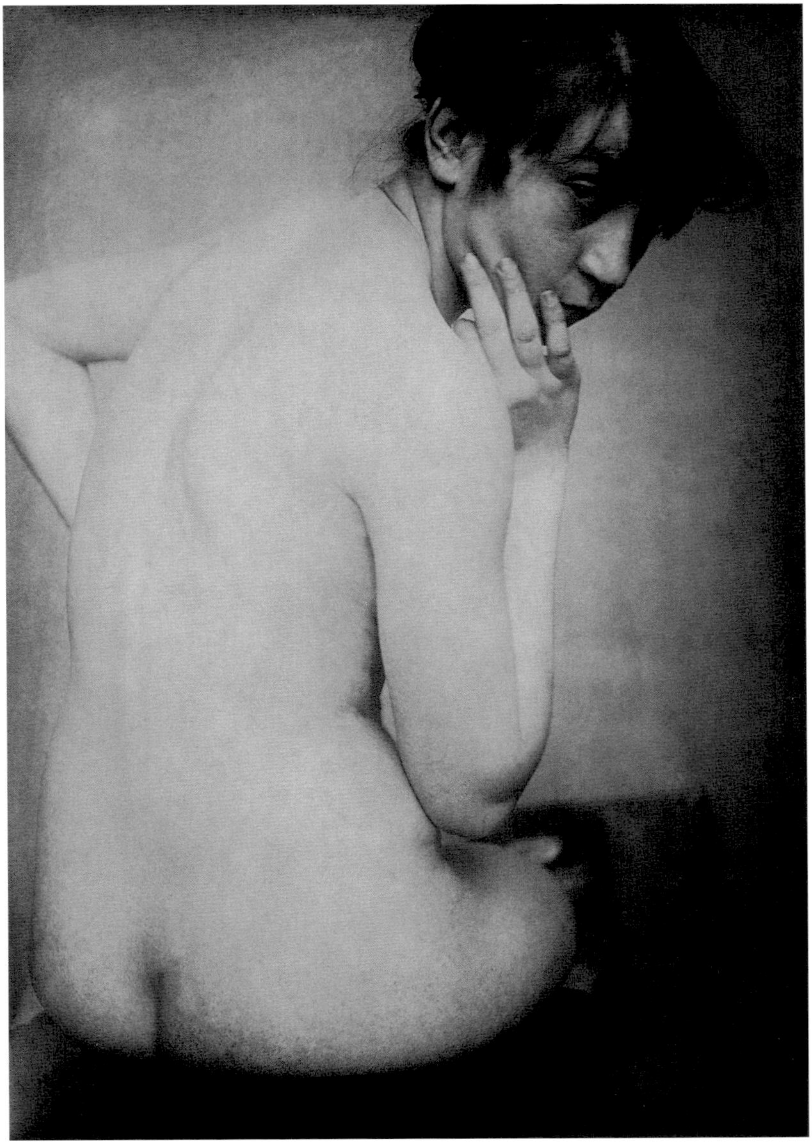

80 **Prague / Praha** c. 1913

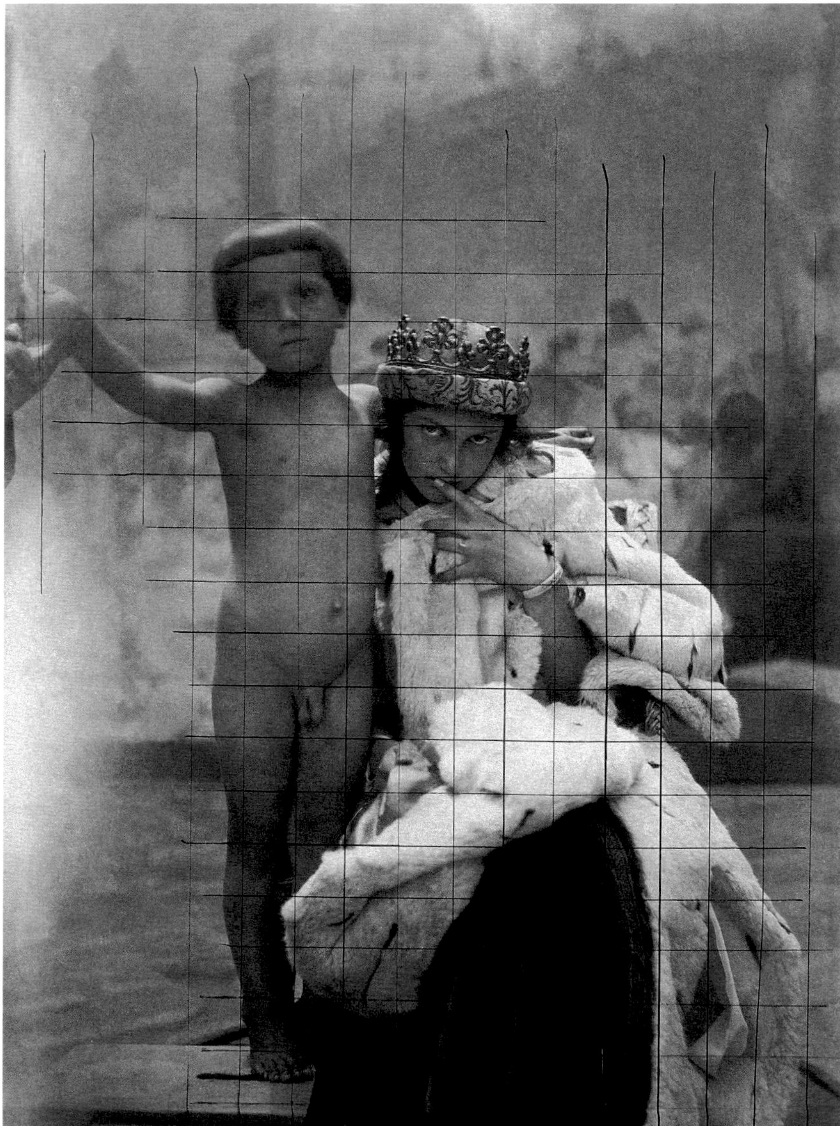

81 **Zbiroh, Bohemia** c. 1921

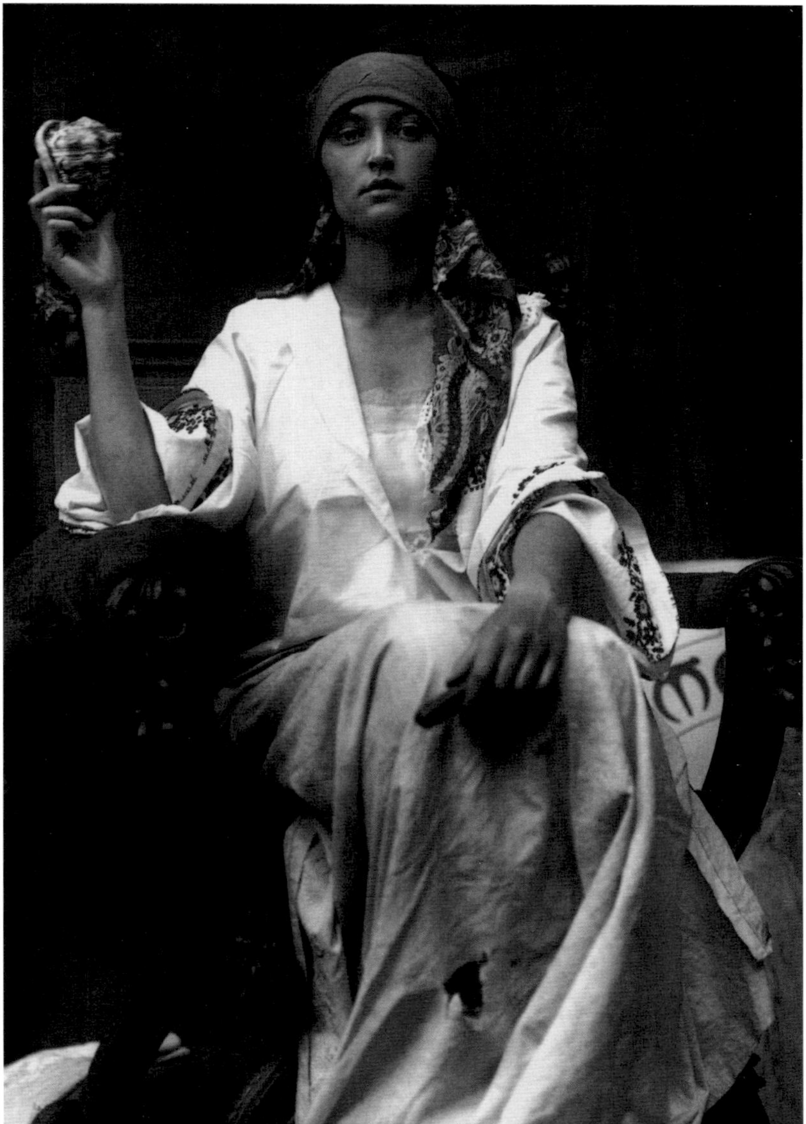

82 **Prague / Praha** c. 1920

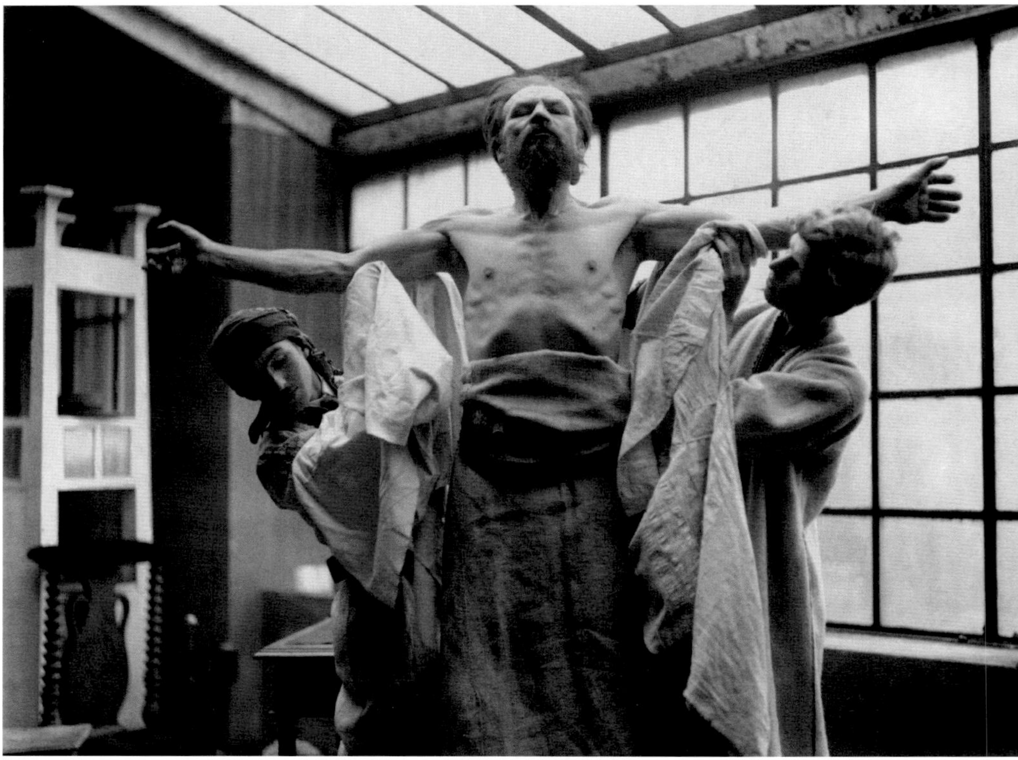

83 **Zbiroh, Bohemia** c. 1926

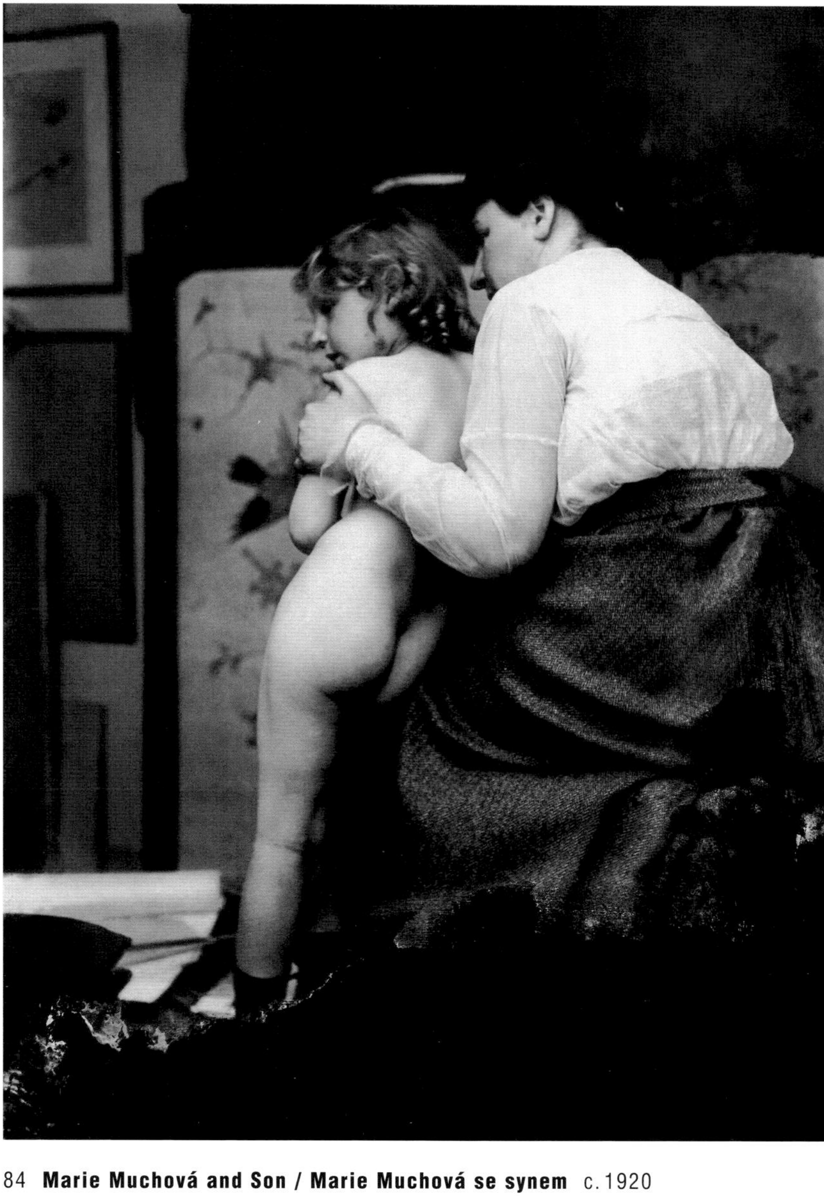

84 **Marie Muchová and Son / Marie Muchová se synem** c. 1920

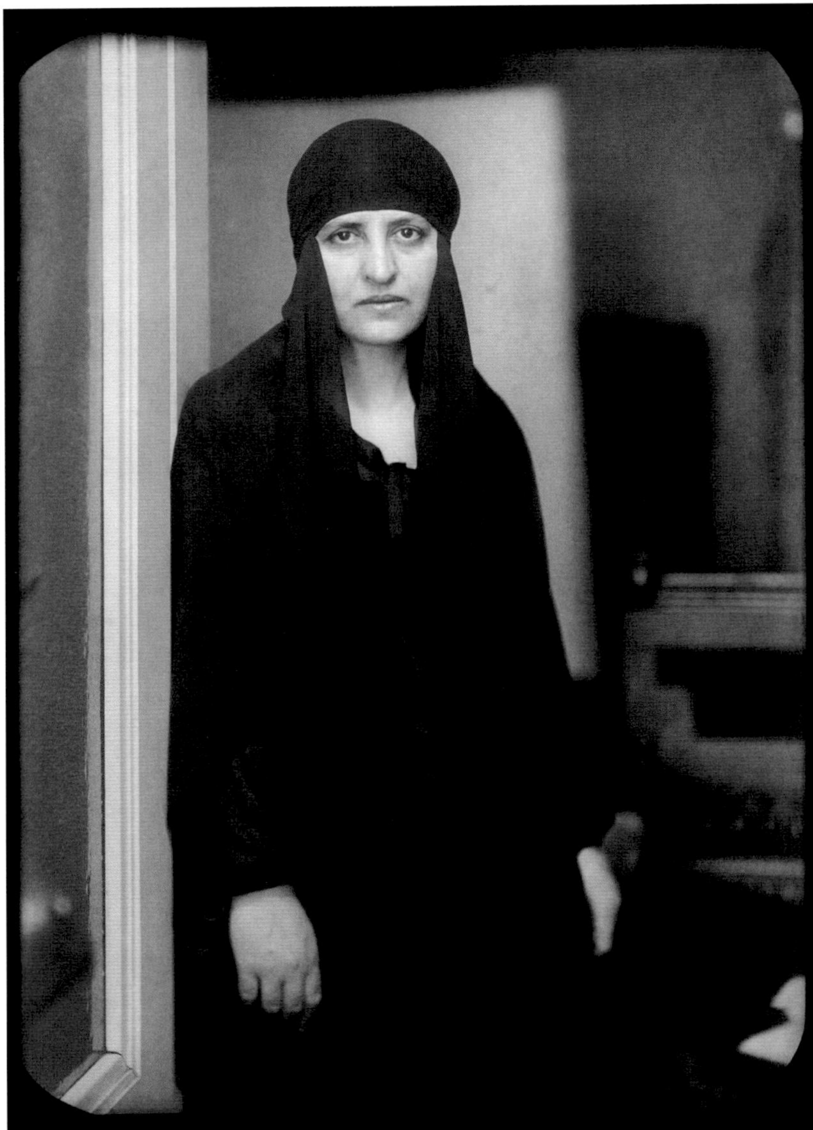

85 **Zbiroh, Bohemia** 1925

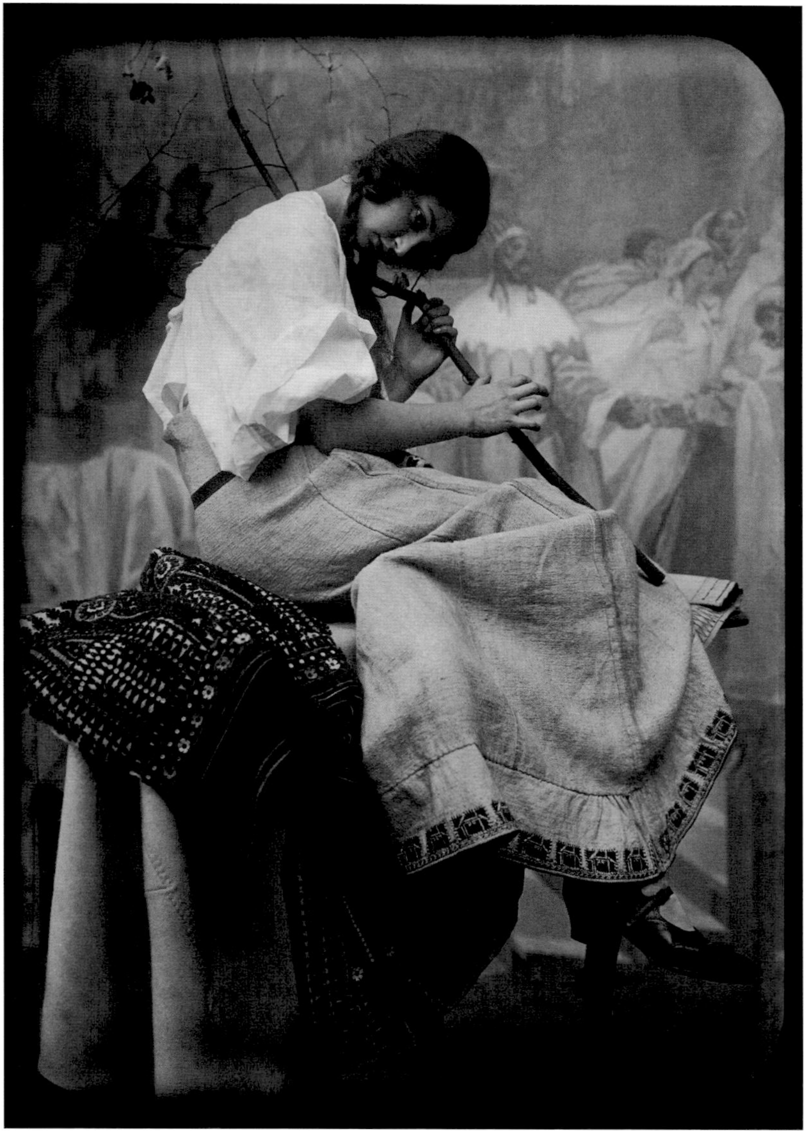

86 **Zbiroh, Bohemia** 1926

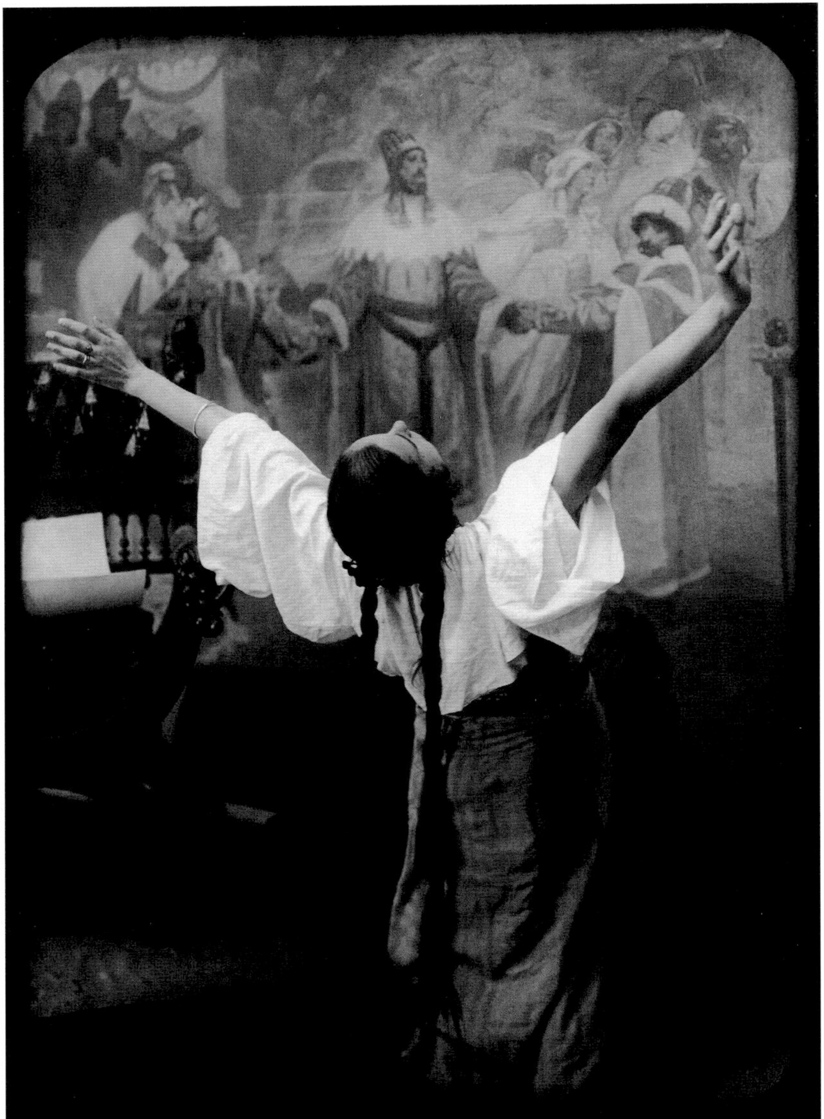

87 **Zbiroh, Bohemia** 1926

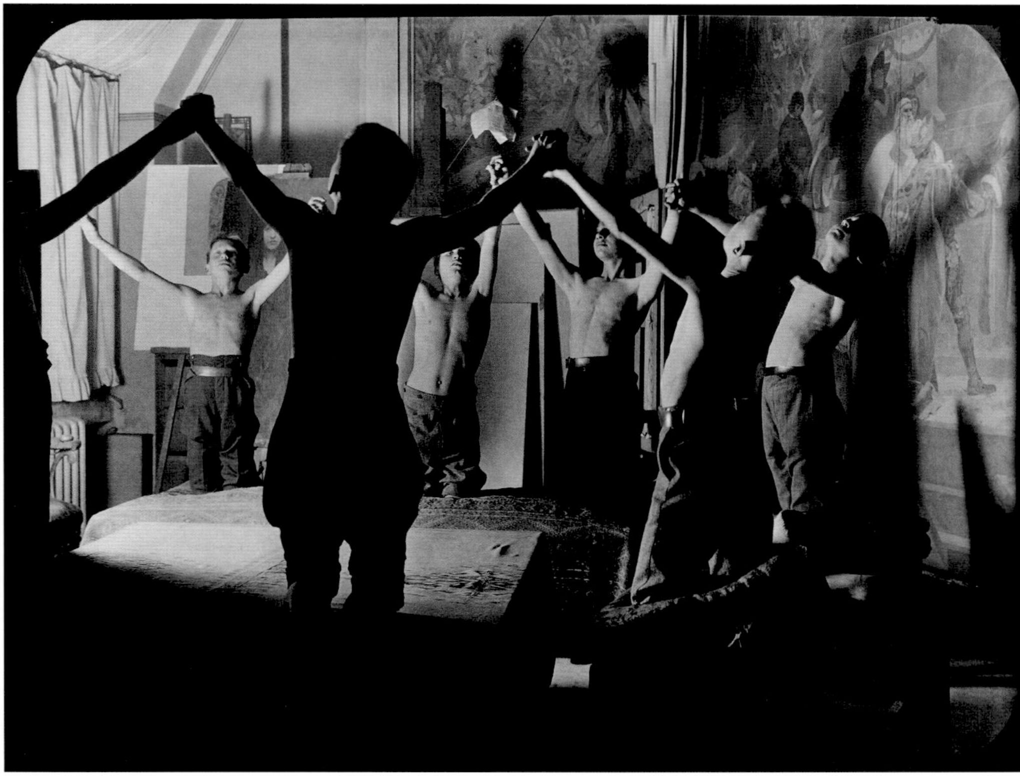

88 **Zbiroh, Bohemia** 1926

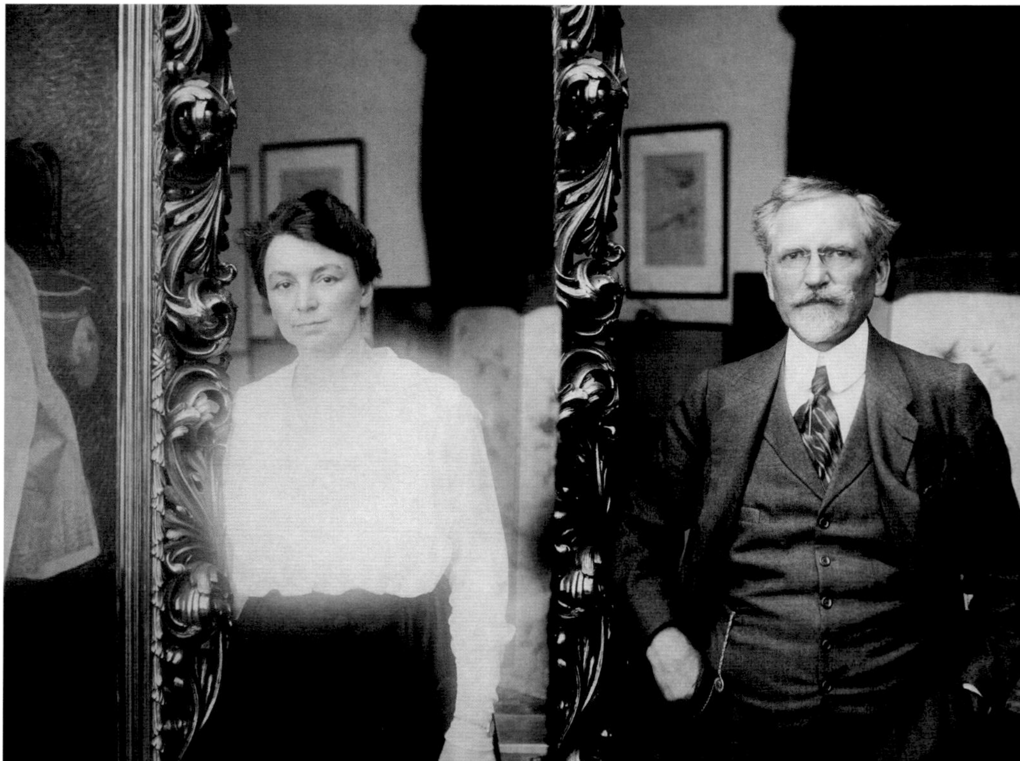

89 **Prague / Praha** c. 1920

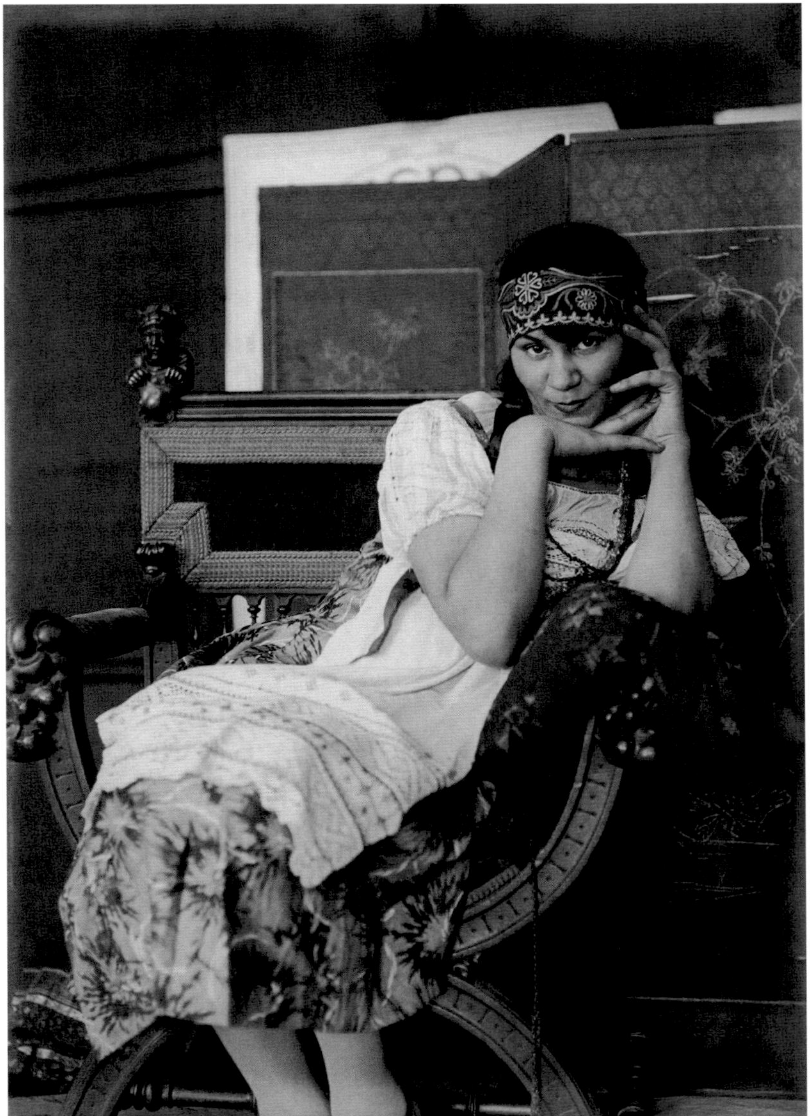

90 **Zbiroh, Bohemia** c. 1923

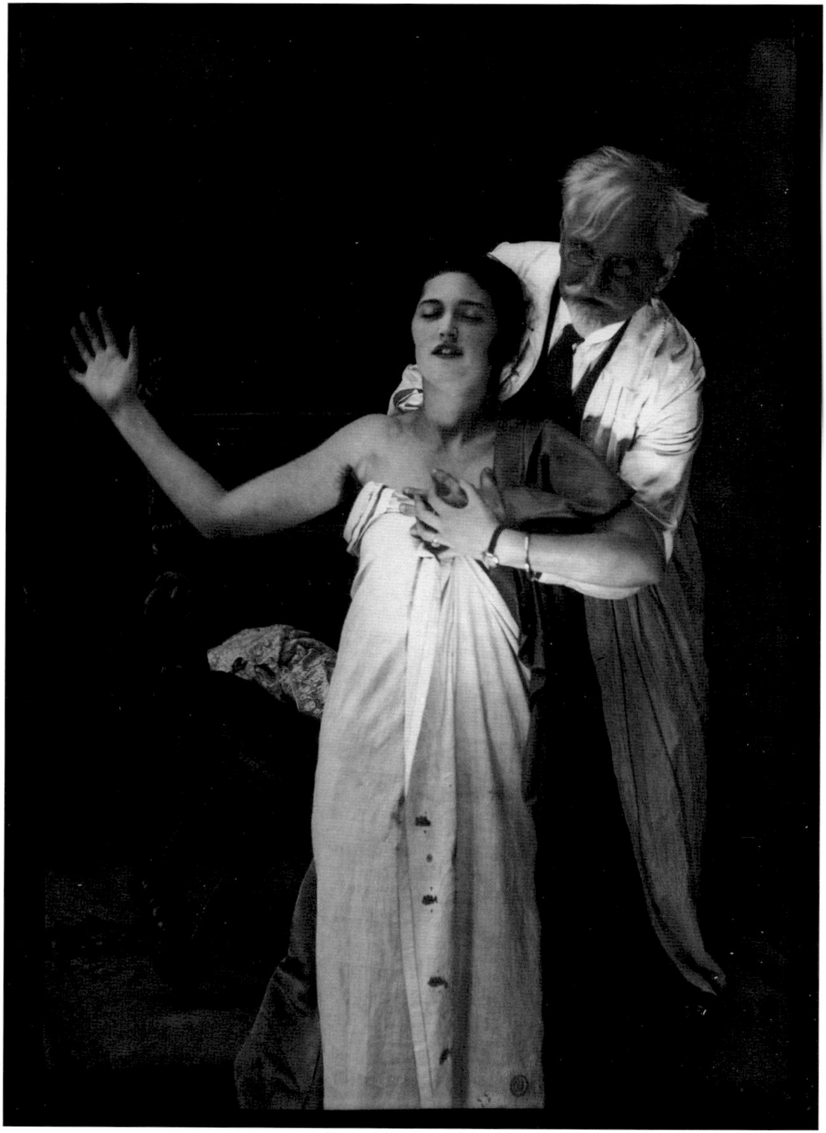

91 **Zbiroh, Bohemia** 1927

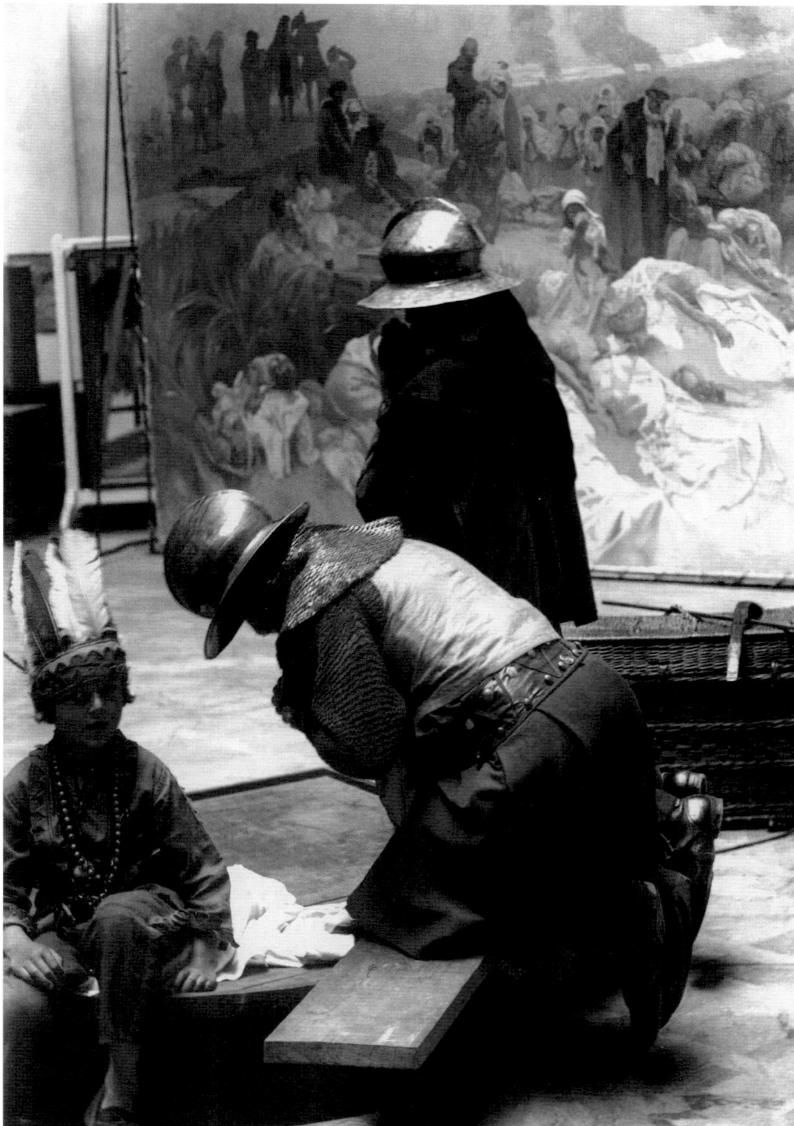

92 **Zbiroh, Bohemia** c. 1919

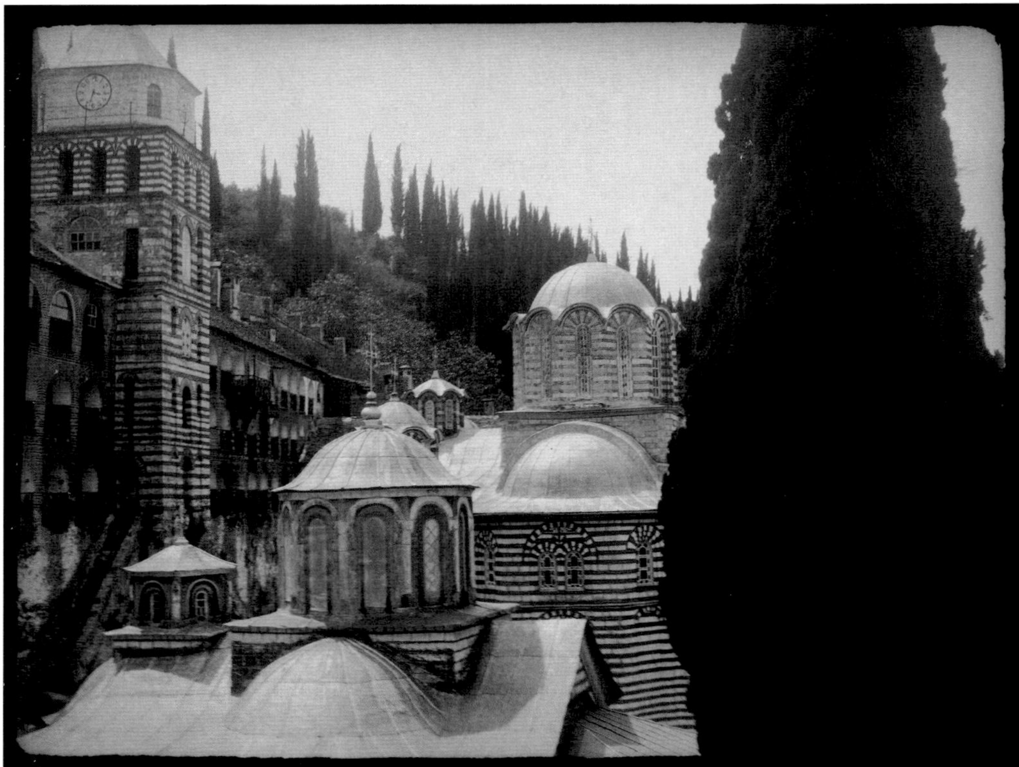

93 **Mount Athos / Mont Athos** 1924

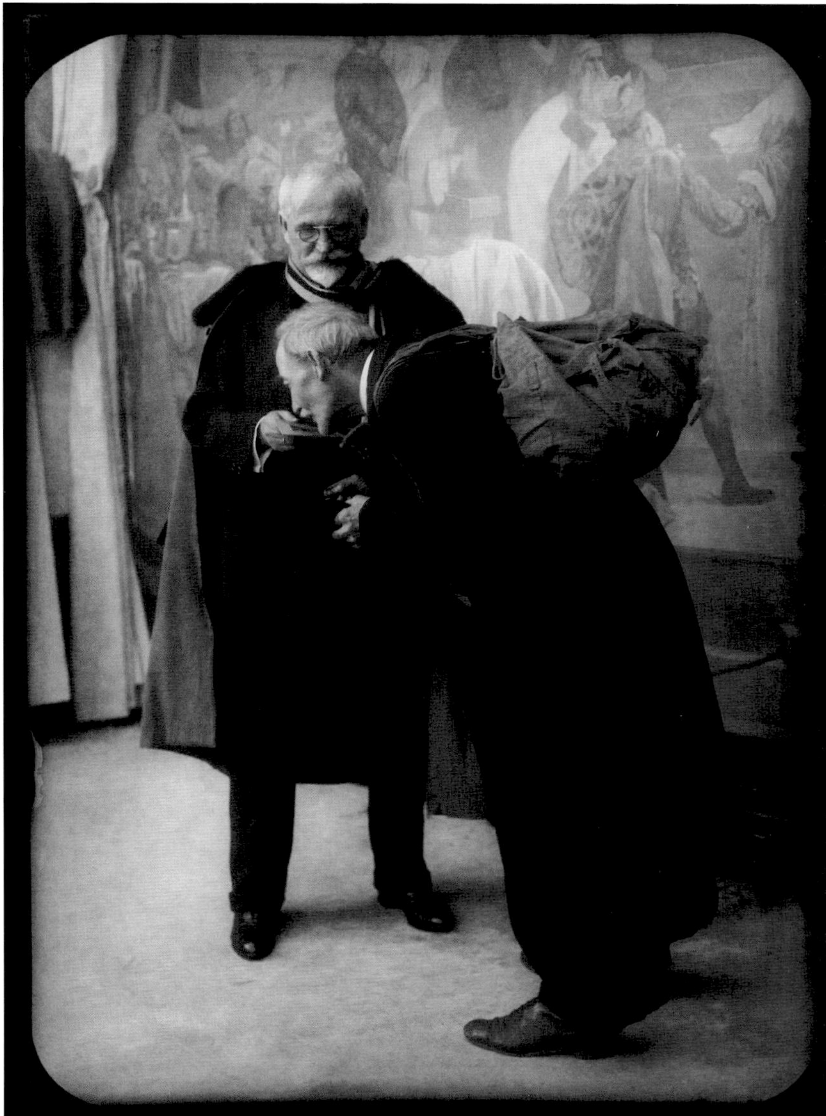

94 **Zbiroh, Bohemia** 1926

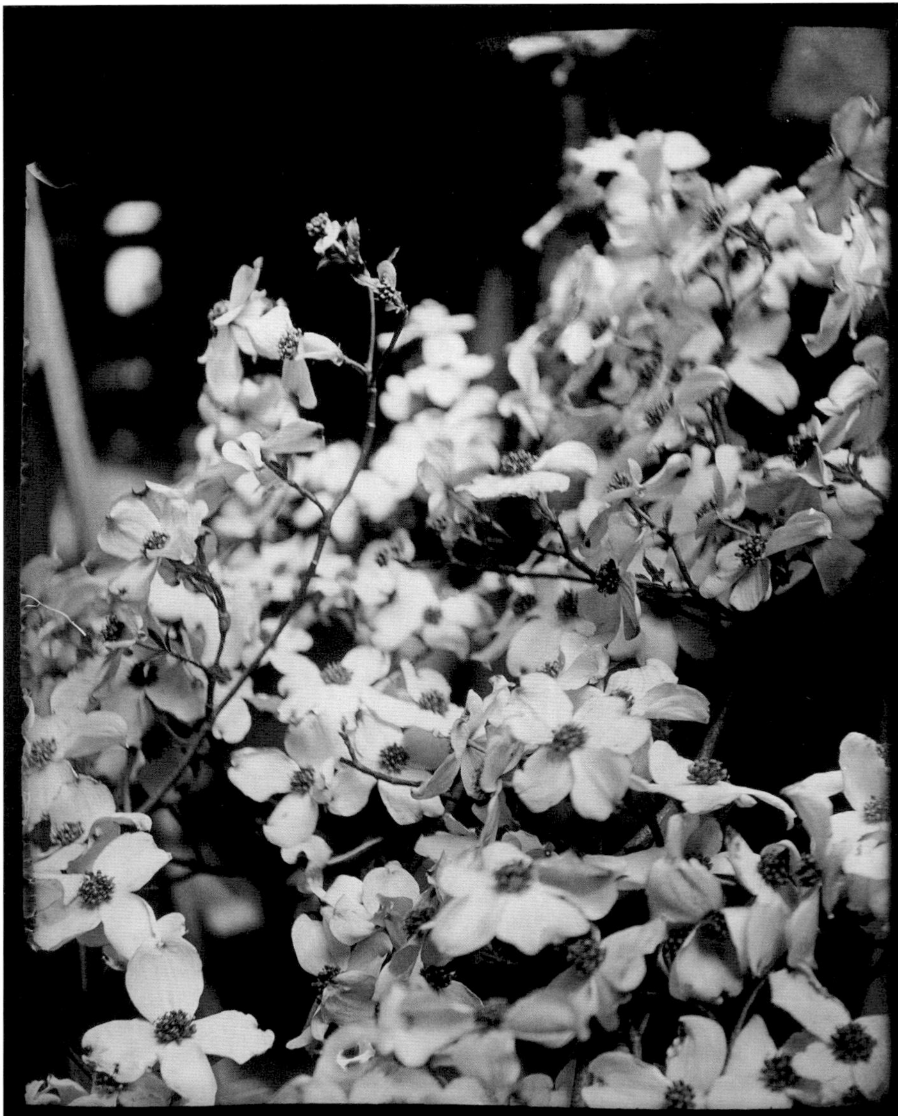

95 **Bush in Bloom / Kvetoucí keř**

Biographical Chronology

1860 Born on 24 July, in Ivančice, south Moravia, the son of Ondřej and Amálie Mucha. Even in childhood displayed talent for drawing.

1872 On 1 October, began the Slavic Secondary School, Brno, with a scholarship from the church in Petrov; sang in the choir, whose master was Leoš Janáček, six years his senior. Perfected his drawing skills under the painter Josef Zelený, who encouraged him to become a professional artist.

1877 Owing to poor results, expelled from school; became a court stenographer in Ivančice.

1878 In September, not accepted to the Academy of Fine Art, Prague, allegedly because of a lack of talent.

1881 Owing to unsatisfactory work, was dismissed from position of stenographer. In the autumn, left for Vienna to work for Kautski-Brioschi-Burghardt, a manufacturer of stage sets; on 10 December, fire destroyed the Ringtheater and Mucha lost his job.

1882–5 Made a figural wall painting in the château at Hrušovany nad Jevišovkou for Count Khuen-Belasi, who becomes Mucha's patron for seven years, and worked on frescoes in the Khuen ancestral home, Castle Gandegg, in the Tyrol.

1885 Study trip through the Tyrol and north Italy – Venice, Florence, Bologna, and Milan. In the autumn, admitted to the Munich Academy, from which was soon expelled for not paying school fees.

1886 In Munich, made a series of photographs on 7 x 7 cm negatives. Lived with a large colony of Slav students, for whom he founded what was initially a Czech club, Škréta; became its Chairman.

1887 Left Munich for Paris with Karel Václav Mašek; both men became students at the Académie Julian. Experienced the beginning of Symbolism, whose manifesto had been published by Jean Moréas the year before.

1888 Spent the summer and part of the autumn at the Hrušovany estate, where continued to work as a decorator for his patron. Upon returning to Paris, enrolled at the Académie Colarossi in rue de la Grande Chaumière. Remained faithful to the Latin Quarter, where he lived.

1889 Support from the count ended, which meant abandoning studies and beginning large-scale collaboration as an illustrator with French and Czech publishers of periodicals and books.

1890 In the summer he settled down for six years in rue de la Grande Chaumière (nos. 13, 12, and 8); here he made a number of photographs of places he had lived in, models, and remarkable visitors, including the famous photos with Paul Gauguin.

1893 In this year, at the latest, acquired a 10 x 13 cm camera, and used it till the Great War, together with other rectangular-format cameras, which he continued to use later, whether with glass negatives or, eventually, with celluloid. Eugène Manuel's *Poésies du foyer et de l'école* was published with Mucha's illustrations (reprinted, again in Paris, in 1903 and 1908).

1894 During the Christmas holidays, designed the poster *Gismonda* for Sarah Bernhardt's Théâtre de la Renaissance.

1895 Sarah Bernhardt persuaded "her discovery" to sign a contract for six years, and ordered not only posters but also consultations concerning her own stage designs.

1896 With the printing of the poster for the twentieth exhibition of the Salon des Cent, the gallery of the art journal *La Plume* made Mucha a member of its circle (which included Toulouse-Lautrec, Grasset, De Fevre, Berthon, Bonnard, Ensor, Evenepoel, Rassenfosse, and van Rysselberghe). Illustrated the medieval legend *La princesse Lointaine* retold by Robert de Flers (134 reproductions were published the following year in Paris as *Ilsée, Princesse de Tripoli*; the Czech edition, *Ilséa, princezna Tripolská*, and the German, were published in Prague in 1901); while working on this project, developed a method for the monumental personification of spiritual and natural energies, which then used in his *Epic of the Slavs*. Moved into a studio in rue du Val-de-Grâce, at the upper end of the Boulevard Saint Michel. Here, he had considerably more light: for the first time, he had large windows and a glass ceiling. Here, too, was the printing press of the Champenois company, with whose owner Mucha signed a contract for the next several years. Jiří Mucha figured out from his father's diary, Alfons Mucha had by this time begun to take photographs almost every day. In this new workplace he discovered the studio of the sculptor August Seysses, who led him to sculpt, and, he also began to work in pastels.

1897 First two independent exhibitions were held in Paris: beginning on 15 February, exhibited 107 works in the Galerie de la Bodinière, and, on 24 May, opened a large, representative collection of 448 work in the Salon des Cent, to which the journal *La Plume* dedicated an entire issue. During this year and the next, Mucha's work was sent to Vienna, Prague, Hradec Králové, Budapest, Munich, Brussels, London, and New York (and he twice installed them in independent exhibitions in the East Bohemian Museum of Industry, Chrudim). Champenois commenced the mass production of Mucha postcards, decorative *panneaux*, and prints (both mass produced and as limited editions). The *Zodiac* calendar (designed, in 1896, originally for a company), was taken over and popularized by the magazine *La Plume*; the calendar became so popular that in subsequent years it was reprinted several times for various purposes. Became a member of the Société Internationale de l'Art Populaire and designed the *Pavillion de l'Homme* for the Paris International Exhibition of 1900. In Prague, Svatopluk Čech's *Adamité* was published, illustrated by Mucha, for which he had begun work back in 1893.

1898 In January, made an apprentice member of the Paris lodge of Freemasons called Les inséparables du progrés (after the First World War, became a Grandmaster of the Freemasons in Czechoslovakia, and in the 1920s designed badges for the first Czech lodge, Jan Amos Komenský). Beginning with his participation in the exhibition of the Viennese Sezession, became a member for three years of the Vereinigung bildender Künstler Oesterreichs. An exquisite edition of Charles Seignobos's *Scènes et Episodes de l'Histoire d'Allemagne* was published with illustrations by Mucha and Georges Rochegross, which they had been working on since 1892. Completed a three-panel stained-glass window for the chapel of the Assumption, in the rue François I, Paris, and continued to work on a contractual basis with various publishing houses and the printer Champenois.

1899 Prepared a wide range of projects for the Paris International Exhibition and completed the designs for the decoration of a pavilion promoting the Austro-Hungarian administration of Bosnia and Herzegovina. In the midst of the disruptions at the turn of the century, and pampered by the milieu that liked the popular art of the poster, Mucha decided to dedicate the second half of his life to serious work, in an effort to surmount the reputation of an ingenious graphic designer. Published *Le Pater*, an exquisite edition of the Lord's Prayer in French. (A Czech version was published two years later.)

1900 Art Nouveau came to a peak at the Paris International Exhibition, where Mucha was well represented in a number of departments. Anatole France's Clio and a limited edition of *Cloches de Noël et de Pâques* by Emil Gebhart were published with Mucha's illustrations. Dubbed a Knight of the Order of Franz Joseph I.

1901 Conferred the Order of the Legion of Honor, France, and elected a member of the Bohemian Academy of Arts and Sciences. Georges Fouquet's jewelry shop, designed by Mucha, opened in the rue Royal (the Parisian Musée Carnavalet owns a replica of its extraordinarily complete Art Nouveau interior).

1902 Seventy-two plates called *Documents décoratifs* were published. Forty prints, *Figures décoratives*, appeared three years later; eventually Mucha bought back from the publisher Émil Lévy all the original designs of what amounted to instructions for general use of "le style Mucha." In the summer, accompanied August Rodin to Rodin's Prague exhibition and made a number of enemies in his homeland by declaring, "I see nothing here but the aping of Vienna, Munich, and Paris."

1903 On the windy afternoon of 17 October, in Paris, became acquainted with Marie Chytilová of Chrudim, Bohemia; on 10 June 1906 they were married in the chapel of St Roche at the Strahov Monastery, Prague. The marriage resulted in two children – Jaroslava (1909) and Jiří (1915).

1904 On 5 March, disembarked in the United States of America for the first time. By the outbreak of the First World War (which he anticipated in a statement to the *Chicago Examiner*, on 24 February 1913), Mucha had visited the USA a total of six times.

1905 While on a second visit to the USA, chaired a jury judging designs for a poster advertising photographic equipment and optical instruments.

1906 On 3 April, opened his New York exhibition. While on his honeymoon in the south Bohemian town of Pec near Domažlice, took photographs using Kodak roll-film. In the autumn, moved his studio from Paris to New York.

1908 In the spring, began work on pictures for the decoration of the German Theater in New York, which was ceremoniously presented to the public on 1 October (and closed eight months later). Mrs. Leslie Carter persuaded him to design the scenery, costumes, and poster for *Kassa* (which was a dismal failure in the dramatic sense).

1909 Designed a poster for Maud Adams's performance in Schiller's *Joan of Arc*. Completed his plans for twenty scenes symbolizing the Slavs from prehistory to the modern age, which he intended to present as a gift to the metropolis of the Bohemian Lands. "My work," he said, "has to be like isolated cries free of affectation [...]." At Christmas he obtained a promise of financial support for his *Epic of the Slavs* from the Chicago Slavonophile Charles R. Crane, whose daughters he had portrayed: Josephine, for instance, posed as Slavie for him in 1907, and also appeared on the Czechoslovak hundred-crown note in 1919.

1910 Upon his return to Bohemia he rented a studio in the Zbiroh château, west Bohemia, where he moved with his family and made his base for almost eighteen years; carried out the decoration of the Lord Mayor's Salon in the Municipal House (Obecní dům), Prague, and designed its stained-glass.

1911 Completed his first canvas of the *Epic of the Slavs*, which measures 610 x 810 cm, in egg tempera and oil. For further inspiration, traveled to the Balkans. Also continued in applied arts, and to this end kept a studio on Wenceslas Square, Prague, where he worked on smaller orders, drew, took photographs, and painted.

1912 On 6 December, presented the city of Prague with the first three canvases of his *Epic of the Slavs*.

1913 On 17 February, in New York, participated in the opening of the Armory Show: "A typical psychological phenomenon of all revolutions," he remarked. "The great men began them from an inner need, and the lesser men, in the assumption that they had to continue, got bogged down in eccentricity, because they were not standing on the firm ground of an inner need." Through Warsaw, traveled to Moscow and St Petersburg in order to find models for *Zrušení nevolnictví na Rusi* [The abolition of serfdom in Russia] (1914).

1918 With the break-up of the Austro-Hungarian Monarchy, designed the coat-of-arms of the Czechoslovak Republic, its postage stamps, and banknotes.

1919 Exhibited eleven pictures of the still incomplete *Epic of the Slavs* at the Klementinum, Prague.

1920 In the summer, opened a retrospective exhibition in the Art Institute of Chicago, which was visited by 600,000 people.

1921 On 19 January, an exhibition of his work opened in the Brooklyn Museum, New York. Insisted that admission should be free of charge, but despite the great attendance, refused to allow the show to travel elsewhere in the United States, for fear that the work would be damaged.

1924 At Easter, undertook a pilgrimage to the easternmost of the three Greek peninsulas running from Khalkidike to the Aegean. Full of impressions from the journey, made another painting for the *Epic of the Slavs – Mont Athos* (the "Vatican" of the Orthodox Church and cradle of the oldest Slavic monuments).

1925 To mark the 333rd anniversary of the birth of Jan Amos Komenský (Comenius), published his work on Freemasonry, *Svobodné zednářství* (Prague: Volné myšlenky československé).

1926 Published his credo *O Lásce, Rozumu a Moudrosti* [On Love, Reason, and Wisdom] (reprinted by Volvox Globator, Prague 1992): "To a man, woman means the first stage of sublime love and the last stage of material love."

1928 In the autumn, presented the whole *Epic of the Slavs* to the city of Prague at an exhibition in the Trade Fair Palace. His family moved to Prague.

1931 Completed his stained-glass window for St Vitus's Cathedral, Prague Castle. In the 1930s, continued his diverse activity, including Freemasonry, monumental art, and photography.

1932 Moved with his family to Nice, France, for two years.

1933 Retrospective shows in Brno, Hradec Králové, Pilsen, and Chrudim. An exhibition at the Musée des Arts décoratifs, Paris, titled "Le décor de la vie sous la troisième République."

1934 The Government of France raised him to the rank of Officer of the Legion of Honor.

1936 In June, a retrospective of 139 of his works took place in the Musée des Écoles étrangères contemporaines, Jeu de Paume des Tuileries, Paris, together with an exhibition of the collected works of the great abstract painter František Kupka. Conceived *Tři projevy o životě a díle* [Three speeches about life and work], in which he cautioned that war was imminent and appealed to "international Solidarity." (The essay was published privately by the Rotary Club for an exhibition in the Moravian Museum of Applied Arts, Brno.)

1938 In the autumn, caught pneumonia. Worked on his memoirs.

1939 In the spring, arrested by the Gestapo on account of his being a Freemason; returned home after several days of interrogation and then died in Prague, on 14 July. Buried at the Slavín cemetery, Vyšehrad, Prague.

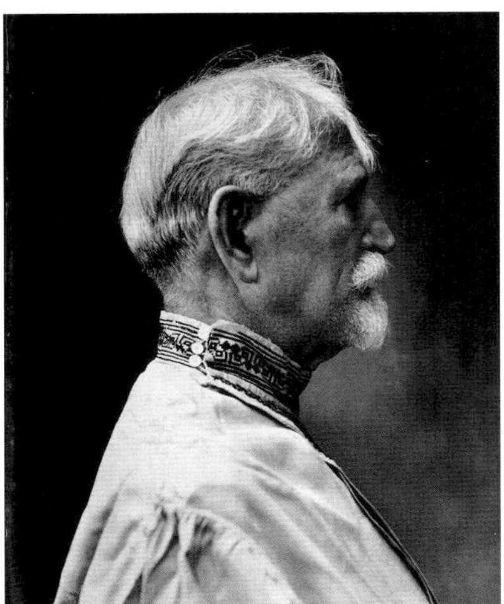

Self-Portrait / Autoportrét c. 1937

Životopisná data

1860 24. července přichází na svět v Ivančicích na jižní Moravě jakožto potomek Ondřeje a Amálie Muchových. Od dětství projevuje kreslířské nadání.

1872 1. října nastupuje v Brně studia na Slovanském gymnáziu coby stipendista chrámu na Petrově a zpívá ve sboru, dirigovaném o šest let starším Leošem Janáčkem. V kreslení se zdokonaluje pod vedením malíře Josefa Zeleného, jenž ho nabádá k profesionalizaci.

1877 Z prospěchových důvodů je ze školy vyloučen, stává se soudním písařem v Ivančicích.

1878 V září je odmítnut pražskou Akademií výtvarných umění pro údajnou nevýraznost talentu.

1881 V důsledku ledabylého zastávání svěřeného úřadu písaře je propuštěn ze státních služeb. Na podzim odchází do Vídně k firmě Kautski – Brioschi – Burghardt, vyrábějící divadelní kulisy. 10. prosince zničí požár vídeňský Ringtheater a Mucha přichází o práci.

1882–85 Provádí nástěnné figurální malby na zámku v Hrušovanech nad Jevišovkou pro hraběte Khuena-Belasiho, jenž mu bude po sedm let mecenášem, a pracuje na freskách v rodovém sídle Khuenů, hradu Gandegg v Tyrolích.

1885 Studijní cesta po Tyrolích a severu Itálie – Benátky, Florencie, Bologna, Milán. Na podzim je přijat na mnichovskou Akademii, z níž je záhy vyškrtnut pro neplacení školného.

1886 V Mnichově vzniká série snímků na negativy formátu 7 x 7 cm. Sžívá se s početnou studentskou kolonií Slovanů, jimž otevírá původně český klub Škréta, jehož předsednictví přebírá.

1887 Uzavírá mnichovské období, aby společně s Karlem Václavem Maškem zamířil do Paříže, kde se oba stanou žáky Académie Julian. Zastihují nástup symbolismu, jehož manifest zveřejnil roku 1886 Jean Moréas.

1888 Léto a část podzimu tráví v panství Hrušovany, kde pokračuje ve výzdobě nemovitostí svého podpůrce. Po návratu do Paříže se zapisuje na Académie Colarossi v rue de la Grande Chaumière. Latinské čtvrti zůstane napříště věrný i občanskou adresou.

1889 Ustává hraběcí apanáž, což znamená konec studií a počátek rozsáhlé ilustrační spolupráce s francouzskými i českými vydavateli periodik a knih.

1890 V polovině roku se na plných šest let usazuje v rue de la Grande Chaumière (čísla domů 13, 12 a 8); odtud pochází řada snímků muchovsky zabydleného prostředí, modelek a pozoruhodných návštěvníků, včetně slavných záběrů Paula Gauguina.

1893 Nejpozději tohoto roku se vybavuje kamerou na desky 10 x 13 cm, kterou používá do první světové války spolu s dalšími přístroji obdélníkového formátu, jejž se už navždy přidrží, ať bude negativ skleněný nebo posléze celuloidový. Vychází Muchou ilustrovaná kniha Poésies du foyer et de l'école Eugèna Manuela (další – rovněž pařížská – vydání 1903 a 1908).

1894 O Vánocích navrhuje plakát Gismonda pro Théâtre de la Renaissance Sarah Bernhardtové.

1895 Sarah Bernhardtová si „svůj objev“ smluvně zavazuje na šest let, v nichž nepožaduje pouze další plakáty, nýbrž i konzultace vlastního výtvarného řešení inscenací.

1896 Tiskem plakátu pro XX. výstavu Salon des Cent jej bere za svého okruh galerie umělecké revue La Plume (Toulouse-Lautrec, Grasset, De Fevre, Berthon, Bonnard, Ensor, Evenepoel, Rassenfosse, van Rysselberghe). Ilustruje převyprávění středověké legendy La princesse

Lointaine Robertem de Flersem (následujícího roku vyjdou 134 reprodukce v pařížském vydání Ilsée, Princesse de Tripoli; české Ilséa, princezna Tripolská a německé následují v Praze roku 1901); při vypracování Mucha rozvíjel metodu monumentálních personifikací duchovních a přírodních sil, kterou užije i ve Slovanské epopeji. Poprvé se stěhuje do ateliéru s velkými okny a s proskleným stropem; v rue du Val-de-Grâce na horním konci bulváru St-Michel (kde sídlila tiskárna firmy Champenois, s jejímž majitelem uzavřel pro příští léta paušální smlouvu) má výrazně lepší světelné podmínky. Jiří Mucha vyčetl z otcova diáře, že v tomto období fotografuje téměř denně. V novém působišti nalézá dílnu sochaře Auguste Seyssese, což ho přivede k realizacím plastik. Přistupuje k pastelům.

1897 Uskuteční prvé dvě samostatné expozice v Paříži: od 15. února vystavuje 107 děl v Galerie de la Bodinière, 24. května zpřístupní v Salon des Cent velkou reprezentativní kolekci 448 prací, které je věnováno monografické číslo La Plume. V tomto a následujícím roce putují Muchovy práce do Vídně, Prahy, Hradce Králové, Budapešti, Mnichova, Bruselu, Londýna, New Yorku – a podvakrát je instaluje v samostatných výstavách Průmyslové muzeum pro východní Čechy v Chrudimi. F. Champenois zahajuje velkovýrobu muchovských pohlednic, dekorativních panneau a sériových i sběratelských tisků. Původně firemní kalendář, zvaný Zodiac (návrh 1896), převezme a zpopularizuje magazín La Plume natolik, že během následujících let doznají předlohy několika dalších reedic k různým účelům. Stává se členem Société Internationale de l'Art Populaire a navrhuje Pavilon člověka pro Světovou výstavu 1900. V Praze vycházejí Adamité Svatopluka Čecha s Muchovými ilustracemi, rozpracovanými již roku 1893.

1898 V lednu je v Paříži přijat za tovaryše lóže svobodných zednářů Les inséparables du progrés (v Československu se po 1. světové válce stane zednářským velmistrem a ve 20. letech navrhne odznaky pro první česky jednající Lóži Jan Amos Komenský). Od účasti na výstavě vídeňské Secession se počítá jeho tříletá příslušnost k Vereinigung bildender Künstler Oesterreichs. Vychází výpravná kniha Scènes et Episodes de l'Histoire d'Allemagne Charlese Seignobose, jejíž ilustrace pořizoval spolu s Georgesem Rochegrossem od roku 1892. Realizuje třídílnou vitráž pro kapli Nanebevzetí Panny Marie v pařížské rue François I. a dále naplňuje smluvní povinnosti různým nakladatelstvím a tiskárně Champenois.

1899 Připravuje různorodé projekty na Světovou výstavu v Paříži a uskutečňuje návrhy výzdoby pavilonu propagujícího správu Bosny a Hercegoviny Rakouskem-Uherskem. Uprostřed třeštění kolem změny století, hýčkán prostředím, které přeje populárnímu umění plakátu, rozhodne se zasvětit druhou polovinu života vážné tvorbě, která by mu dovolila překonat pověst geniálního dekoratéra. Vydá výpravnou oslavu základní křesťanské modlitby Le Pater (první česká mutace Otčenáše vyjde roku 1901).

1900 Na Světové výstavě v Paříži kulminuje secese, přičemž Mucha je bohatě zastoupen v mnoha různých sekcích. Vycházejí jeho ilustrace k povídkám Anatole France Clio a bibliofilie Cloches de Noël et de Pâques s textem Emila Gebharta. Je pasován na rytíře Řádu Františka Josefa I.

1901 Vyznamenán Řádem Čestné legie a zvolen členem České akademie věd a umění. Georges Fouquet otevírá v rue Royal Muchou navržené klenotnictví (pařížské Musée Carnavalet vlastní repliku tohoto mimořádně celistvého secesního interiéru).

1902 Vycházejí 72 tabule Documents décoratifs. 40 listů Figures décoratives se objeví o tři roky později, nakonec všechny originály předloh těchto návodů k všeobecnému užití muchovského stylu vykoupí od nakladatele Émile Lévyho zpět. V létě provází Augusta Rodina na jeho pražskou výstavu a ve vlasti si vyrábí řadu zavilých nepřátel jednoduchým prohlášením: „Vidím jen samé opičení se po Vídni, Mnichově a Paříži."

1903 17. října poznává v Paříži slečnu Marii Chytilovou z Chrudimi: 10. června 1906 se s ní ožení v kapli svatého Rocha při Strahovském klášteře. Z manželství vzejdou děti Jaroslava (1909) a Jiří (1915).

1904 5. března se poprvé vylodí ve Spojených státech amerických. Do 1. světové války (jejíž rozpoutání předjímá v Chicago Examiner 24. února 1913) navštíví USA šestkrát.

1905 Při druhé cestě do USA předsedá porotě pro vyhodnocení návrhů reklamního plakátu na fotografické a optické přístroje.

1906 3. dubna zahajuje newyorskou výstavu. Na svatební cestě v Peci u Domažlic fotografuje aparátem na svitkové filmy Kodak. Na podzim přestěhuje do New Yorku svůj pařížský ateliér.

1908 Zjara začíná pracovat na obrazech k výzdobě hlediště Německého divadla v New Yorku, slavnostně předaného veřejnosti 1. října (a uzavřeného osm měsíců poté). Leslie Carterová jej získá k výtvarnému řešení scény, kostýmů i plakátu neúspěšné romantické hry Kassa.

1909 Navrhuje plakát pro vystoupení Maud Adamsové v schillerovské roli Johanky z Arku. Uzrává předsevzetí na dvacítku výjevů symbolizujících rozvoj Slovanstva od prehistorie k novověku, jiż plánuje jako dar metropoli zemí Koruny české: „Má práce musí být jako jednotlivé výkřiky bez vší hledanosti..." O Vánocích získává příslib financování Slovanské epopeje od chicagského slovanofila Charlese R. Cranea, jehož dcery portrétoval: Josephine se mu roku 1907 stala představitelkou Slavie – znovu se objeví na československé stokoruně (1919).

1910 Po návratu do Čech najímá ateliér na západočeském zámku Zbiroh, kam stěhuje na bezmála osmnáct let také rodinu; provádí výzdobu Primátorského salonku Obecního domu v Praze a navrhuje jeho vitráže.

1911 Dokončí první plátno Slovanské epopeje o rozměrech 610 x 810 cm, pojednané vaječnými temperami a olejovými barvami. Za další inspirací cestuje na Balkán. Pokračuje také v užité tvorbě, a drží si proto ateliér na Václavském náměstí v Praze, kde realizuje menší zakázky a kreslí, fotografuje i maluje.

1912 6. prosince předává městu Praze první tři plátna Slovanské epopeje.

1913 17. února se účastní vernisáže newyorské Armory Show: „Typický psychologický zjev všech dob velkých převratů," poznamenává. „Ti velcí převrat začali z vnitřní nutnosti a ti malí, v domnění, že musí pokračovat, zabředli do výstředností, protože jim pod nohama scházela pevná půda vnitřní nutnosti." Přes Varšavu cestuje do Moskvy a Petrohradu, aby našel představitele k Zrušení nevolnictví na Rusi (1914).

1918 V souvislosti s rozpadem Říše rakousko-uherské navrhuje státní znak Československé republiky, její známky a bankovky.

1919 Vystavuje dílčí bilanci jedenácti obrazů Slovanské epopeje v pražském Klementinu.

1920 V létě zahajuje retrospektivu v Art Institute of Chicago, kterou navštíví 600 000 diváků.

1921 Od 19. ledna vystavuje v newyorském Brooklyn Museum. Odmítá vybírání vstupného, ale vzdor masovým návštěvám se zříká dalšího putování přehlídky po Spojených státech, obávaje se poškození exponátů.

1924 Velikonoční pouť do Řecka na nejvýchodnější ze tří poloostrovů vybíhajících z Chalkidiki do Egejského moře, pod jejímž dojmem vzniká další položka slovanské série Mont Athos (Vatikán pravoslavných, schránka nejstarších slovanských památek).

1925 K 333. výročí narození Jana Amose Komenského vychází ve vydavatelství Volné myšlenky československé Muchův spis Svobodné zednářství.

1926 Vydává vyznání O Lásce, Rozumu a Moudrosti (reprint Volvox Globator, Praha 1992): „Žena znamená muži první stupeň lásky nebeské a poslední stupeň lásky hmotné."

1928 Na podzim odevzdává celek Slovanské epopeje hlavnímu městu Praze na výstavě ve Veletržním paláci. Rodina se stěhuje do metropole.

1931 Realizace vitráže ve svatovítské katedrále na Pražském hradě. Ve 30. letech pokračuje všestranná aktivita, nevyjímaje zednářství, monumentální tvorbu ani fotografii.

1932 Stěhuje se s celou rodinou na dva roky do francouzské Nice.

1933 Retrospektivy v Brně, Hradci Králové, Plzni a Chrudimi. V Paříži připomenut v Musée des Arts décoratifs výstavou Le décor de la vie sous la troisième République.

1934 Francouzskou vládou povýšen na důstojníka Čestné legie.

1936 V červnu retrospektiva 139 děl v pařížském Musée des Écoles étrangeres contemporaines, Jeu de Paume des Tuileries spolu se soubornou výstavou velikána abstrakce Františka Kupky. Koncipuje Tři projevy o životě a díle, v nichž konstatuje hrozbu nadcházející války a vyzývá k „mezinárodní Svornosti" (soukromý tisk Rotary klubu u příležitosti výstavy v Moravském uměleckoprůmyslovém muzeu v Brně).

1938 Na podzim prodělá zápal plic. Sepisuje paměti.

1939 Na jaře jakožto zednář zatčen gestapem, po několika dnech výslechů se vrací domů a 14. července v Praze umírá. Pohřben je na vyšehradském Slavíně.

Photography Exhibitions / Výstavy fotografií

1939 *Sto let České fotografie 1839–1939*, Uměleckoprůmyslové museum v Praze. Kurátor Zdeněk Wirth.

1973 *Osobnosti České fotografie I/ze sbírek UmûleckoprÛmyslového musea v Praze*, Galerie výtvarného umění v Roudnici nad Labem; Uměleckoprůmyslové museum v Praze (1974). Kurátorka Anna Fárová.

1977 *Malerei und Photographie im Dialog*, Kunsthaus, Zürich. Kurátorka Erika Billeter.

1978 Instituto Italiano di Cultura, Praha. Kurátor Paolo Porthoghesi.

1980 *Alfons Mucha 1860–1939; peintures, illustrations – affiches, arts décoratifs*, Grand Palais, Paris; Mathildenhöhe, Darmstadt; Jízdárna Pražského hradu. Kurátorka Jana Brabcová.

1981 Fotografie a plagáty A. Muchu, Galéria F, Banská Bystrica.

1982 *Alfons Mucha fotografem*, Chebské muzeum v Chebu. První reprízu uskutečnilo Muzeum v Ivančicích s převzatým plakátem i katalogem. Premiéra měla být původně v dubnu až květnu 1982 v Roztokách u Prahy, nebyla však povolena a neuskutečnila se, ačkoli existuje její plakát. V 80. letech soubor prošel řadou měst, termíny a hostitelské instituce však nebyly – s výjimkou Itálie – evidovány. Kurátor Jiří Řapek uvádí Budapešť, Havanu, Krakov, Mnichov a pro rok 1989 východní Berlín, Valencii a Moskvu.

1983 *Alphonse Mucha*, Isetan Museum of Art, Tokyo. Kurátorka Jana Brabcová.

1986 *Fotografie v Praze 1839–1914*, Muzeum hlavního města Prahy. Kurátor Pavel Scheufler.

1988 *Alfons Mucha fotografem*, Památník národního písemnictví, Praha. Kurátor Jiří Řapek.

1988 *Alfons Mucha 1860–1939*, Chudožestvena galerija pri meždunarodnata fondacija Ljudmila Živkova, Sofia. Kurátorka Jana Brabcová.

1988 *Alfons Mucha fotografo*, Cittą di Castello; Galleria del l'immagine, Cesena; La Salara, Bologna (1989). Kurátor Jiří Řapek.

1989 *The 50th Year Anniversary Exhibition of Alphonse Mucha*, Takashimaya Gallery, Nihombashi. Kurátorka Jana Brabcová.

1989 *Czech Modernism: 1900–1945*, The Houston Museum of Fine Arts. Kurátoři Jaroslav Anděl, Anne Wilkes Tucker, Alison de Lima Greene, Ralph McKay a Willis Hartshorn.

1989 *Cesty Československé fotografie*, Galerie hlavního města Prahy, Dům U kamenného zvonu. Komisaři Daniela Mrázková a Vladimír Remeš.

1990 *Fotografie v Čechách 1839–1914*, Galerie hlavního města Prahy, Zámek Trója. Kurátor Pavel Scheufler.

1994 *Alfons Mucha. Pastely, plakáty, kresby a fotografie*, Císařská konírna Pražského hradu. Kurátor Petr Wittlich.

1998 *Alfons Mucha: Fotografické studie*, Galerie Josefa Sudka v Praze. Kurátoři Jan Mlčoch a Petr Štembera.

1998 *Alfons Mucha fotografem*, Egon Schiele Centrum, Český Krumlov. Kurátor Jiří Řapek.

1998 *Alphonse Mucha: The Spirit of Art Nouveau*, americké turné: premiéra v San Diego Museum of Art, poslední instalace v Dixon Gallery and Gardens, Memphis (2000). Kurátoři Victor Arwas, Jana Brabcová-Orlíková, Anna Dvořák a další.

1999 *Alfons Mucha – fotografie*, Okresní muzeum Brno – venkov, Muzeum v Ivančicích.

2002 *Alfons Mucha: Fotografien*, Tscheschises Zentrum & Institut Français, Berlin. Kurátor Jiří Řapek.

Bibliography / Literatura

Books / Knihy

de Rochas d'Aiglun, Albert: *Les sentiments, la musique et le geste*, Grenoble, H. Falque et F. Perrin 1900.

Mucha, Jiří: *Alphonse Mucha. The Master of Art Nouveau*, Praha-London, Artia-Paul Hamlyn 1966.

Mucha, Jiří: *Kankán se svatozáří. Život a dílo Alfonse Muchy*, Praha, Obelisk 1969.

Mucha, Jiří; Henderson, Marina & Scharf, Aaron: Alphonse Mucha: *Posters and Photographs*, London, Academy Editions 1971.

Ovenden, Graham: *Alphonse Mucha Photographs*, London, Academy Editions 1974; New York, St. Martin's Press Inc. 1974.

Krichbaum, Jörg: *Lexikon der Fotografen*, Frankfurt a. M., Fischer 1981.

Mucha, Jiří: *Alfons Mucha*, Praha, Mladá fronta 1982 (4. vydání Eminent 1999).

Mrázková, Daniela & Remeš, Vladimír: *Tschechoslowakische Fotografen 1900–1940*, Leipzig, VEB Fotokinoverlag 1983.

Auer, Michèle & Michel: *Encyclopédie internationale des photographes 1839–1984*, Hermance, Editions Camera Obscura 1985.

Mrázková, Daniela: *Příběh fotografie*, Praha, Mladá fronta 1985.

Hlaváč, Ľudovít: *Dejiny fotografie*, Martin, Osveta 1987.

Mucha, Jiří: *Alphonse Maria Mucha. His Life and Art, London*, Academy Editions 1989.

Mrázková, Daniela & Remeš, Vladimír: *Cesty Československé fotografie*, Praha, Mladá fronta 1989.

Scheufler, Pavel: *Pražské fotografické ateliéry 1839–1918. II/ 1889–1918*, Praha, Muzeum hlavního města Prahy 1989.

Scheufler, Pavel: *Přehled vývoje fotografie v Praze v letech 1839–1918. II/ 1889–1918*, Praha, Státní pedagogické nakladatelství 1991.

Ellridge, Arthur: *Mucha. Le triomphe du Modern Style*, Paris, Finest S. A. – Editions Pierre Terrail 1992.

Scheufler, Pavel: Mucha Alfons, in: *Encyklopedie českých a slovenských fotografů*, Praha, ASCO 1993.

Frizot, Michel (ed.): *Nouvelle Histoire de la Photographie*, Paris, Bordas S. A. 1994.

Ulmer, Renate: *Alfons Mucha. Master of Art Nouveau*, Köln, Taschen 1994.

Dufek, Antonín: Fotografie 1890–1918, in: *Dějiny českého výtvarného umění 1890–1938 (IV/1)*, Praha, Academia 1998.

Bajac, Quentin: Mucha and Photography, in: Arwas, Victor & Brabcová-Orlíková Jana & Dvořák, Anna et al.: *Alphonse Mucha: The Spirit of Art Nouveau*, Alexandria, Virginia, Art Services International in association with Yale University Press 1998.

Scheufler, Pavel: Počátky fotografie aktu v Čechách, na Moravě a ve Slezsku, in: *Sex a tabu v České kultuře 19. století*, Praha, Academia 1999.

Scheufler, Pavel & Birgus, Vladimír: *Fotografie v českých zemích* 1839–1999, Praha, Grada Publishing 1999.

Mlčoch, Jan: Muchův odkaz ve fotografiích, in: Muchová, Sarah (ed.): *Alfons Mucha*, London, Mucha Ltd. 2000.

Exhibition Catalogues / Katalogy výstav

Fárová, Anna: *Osobnosti české fotografie I/ ze sbírek Uměleckoprůmyslového musea v Praze*, Galerie výtvarného umění v Roudnici nad Labem 1973 a Uměleckoprůmyslové museum v Praze 1974.

Brabcová, Jana et al.: *Mucha 1860–1939; peintures, illustrations – affiches, arts décoratifs*, Paris, Éditions des musées nationaux – Spadem 1980.

Brabcová Jana, et al.: *Mucha 1860–1939*, München, Prestel Verlag 1980.

Kotalík, Jiří (ed.): *Alfons Mucha (1860–1939)*, Praha, Národní galerie 1980.

Řapek, Jiří (ed.): *Alfons Mucha fotografem*, Cheb, Chebské muzeum 1982.

Brabcová, Jana & Kotalík, Jiří & Mucha, Jiří & Čiháková, Vlasta & Shimada, Norio: *The Spiritof Art Nouveau Alphonse Mucha*, Tokio, Otsuka Kogei-sha 1983.

Mucha, Jiří: *Alfons Mucha fotografem*, Praha, Památník národního písemnictví 1988.

Čiháková, Vlasta: Light and Photography in the Work of Alphonse Mucha, in: Brabcová, Jana (ed.): *The 50th Year Anniversary Exhibition of Alphonse Mucha*, Nihombashi, Shuko-sha 1989.

Řapek, Jiří & Mucha, Jiří: *Grafica e fotografie nel periodo della Secessione*, Bologna, Comune di Bologna 1989.

Andel, Jaroslav & Tucker, Anne W. (ed.): *Czech Modernism: 1900–1945*, Houston, The Houston Museum of Fine Arts – Bullfinch Press (USA), Little, Brown & Company (Canada) 1989.

Faber, Monika: *Tanz. Foto. Annäherungen und Experimente 1880–1940*, Wien, Museum moderner Kunst 1990.

Scheufler, Pavel: *Fotografie v Čechách 1839–1914*, Praha, Galerie hlavního města Prahy 1990.

Wittlich, Petr: *Alfons Mucha. Pastely, plakáty, kresby a fotografie*. Výstava v Císařské konírně Pražského hradu, London, Nadace Mucha 1994.

Fischer, Andreas & Loers, Veit: *Fotografie des Unsichtbaren*, Städtisches Museum Abteiberg, Mönchengladbach 1997.

Birgus, Vladimír & Mlčoch, Jan: *Česká fotografie 20. století*, Praha, Kant & Uměleckoprůmyslové museum v Praze 2005.

Articles / Články

Mucha, Jiří: Alfons Mucha, *Camera* 48, 1969, č. 11, s. 18–29.

Mucha, Jiří: Alfons Mucha, *Československá fotografie* 21, 1970, č. 7, s. 302–303.

Fárová, Anna: Alfons Mucha, *Československá fotografie* 24, 1973, č. 1, s. 20–21.

Gilles, Xavier: Mucha. Peintre et photographe, *L'Oeil*, 1975, č. 236, s. 38–43.

Remeš, Vladimír: Alfons Mucha jako fotograf, *Revue Fotografie* 21, 1977, č. 4, s. 23–26.

Mrázková, Daniela: Fotografické dědictví, *Československá fotografie* 29, 1978, č. 6, s. 261.

Anonym: Pražští příznivci art nouveau... *Československá fotografie* 29, 1978, č. 6, s. 242.

Mucha, Jiří: Alfons Mucha, *Fotografie* 23, 1979, č. 3, s. 53–65.

Mrázková, Daniela: Alfons Mucha. Bilder aus einem fotografischen Skizzenbuch, *Fotografie* 25, 1981, č. 2, s. 68–75.

Moucha, Josef: Déjà vu, *Fotograf* 4, 2005, č. 5, s. 104–107.

List of Published Photographs

p. 2 Alphonse Mucha with Masonic Regalia (cropped photo), c. 1925
1 Skating in Austria, 1887
2 View from a window of Mucha's apartment near Amalienstraße, Munich, 1886
3 View from a window of Mucha's apartment near Amalienstraße, Munich, 1886
4 Munich, 1886
5 Karel Václav Mašek, painter, c. 1887
6 Paul Gauguin at the harmonium in Mucha's studio, Paris, c. 1895
7 Paul Gauguin, Alphonse Mucha, Luděk Marold, and Annah la Javanaise in Mucha's studio, Paris, 1896
8 Annah la Javanaise, c. 1896
9 Alphonse Mucha and Annah la Javanaise, c. 1896
10 Mucha with a model for a poster for Cassan fils, printers in Toulouse, Paris, 1897 (GF UPM 1179)
11 Model for the decorative panel *Roses* from the *Flowers* series, Paris, 1897 (GF UPM 1197)
12 Model with a headband, Paris, 1899
13 Model with a headband, Paris, 1899
14 Nude with a spear, Paris, 1899
15 Paris, 1899
16 Model on a sofa, Paris, 1899
17 Model in front of a mirror, Paris, 1899
18 Model for an allegorical figure from the series of the twelve months for the journal *Cocorico*, Paris, 1899 (GF UPM 1183)
19 One of two models for a theatre production of *Medea*, Paris, 1898 (GF UPM 1184)
20 Model for a banquet menu envelope of the Société de bienfaisance austro-hongroise, Paris, 1899 (GF UPM 1175)
21 Model for the decorative panel *Primrose*, Paris, 1899 (GF UPM 1173)
22 Model for an illustrations to Émile Gebhart's *Cloches de Noël et de Pâques*, Paris, 1900
23 Model, originally intended for a poster, used on the cover of a special issue of the student journal *Au Quartier latin*, 1898; it later served as the model for a catalogue and banquet invitation at the 1900 Paris Exhibition, and also for *Documents décoratifs* and the cover of the Christmas 1903 issue of *Paris Illustré*, Paris, 1898 (GF UPM 1192)
24 Model used in the interior decoration of the German Theatre in New York in 1908, Paris, 1899
25 Seated model with a little laurel branch, Paris, 1899
26 Model for a decorative panel, Paris, c. 1899
27 Model in a white gown and a hat with ribbons, Paris, 1899
28 Model used in 1917 for a bookplate for a certain Vostřebal, Paris, 1899
29 Model in Mucha's studio in the rue du Val de Grâce for *Documents décoratifs*, Paris, 1899 (GF UPM 1176)
30 Model in Mucha's studio in the rue du Val de Grâce, Paris, 1899
31 Semi-nude woman bending backwards, Paris, 1899

32 Model for illustrations to Émile Gebhart's *Cloches de Noël et de Pâques*, Paris, 1900
33 Model in a striped skirt, Paris, 1899
34 Model for the cover of the November 1903 issue of *La Chronique de Paris*, Paris, 1899
35 Model for the decorative panel *Emerald*, used in the early 1930s for a number of other drawings and paintings, Paris, c. 1900
36 Model in an armchair, Paris, 1903
37 Model for the hand-colored lithograph *Brunette* and the pattern book *Documents décoratifs*, Paris, 1901 (GF UPM 1172)
38 Study for *Iris*, Paris, 1897
39 Study for *Woman with Poppies*, Paris, 1897
40–43 Model posing as a ballerina, Paris, 1901
44 Model for the allegorical figure from the series of the twelve months for the journal *Cocorico*, Paris, 1899 (GF UPM 1180)
45 Lina de Ferkel as a medium at a séance, at which Judith seduces Holofernes, in Mucha's studio in the rue du Val de Grâce, Paris, 1899 (GF UPM 1174)
46 Model for a sculpture, Paris, 1899
47 Model for the decorative panel *North Star*, Paris, 1902 (GF UPM 1193)
48 Model for the decorative panel *The Moon*, Paris, 1902 (GF UPM 1186)
49 Violinist Mme Marguerite Syamour, Paris, c. 1900
50 Mucha's studio in the rue du Val de Grâce, Paris, 1990
51 Alphonse Mucha in his studio in the rue du Val de Grâce, Paris, 1899
52 Marie Chytilová, Chrudim, 1905
53 Landscape, the South of France from a train, c. 1900
54 Harbor, c. 1900
55 Model for the painting *Madonna of the Lilies*, New York, 1904 (GF UPM 1171)
56 Model for the painting *Tragedy* for the German Theatre in New York, New York, 1908 (GF UPM 1195)
57 Man leaning over a woman in an armchair, a study for an unknown work, New York, 1908 (GF UPM 1198)
58 Model for the painting *Comedy* for the German Theatre in New York, New York, 1908 (GF UPM 1194)
59 Model for the painting *Tragedy* for the German Theatre in New York, New York, 1908 (GF UPM 1196)
60 Model for the painting *Tragedy* for the German Theatre in New York, New York, 1908 (GF UPM 1202)
61 Children models for the painting *Harmony*, New York, 1908
62 New York, 1908
63 Miss Reichl, a leading tragic actress of the Reinhardt Theatre, as a model for the painting *Tragedy*, part of the interior decoration of the German Theatre, New York, 1908
64 Mucha sitting in the front of *Madonna of the Lilies*, New York, c. 1905
65 Mucha at work on the lunette *Liberty through Strength, Unity through Love!* for the Mayor's Hall in the Municipal House, Prague, 1911

66 Marie Muchová with her daughter Jaroslava in the park, Zbiroh, 1913

67 Study for *The Slav Epic, The Oath of the Omladina*, near Žamberk, 1925

68 Alphonse Mucha with his sisters Anna and Anděla and Anděla's husband Jan Remunda, Rosice near Brno, c. 1911

69 Marie Muchová with her children Jaroslava and Jiří, Zbiroh, 1919

70–75 Photographs from a trip to Russia to make preparatory studies for the painting *The Abolition of Serfdom in Russia* (1914) from the *Slav Epic* series, Moscow, 1913

76 Marie Muchová sitting for the painting *Winter Night*, Prague, c. 1920

77 Study for the poster *Russia restituenda* in support of Russian children, which was printed by Melantrich in 1922, Prague, c. 1921

78 Sketch for the poster *Zdeňka Černý: The Greatest Bohemian Violoncellist*, which was printed by Václav Neubert in 1913, Chicago, 1913

79 Model for a painting of a girl with a jug, 1927

80 Seated nude as a model for a painting, Prague, c. 1913 (GF UPM 1191)

81 Mucha's daughter Jaroslava and son Jiří as models for the cover of the January 1922 issue of *Hearst's International*, Zbiroh, c. 1921

82 Woman with a shell, Prague, 1920

83 Model for the chief figure of the painting *The Apotheosis of the Slavs* from the *Slav Epic* series, Zbiroh, c. 1926

84 Marie Muchová with her son Jiří, c. 1920

85 Study for a portrait of Halidé Edip, the most important woman in modern Turkish history, Zbiroh, 1925

86 Mucha's daughter Jaroslava as a model for the picture *Taking an Oath under the Lime of the Slavs* form the *Slav Epic* series. Mucha used the same motif in the poster for an exhibition of the completed series of twelve monumental pictures in their official presentation to the City of Prague in 1928, Zbiroh, 1926

87 Mucha's daughter Jaroslava as a model for the painting *Apotheosis of the Slavs* from the *Slav Epic* series, Zbiroh, 1926

88 Models for a symbolic group in the painting *Taking an Oath under the Lime of the Slavs* from the *Slav Epic* series, Zbiroh, 1926

89 Marie and Alphonse Mucha, Prague, c. 1920

90 Model for the painting *Girl in Traditional Costume*, Zbiroh, c. 1923

91 Mucha with his daughter Jaroslava as a model for a poster for De Forest Phonofilm for the first "talkie," which was screened in the Bio Adria cinema in Prague, Zbiroh, 1927

92 Jiří Mucha as a Native American with models, Zbiroh, c. 1919

93 The Chilandar monastery, Mount Athos, 1924

94 Mucha and his assistant Knap as models for the painting *Mount Athos* from the *Slav Epic* series, Zbiroh, 1926

95 Bush in bloom

The photographs from the collections of the Museum of Applied Arts in Prague are marked GF UPM; all others are from the archives of the Mucha Trust, London.

Soupis publikovaných fotografií

s. 2	Alfons Mucha se zednářskými regáliemi (výřez), c. 1925
1	Bruslení v Rakousku, 1887
2	Pohled z okna Muchova bytu v sousedství Amalienstraße, Mnichov, 1886
3	Pohled z okna Muchova bytu v sousedství Amalienstraße, Mnichov, 1886
4	Mnichov, 1886
5	Malíř Karel Václav Mašek, c. 1887
6	Paul Gauguin u harmonia v Muchově ateliéru, Paříž, c. 1895
7	Paul Gauguin, Alfons Mucha, Luděk Marold, Annah la Javanaise v Muchově ateliéru, Paříž, 1896
8	Annah la Javanaise, c. 1896
9	Alfons Mucha a Annah la Javanaise, c. 1896
10	Alfons Mucha s modelkou pro plakát tiskárny Cassan fils v Toulouse, Paříž, 1897 (GF UPM 1179)
11	Model pro dekorativní panneau Růže z cyklu Květiny, Paříž, 1897 (GF UPM 1197)
12	Model s čelenkou, Paříž, 1899
13	Model s čelenkou, Paříž, 1899
14	Ženský akt s kopím, Paříž, 1899
15	Paříž, 1899
16	Model na pohovce, Paříž, 1899
17	Model před zrcadlem, Paříž, 1899
18	Model pro alegorickou postavu z cyklu dvanácti měsíců pro časopis Cocorico, Paříž, 1899 (GF UPM 1183)
19	Jeden ze dvou modelů pro divadelní plakát Medea, Paříž, 1898 (GF UPM 1184)
20	Model pro obálku menu banketu Société de bienfaisance austro-hongroise, Paříž, 1899 (GF UPM 1175)
21	Model pro dekorativní panneau Prvosenka, Paříž, 1899 (GF UPM 1173)
22	Model pro ilustrace knihy Emila Gebharta Cloches de Noël et de Pâques, Paříž, 1900
23	Model, původně určený pro plakát použitý na obálce zvláštního čísla studentského časopisu Au Quartier latin r. 1898; později posloužil nejen jako předloha pro katalog a pozvánku na banket Světové výstavy v Paříži r. 1900, ale i pro Documents décoratifs a titul vánočního čísla Paris Illustré r. 1903 – Paříž, 1898 (GF UPM 1192)
24	Model využitý při výzdobě Německého divadla v New Yorku r. 1908, Paříž, 1899
25	Sedící model se snítkou vavřínu, Paříž, 1899
26	Model pro dekorativní panneau, Paříž, c. 1899
27	Model v bílé říze s kloboukem se stuhami, Paříž, 1899
28	Model použitý r. 1917 pro Ex libris Vostřebala, Paříž, 1899
29	Model v ateliéru v rue du Val de Grâce pro Documents décoratifs, Paříž, 1899 (GF UPM 1176)
30	Ženský model v ateliéru v rue du Val de Grâce, Paříž, 1899
31	Ženský poloakt v záklonu, Paříž, 1899

32 Model pro ilustrace knihy Emila Gebharta Cloches de Noël et de Pâques, Paříž, 1900
33 Model v pruhované sukni, Paříž, 1899
34 Model pro záhlaví časopisu La Chronique de Paris z listopadu 1903, Paříž, 1899
35 Model pro dekorativní panneau Smaragd, použitý počátkem 30. let pro řadu dalších kreseb a obrazů, Paříž, c. 1900
36 Model v křesle, Paříž, 1903
37 Model pro kolorovanou litografii Brunetka a sborník předloh Documents décoratifs, Paříž, 1901 (GF UPM 1172)
38 Studie pro Iris, Paříž, 1897
39 Studie k obrazu Žena s máky, Paříž, 1897
40–43 Model baletky, Paříž, 1901
44 Model pro alegorickou postavu z cyklu dvanácti měsíců pro časopis Cocorico, Paříž, 1899 (GF UPM 1180)
45 Lina de Ferkel jako médium při spiritistické seanci Judita okouzluje Holoferna v ateliéru v rue du Val de Grâce, Paříž, 1899 (GF UPM 1174)
46 Model pro sochu, Paříž, 1899
47 Model pro dekorativní panneau Severka, Paříž, 1902 (GF UPM 1193)
48 Model pro dekorativní panneau Měsíc, Paříž, 1902 (GF UPM 1186)
49 Houslistka Mme Marguerite Syamour, Paříž, c. 1900
50 Ateliér v ulici Val de Grâce, Paříž, 1900
51 Alfons Mucha v ateliéru v rue du Val de Grâce, Paříž, 1899
52 Marie Chytilová, Chrudim, 1905
53 Jihofrancouzská krajina z vlaku, c. 1900
54 Přístav, c. 1900
55 Model k obrazu Madona v liliích, New York, 1904 (GF UPM 1171)
56 Model k obrazu Tragédie pro newyorské Německé divadlo, New York, 1908 (GF UPM 1195)
57 Muž sklánějící se nad ženou v křesle. Studie k neznámému dílu, New York, 1908 (GF UPM 1198)
58 Model k obrazu Komedie pro newyorské Německé divadlo, New York, 1908 (GF UPM 1194)
59 Model k obrazu Tragédie pro newyorské Německé divadlo, New York, 1908 (GF UPM 1196)
60 Model k obrazu Tragédie pro newyorské Německé divadlo, New York, 1908 (GF UPM 1202)
61 Dětské modely pro obraz Harmonie, New York, 1908
62 New York, 1908
63 Slečna Reichlová, hlavní tragédka Reinhardtova divadla, jako model k obrazu Tragédie, součásti výzdoby interiéru newyorského Německého divadla, New York, 1908
64 Mucha sedící před obrazem Madona v liliích, New York, c. 1905
65 Alfons Mucha při práci na lunetě Silou ke svobodě, láskou k jednotě! pro primátorský sál Obecního domu, Praha, 1911
66 Marie Muchová s dcerou Jaroslavou v parku, Zbiroh, 1913
67 Studie k obrazu Přísaha Omladiny pod slovanskou lípou z cyklu Slovanská epopej, Žambersko, 1925

68 Alfons Mucha se sestrami Annou a Andělou a s jejím manželem Janem Remundou, Rosice u Brna, c. 1911

69 Marie Muchová s dětmi Jaroslavou a Jiřím, Zbiroh, 1919

70–75 Fotografie ze studijní cesty do Ruska jako příprava obrazu Zrušení nevolnictví na Rusi (1914) z cyklu Slovanská epopej, Moskva, 1913

76 Marie Muchová pózující pro obraz Zimní noc, Praha, c. 1920

77 Studie k plakátu Russia restituenda na pomoc ruským dětem – tiskárna Melantrich 1922, Praha, c. 1921

78 Skica k plakátu Zdeňka Černý: The Greatest Bohemian Violoncellist – tiskárna V. Neubert 1913, Chicago, 1913

79 Model pro obraz Dívka se džbánem, 1927

80 Sedící ženský akt jako model pro obraz, Praha, c. 1913 (GF UPM 1191)

81 Dcera Jaroslava se sourozencem Jiřím jako modelka pro obálku časopisu Hearst's International z ledna 1922, Zbiroh, c. 1921

82 Žena s mušlí, Praha, c. 1920

83 Model pro dominantní postavu obrazu Apotheosa z dějin Slovanstva z cyklu Slovanská epopej, Zbiroh, c. 1926

84 Marie Muchová se synem Jiřím, c. 1920

85 Studie k portrétu Halidé Edip, nejvýznamnější ženské postavy moderních tureckých dějin, Zbiroh, 1925

86 Muchova dcera Jaroslava jako model k obrazu Přísaha Omladiny pod slovanskou lípou z cyklu Slovanská epopej. Stejný motiv autor uplatnil i na plakátu k výstavě dovršeného souboru dvaceti monumentálních obrazů při jejich předání městu Praze roku 1928, Zbiroh, 1926

87 Dcera Jaroslava jako modelka k obrazu Apotheosa z dějin Slovanstva z cyklu Slovanská epopej, Zbiroh, 1926

88 Modely pro symbolickou skupinu obrazu Přísaha Omladiny pod slovanskou lípou z cyklu Slovanská epopej, Zbiroh, 1926

89 Marie a Alfons Muchovi, Praha, c. 1920

90 Model pro obraz Dívka v kroji, Zbiroh, c. 1923

91 Alfons Mucha s dcerou Jaroslavou jako modelem pro plakát De Forest Phonofilm k prvnímu zvukovému filmu, promítanému v Biu Adria v Praze, Zbiroh, 1927

92 Jiří Mucha v indiánském převleku s modely, Zbiroh, c. 1919

93 Klášter Chilandar, Mont Athos, 1924

94 Alfons Mucha s pomocníkem panem Knapem jako modely pro obraz Mont Athos z cyklu Slovanská epopej, Zbiroh, 1926

95 Kvetoucí keř

Fotografie ze sbírek Uměleckoprůmyslového musea v Praze jsou označeny GF UPM, ostatní fotografie jsou z archívu Mucha Trust v Londýně.

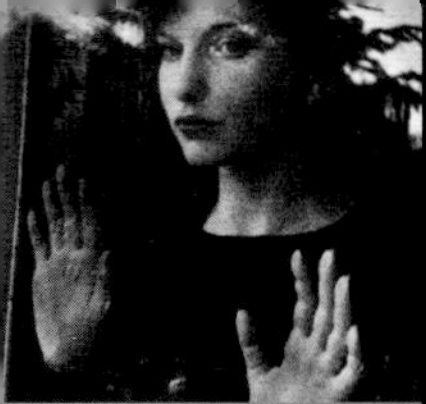

Alexandr **Hackenschmied**

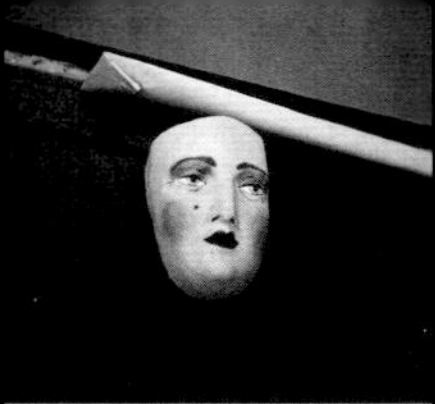

Jindřich **Štyrský**

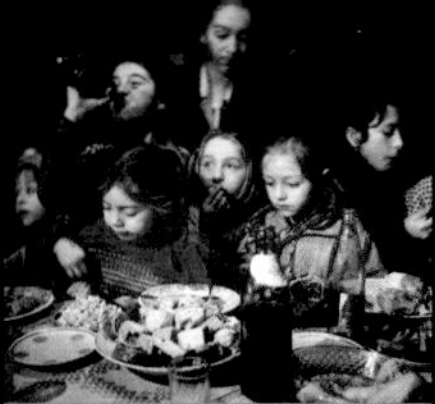

Karel **Cudlín**

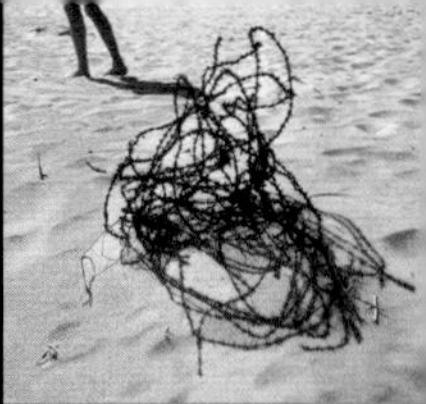

Josef **Koudelka**

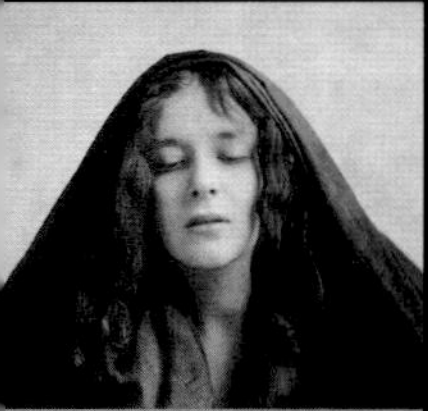

Alfons **Mucha**

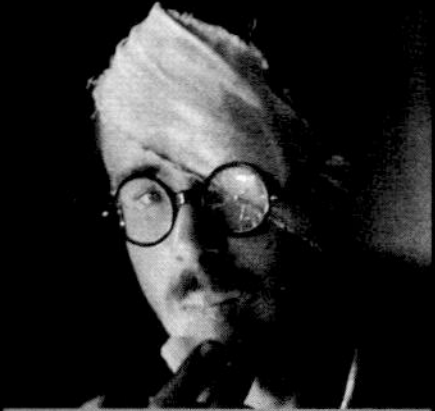

Zdeněk **Tmej**

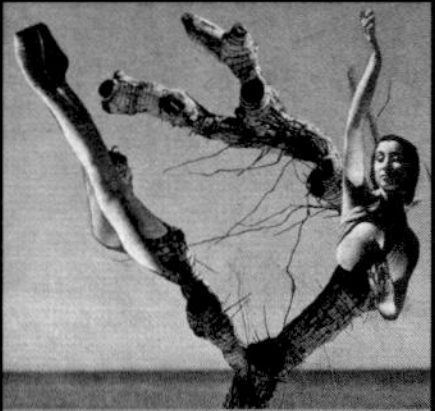

Karel **Teige**

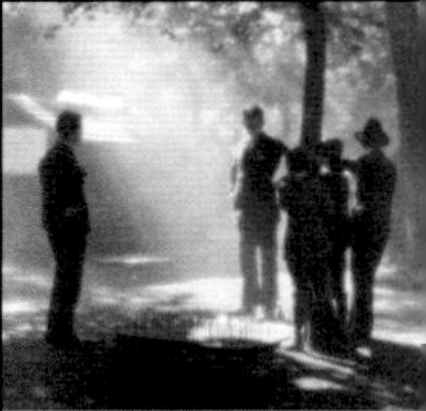

Josef **Sudek**

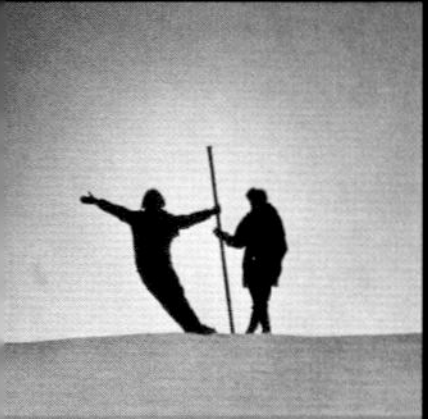

Bohdan **Holomíček**

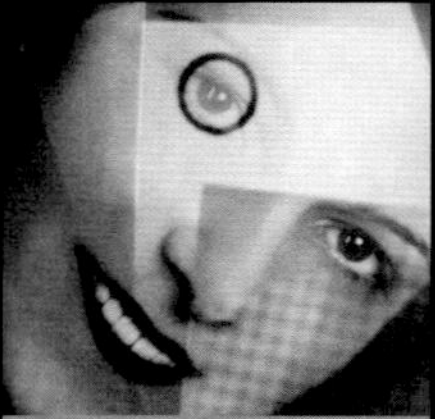

Jaroslav **Rössler**

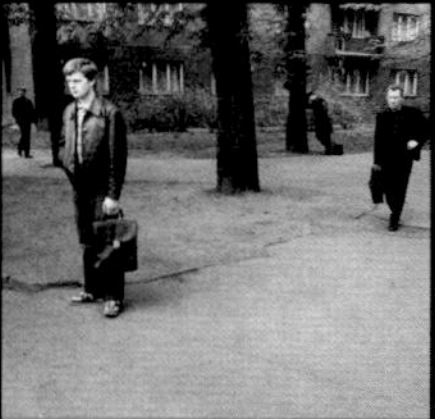

Viktor **Kolář**

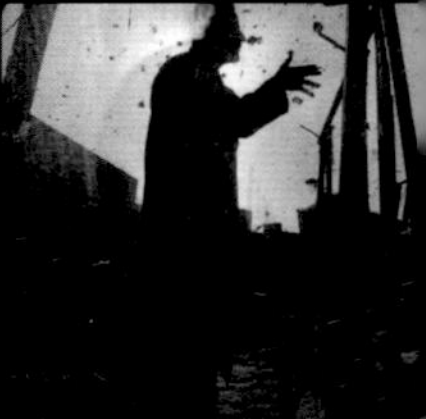

Antonín **Kratochvíl**

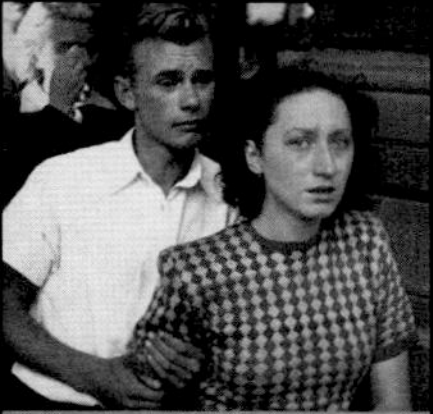

Jan **Lukas**

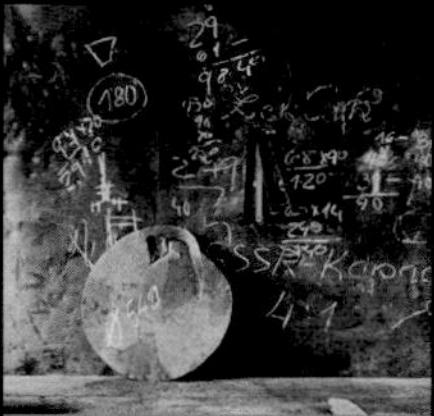

Ivo **Přeček**

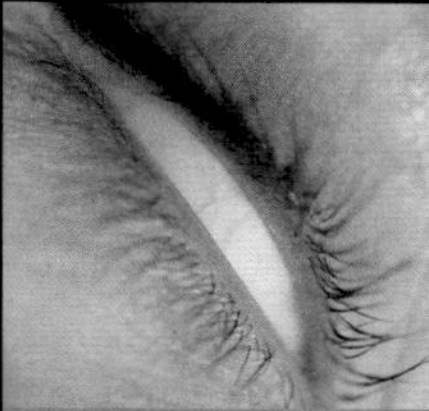

Tono **Stano**

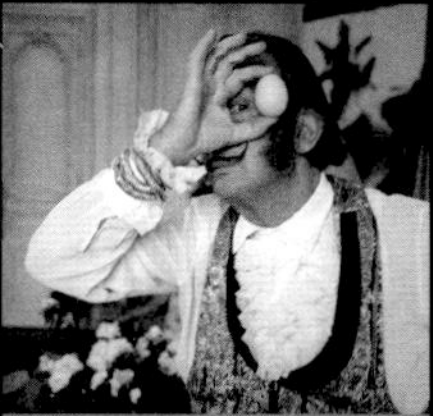

Václav **Chochola**

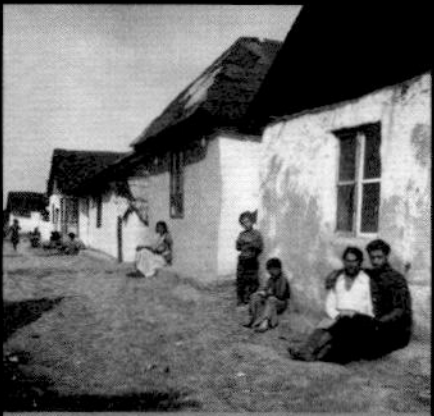

Eva **Davidová**

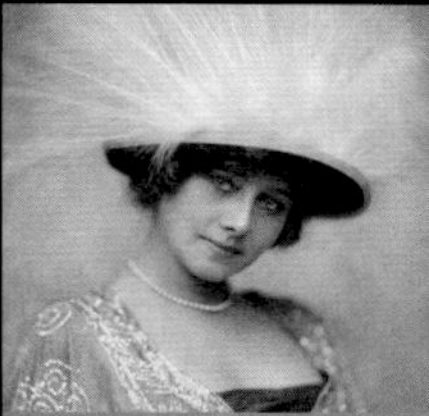

Jan **Langhans**

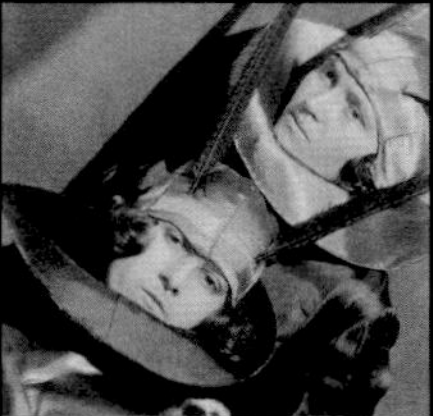

Jaromír **Funke**

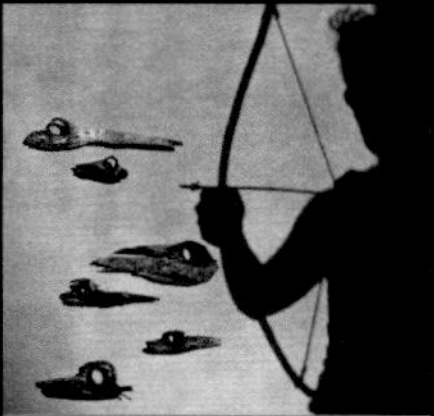

Emila **Medková**

FOTO**TORST**

Published to date / Dosud vyšlé svazky:

1 **Alexandr Hackenschmied**
2 **Bohdan Holomíček**
3 **Alfons Mucha**
4 **Jindřich Štyrský**
5 **Zdeněk Tmej**
6 **Jaroslav Rössler**
7 **Karel Cudlín** (Out of print / Vyprodáno)
8 **Karel Teige**
9 **Viktor Kolář**
10 **Josef Koudelka**
11 **Josef Sudek**
12 **Antonín Kratochvíl**
13 **Jan Lukas**
14 **Václav Chochola**
15 **Jaromír Funke**
16 **Ivo Přeček**
17 **Eva Davidová**
18 **Emila Medková**
19 **Tono Stano**
20 **Jan Langhans**

Soon to be published / Připravujeme:

Eugen Wiškovský
Josef Binko
František Drtikol

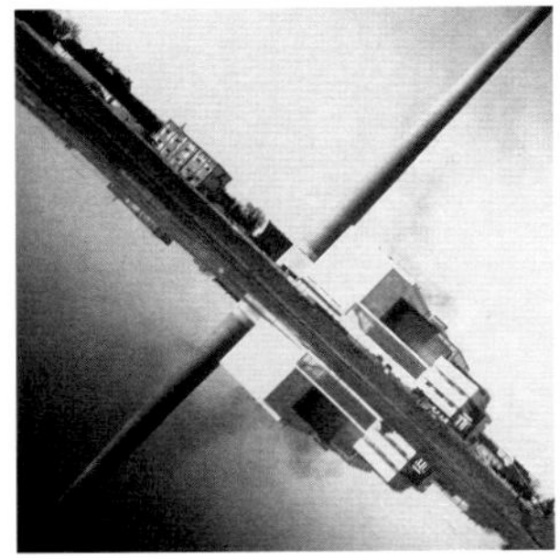

Eugen Wiškovský

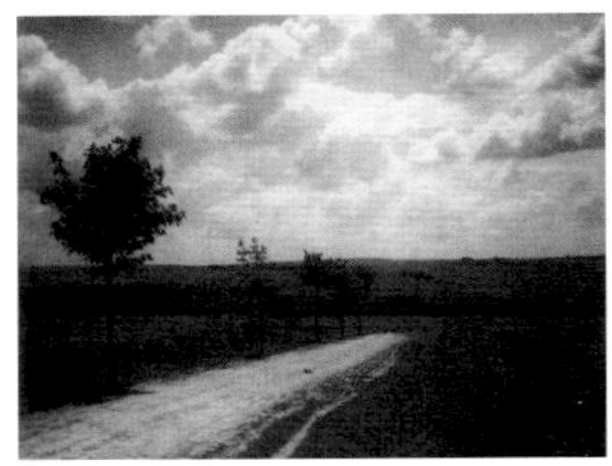

Josef Binko

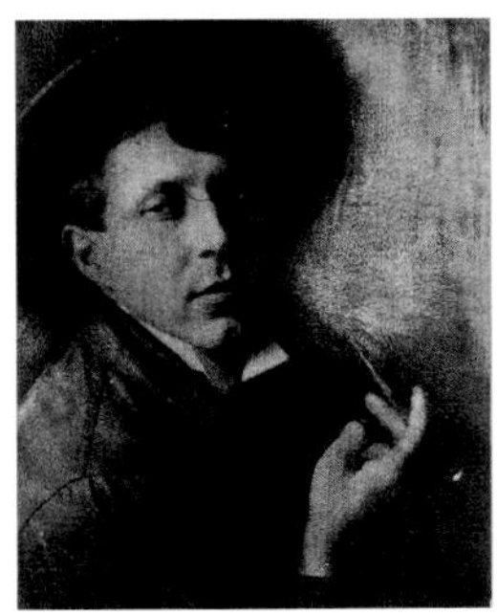

František Drtikol

Also available through D. A. P. / Distributed Art Publishers
155 Sixth Avenue, 2nd Floor, New York, N.Y. 10013, USA
Tel: ++1 (212) 627-1999 Fax: ++1 (212) 627-9484

Alfons **Mucha**

by Josef Moucha
Translation: Derek Paton
Graphic concept: Studio Najbrt, Prague
Graphic design: Pavel Lev, Studio Najbrt
Lithography: ArtD, Prague
Printed by Trico, Prague
Copy editors: Jan Šulc, Jan Zelenka, and Derek Paton
Published by TORST
Address: Opatovická 24, Prague 1,
CZ–110 00, Czech Republic
torst@torst.cz
Second, enlarged edition, 2005

Available through D.A.P./Distributed Art Publishers
155 Sixth Avenue, 2nd Floor, New York, N.Y. 10013
Tel: (212) 627-1999 Fax: (212) 6227-9484